THE GOLDEN LOTUS

Reg. U. S. Pat. Off.

"FOR HOLY VIRTUE, FOR HIGH ENDEAVOR,
FOR SUBLIME WISDOM - FOR THESE
THINGS DO WE WAGE WAR: THEREFORE
ARE WE CALLED WARRIORS."

Gautama Buddha

VOL.4

1947

CONTENTS

VOLUME FOUR

JANUARY to DECEMBER

1947

-*- -*- -*- -*-

	Glossary Term	Page

-*- -*- -*- -*-

-+- -+- -+- -+-

-*- -*- -*- -*-

1944 - 1945 - 1946

	Author	Publisher
FIERY WORLD -1944-	Agni Yoga Series	The Agni Yoga Press
THE VOICE OF THE SILENCE	H. P. Blavatsky	Theos. Univ. Press
THE LIGHT OF ASIA	Sir Edwin Arnold	McKay & Co.
THE DIAMOND SUTRA *	Bhikshu Wai-tao and Dwight Goddard	Dwight Goddard
THE BHAGAVAD GITA (Conflation)	A. E. S. Smythe	The Blavatsky Institute
BUDDHISM, THE SCIENCE OF LIFE	A. L. Cleather and Basil Crump	The H. P. B. Library
THE DEVELOPMENT OF BUDDHISM IN ENGLAND *	T. Christmas Humphreys	The Buddhist Society
THE WINGED PHAROAH	Joan Grant	Harper & Brothers
"THE MIDDLE WAY"	(periodical)	The Buddhist Society
HIERARCHY	Agni Yoga Series	The Agni Yoga Press
SANSKRIT KEYS TO THE -1945- WISDOM RELIGION	Judith Tyberg	Theos. Univ. Press
THE SUTRA OF WEI LANG *	Trans. by Wong Mou-Lam	The Buddhist Society
THE STORY OF ORIENTAL PHILOSOPHY	L. Adams Beck	
KIM	Rudyard Kipling	
FOUNDATIONS OF BUDDHISM	Natalie Rokotoff	The Agni Yoga Press
STUDIES IN OCCULTISM	H. P. Blavatsky	Theos. Univ. Press
EVOLUTION AS OUTLINED IN THE ARCHAIC EASTERN RECORDS	Basil Crump	The H. P. B. Library
DHAMMAPADA *	U. Dhammajoti	
CONCENTRATION AND MEDITATION	The Buddhist Lodge	The Buddhist Society
HEART	Agni Yoga Series	The Agni Yoga Press
THE ESOTERIC CHARACTER OF THE GOSPELS	H. P. Blavatsky	The Blavatsky Institute
TWENTY JATAKA TALES -1946-	Retold by Noor Inayat	McKay & Co.
MOMENTS WITH H. P. B. *	by Two Students	The Harbison Press
KARMA AND REBIRTH	T. Christmas Humphreys	The Buddhist Society
THE GOSPEL OF THE BUDDHA	Paul Carus	Open Court Pub. Co.
BALLANTYNE'S FIRST LESSONS IN SANSKRIT GRAMMAR	Revised by L. A. Ware and Judith Tyberg	Theos. Univ. Press
THE SONG CELESTIAL	Sir Edwin Arnold	McKay & Co.
"THE MAHA BODHI"	(periodical)	The Maha Bodhi Society
WOVEN CADENCES OF THE EARLY BUDDHISTS	Trans. by E. M. Hare	The Oxford Univ. Press
TAO TE CHING	Trans. by Ch'u Ta-Kao	The Buddhist Society
STUDIES IN THE MIDDLE WAY	T. Christmas Humphreys	The Buddhist Society
TRANSACTIONS OF THE BLAVATSKY LODGE	H. P. Blavatsky	Theos. Univ. Press

(* - Now Out of Print)

1947

	Author	Publisher
THE FOUR HOLY TRUTHS	Sister Vajira	Western Women's Buddhist Bureau
SOME SAYINGS OF THE BUDDHA	Trans. by F. L. Woodward	Oxford University Press
THE LIFE OF THE BUDDHA	H. C. Warren	Harvard University Press
THE SECRET DOCTRINE	H. P. Blavatsky	The Theosophy Company
THE HISTORY OF BUDDHIST THOUGHT	E. J. Thomas	Kegan Paul
MYTHS OF THE HINDUS AND BUDDHISTS	Nivedita and Coomaraswamy	Harrap & Co., Ltd.
BUDDHISM IN TRANSLATIONS	H. C. Warren	Harvard University Press
THE THEOSOPHICAL GLOSSARY	H. P. Blavatsky	The Theosophy Company
"NIRVANA"	(periodical)	The Eastern Young Buddhist League
THE SUTRA OF 42 SECTIONS	Trans. by Chu Ch'an	The Buddhist Society

-*- -*- -*- -*-

SHADOWS

Looking backward, as is the custom at the end of the year, events stand out with ominous significance, casting long shadows forward into the approaching days of the new year.   Other events cast bright radiance.   Thie chequered pattern of the past overlays the present and projects itself into the future.

Too many people were disillusioned in the days of 1946.   The resulting mountainous shadow - dark, threatening and sullen - lies across our path. Disillusionment is a corrosive acid, which may be called a national catastrophe if it bites deep enough into the national vitality.   With its coming hope, enthusiasm, spontaneous joyousness and kindly reciprocity are corroded, replaced by a cynical distrustful indifference.   Poison in all the veins of the nation evidences itself in numberless events, much like the miasma of a feverish wound, unpleasant, harmful to the vicinity.

Uncertainty and misgiving arising from the discovery of atomic energy casts another shadow.   Many people find the structure of civilization undermined by this uncertainty.   For the first time the possibility of annihilation without warning, hope of self defense, or retaliation, must be contemplated. This creates a subtle undercurrent of despair and a breathless grasp of pleasure, enjoyment, luxury and personal possessions.   But this shadow is less extensive, as it is possible for many to ignore this less personal threat, whereas millions are directly affected by dissillusionment and disappointment.

Care stalks the highways and the byways.   Want rides the open road in broad daylight.   They strike victims as they please.   The world has indifference to death, deprivation, desolation and disease, since the war years inured the World Conscience to the existence of these conditions everywhere.

Shadows lengthen, while the great powers erect more walls of division, create more laws and more committees to discuss and to complicate the world commerce and the world banking.   Everywhere the cry resounds for more brotherhood, for more understanding, for more liberty, f or more opportunity, and for more justice - only to fall unheeded upon the statesmen's ears.

Sunlight flows in upon the jumbled chequered shadows, causing the fever to lift and lessen, while the restless multitudes look up and take fresh heart again.   But these respites are few, for that which causes rifts and sunshine comes too seldom to be permanent.   The law of opposites prevails, and we must endure the shadows until we learn to create sunshine.

Could it be true that each one is responsible for a share of shadow and a share of sunlight, that each one helps the Light or helps the Shadow, as he chooses, by his actions?   If that were so, would we not look for Light, and hurl the Shadow into its brightness - somehow, sometime, somewhere?

-*- -*- -*- -*- -

THE DHARMA

DUHKHA

Suffering and the Cessation of Suffering should be the most important study of the incarnated being, as it is created by the revolving cycle of becoming. Friction, or suffering, and the elimination of friction, might be termed the business or the concern of all life, were it not that the attention of the multitudes has been diverted by an escape complex, resulting in a hopeless endurance of friction and pain.

Science today seeks remedies and cures for many ills, lifting from mankind much pain of body, but the scientist is unable to control the underlying causes for human misery as these are beyond his control. Disease, death, malnutrition, squalor, congestion, indulgence, pollution of water, earth and air, deterioration and adulteration of food, and the racking inharmonies of modern cities create mass effects, because they are mass causes. These causes are too widespread, too deeply rooted, to be controlled by scientists; they grapple only with the effects.

So also the occultist. He grapples with effects from causes beyond his control. He meets life immured within a body subjected from childhood to conditions favorable to disease and death. He also must submit to mass effects, because he cannot escape mass causes. In addition he must submit to his own limitations and particular handicaps caused by his cyclic progress through the centuries of becoming. Child of his age as he is, he is also the child of previous ages, and he inherits from all of them present tendencies and present abilities.

Suffering, Change, Decay and Dissolution - are they not inherent in all manifested beings? Are they not latent in all unmanifested beings who travel on the pathway toward rebirth? Can they be escaped or evaded, are they not natural and inevitable, can they not be accepted as evidences of life and growth and progress, are they not predestined and proper, should they not be taken without protest, have they no place in the Universal Plan? These and similar questions Man has asked himself, but failed to answer with finality in the past, is unlikely to answer them in the immediate future.

This is because he works with the effects and will not make allowance for the cause. He has too many immediate and pressing problems engrossing his attention, causing him to neglect the long-range view of the underlying causes. He has insufficient understanding of natural forces to remove the effects and prevent recurrence of them. He does not understand himself and his own integrated being; therefore he is compelled to endure friction, unaware that lack of skill in living creates the friction.

He is a tyro at the game of life. He must study rules, methods, skills, timing, precision and the ethics of the game, before he learns to eliminate the strain, the fatigue, and the mistakes responsible for friction or suffering, called by the Buddha in his teachings - DUHKHA.

MYTHOLOGY

THE TITANS

Battlemented and turreted, girded with the magic word-created power of the mighty Zeus, the heights of the great mountain Olympus towered into the sky, aloof, sacrosanct, and apart. Here were the portals to the world of Gods, and here the passageway to what the mortals vaguely thought of as another earth-like realm. And high above Olympus, secure from interruption, safe from any intrusion, far removed from troubles such as mortals must endure, the Gods were angry. But, though the Gods were angry, they were not like men, except that men could only understand them if they appeared somewhat like mortals - and so the legends grew of the Immortals.

The lower world was in rebellious chaos, and the Overlords of Earth were therefore much displeased. Leaving the pleasant places, where they could hold communication with the denizens of other, higher levels, they reluctantly descended to the lower levels below their own, to find the source of the disturbance. They came to earth, they touched their feet to land, they took upon themselves the forms of higher beings and so descended upon Olympus. The mountain became invested with their power; it became a place apart, a sacred mountain.

Here they called the rebellion into order. They asked for reasons for the discontent, and when the tale was told they rendered judgment. The long war of the rebels had left traces. The high Gods were displeased by the disasters. The order of the planet had been disrupted and much had to be done to restore order. The Lords, the most high Gods, were lenient, but angry at the disturbance and resolved to maintain a closer watch upon the rebels in the future.

It was so simple and so naive an explanation. The Titans, huge and powerful, mighty in their strength, these Wardens of the lower levels, these Sons of Earth the Mother, grim and defiant, said briefly they were completely prisoned, they longed for freedom, they thought of freedom, and they sought freedom. They wished to join the Gods above Olympus. They climbed the mountains - not Olympus, girded with magic power - and yet were earthbound. They sought, therefore, to build a bridge into the realm of Gods, and had piled the mountain Pelion upon the mountain Ossa, and looked for other mountains to add - until the Gods appeared. They were determined, not repentant. The mountains trembled, the lower levels shivered, the oceans quivered, and all Earth was threatened with upheaval. For over all the lower level, the Earth Gods have great power. The fate of Earth hung in the balance.

The high Gods laughed, and that was answer - they could be merry. "The road to high above Olympus? Why", they said to the sullen, envious Titans, "did you not know that you are free, the road lies up, the door is wide, the worlds are linked, the portal swings between all levels? How could you be so stupid? The weight you pile is weight, and weight does not scale heaven. Why did you not call for instruction? We, being undisturbed, deemed you were not ready. And we still think so, seeing the disorder."

So they began the long instruction, after the Titans restored the mountains, and smoothed the seas, and filled the hollows, and made the Earth more happy, working as Titans work, with grim and ceaseless effort, with no pause for converse.   And they lingered for no refreshment, for the Lords had said the way was open and the portal swung at a touch, to heaven.

The Lords then showed them what must be accomplished, what work was to be done, how to proceed, how to grow wiser, how to be lighter - less in weight and more translucent.   They promised friendship.   They offered counsel.   They spoke, those most high Gods, of other ages, and all the lower level listened, so that around the Titans still smaller lives remembered and were instructed.

The Gods rose, shining, laughing, happy, friendly, joyous, light and free, into high heaven, leaving Olympus and the magic band of power.   The Titans, wiser and contented, bowed before the benediction of the mighty Zeus, holding the promise of the all-powerful as covenant, able to call for aid and to be guided.   They watched the Gods go with awe and better comprehension.   And silently the clouds closed on their passing, and all was silence in the air above Olympus.

The war was over.   The high Gods, understanding that Life in aspiration had piled the mountains, were no longer angry.   Life flowed on in its accustomed way in heaven, and the Titans - who were once rebels - held the friendship of the mighty Zeus.   They settled down to find the way to scale the magic-girded mountain called Olympus.

-*- -*- -*- -*- -*- -*- -*- -*- -*- -*- -*- -*- -*- -*- -*- -*- -*- -*- -*-

"By the Seven 'Eternities' aeons or periods are meant. ....."

"The Seven Eternities meant are the seven periods, or a period answering in its duration to the seven periods, of a MANVANTARA, and extending throughout a MAHA KALPA or the 'Great Age' - 100 years of Brahma - making a total of 311,040,000,000,000 of years; each year of Brahma being composed of 360 'days' and of the same number of 'nights' of Brahma (reckoning by the Chandrayana or lunar year); and a 'Day of Brahma' consisting of 4,320,000,000 of mortal years.

"These 'Eternities' belong to the most secret calculations, in which, in order to arrive at the true total, every figure must be 7x (7 to the power of x); x varying according to the nature of the cycle in the subjective or real world; and every figure or number relating to, or representing all the different cycles from the greatest to the smallest - in the objective or unreal world - must necessarily be multiples of seven.   The key to this cannot be given, for herein lies the mystery of esoteric calculations, and for the purpose of ordinary calculation it has no sense."

THE SECRET DOCTRINE (Original Edition)
Vol. 1, page 36.

ARHAT

What is the ultimate goal of the Adept or - in Buddhism - ARHAT?

Perfection.   That is, completion and achievement, not flawlessness, or infallibility.

What does he achieve?

A goal, or stage to be reached, before he goes onward to be - more than ARHAT.

Does he travel further?

Ultimately, he reaches larger, wider, loftier spheres of being.   He must first perfect (complete or finish) his growth, must reach full stature before he does this.

Does he renounce humanity, when he reaches Perfection?

All stages renounce other stages.

How does he advance into another stage?

He hovers on the brink of the new stage, half or partially participating, half or partially participating here.   He grasps the new rung of the ladder before he relinquishes the old.

Does he then leave the state of ARHAT?

He need not, for a time, and can prolong that time if he should choose to do so.   He often does.   Ultimately - he goes onward.

Why does he stay?

He has the heart of compassion.   It holds him to the Wheel of Life and Birth, and he must spend himself in aid.   Or he has duties which are undischarged and he must loosen those duties.   Or he chooses to remain for companionship, because of comrades - or he sees no one to take his place - or maybe he loves our Earth, the blue star dim and clouded.

He is not, then, a completely evolved and perfect Being?

To our eyes, yes.   To others, he is incomplete.   He has progressed so far - no further.

What is the reason for this?   Is it our blindness?

No.   It is relativity.   The lower in development can see no flaws; the higher in development observes them.   The equal knows all and may be friend and comrade but not critic.

Do they have special traits, or special powers, or special characteristics - these ARHATS?

> They may be different in essence. They appear similar in body. They do not advertise the difference.

But, are they glad to go?

> Sometimes. Yet others, leaving this world scene, make request to stay. So few may dare the Heights, it seems, though all must progress to the Goal in time.

But can one choose?

> In limits, and in reason, yes. The fate of others is forgotten by those most glad to go. To them, the Goal is most desired. But others seek to aid; and so they choose to stay.

Does all the world reach to the Goal in time?

> In time. MANVANTARA is long "time" - and there is therefore "time" for many yet to reach the Goal. All will be well.

> (to be continued)

-*- -*- -*- -*- -*- -*- -*- -*- -*- -*- -*- -*- -*- -*- -*- -*- -*- -*- -*-

> "He who would be an occultist must not separate either himself or anything else from the rest of creation or non-creation. For, the moment he distinguishes himself from even a vessel of dishonour, he will not be able to join himself to any vessel of honour.

> "He must think of himself as an infinitesimal something, not even as an individual atom, but as a part of the world-atoms as a whole, or become an illusion, a nobody, and vanish like a breath leaving no trace behind. As illusions, we are separate distinct bodies, living in masks furnished by Mâyâ. Can we claim one single atom in our body as distinctly our own? Everything, from spirit to the tiniest particle, is part of the whole, at best a link. Break a single link and all passes into annihilation; but this is impossible.

> "There is a series of vehicles becoming more and more gross, from spirit to the densest matter, so that with each step downward and outward we get more and more the sense of separateness developed in us. Yet this is illusory, for if there were a real and complete separation between any two human beings, they could not communicate with, or understand each other in any way."

> TRANSACTIONS OF THE BLAVATSKY LODGE
> page 138.

There are so many vividly remembered names of gods and goddesses today, still existing in our language, carried as a matter of course in every
dictionary and encyclopedia, and so interwoven still with thought and custom
that this evidence of strength should be considered in an estimate of the
gods of other lands.

Time is an element in favor of the rapid disappearance of outgrown
ideas and festivals, but Time has not destroyed the strength and vigor of the
early gods of any race, for even the unknown idol images of vanished races
are discovered and re-identified if possible. The race regards them as a
child regards its toys of infancy - possessions once treasured, not to be
destroyed, even if other toys replace them.

Altars stand idle everywhere and courts once crowded are deserted, but
still the abstract idea of the worshippers is living in the names and attributes of many, many gods. They have no priests, no power temporal, no
sacrifices, no incense, and no invocations, but still they live within the
minds and memories of men, from whence they sprung, from whence they never
have departed. Men do not call upon their names or speak of them as wit-
nesses to oaths, or seek their blessing on some bond, but they preserve the
gods intact, without apparent disrespect to newer gods and newer priests,
who let the matter pass.

The gracious lines of loveliness called Venus, the slim and youthful
beauty of Apollo, the other-world abstractions of the older Egypt, the
swaying grace of Kali, the mystic flute of Krishna, and the sweet-toned
Valkyries, are they not part of song, tradition, story, epic and the drama,
even today? Where does the many-handed Siva sit, save in the hearts of worshippers? Where is the throne of Jupiter, but in the minds of men?

So none of the old gods depart, for Time cannot destroy them. They
were fashioned of the mental essence, built with power and with aspiration,
ensouled and endowed by the constant impetus of the vital strength of men.
This strength endures. It preserves the thought-concepts of the individuality, the attributes, the jeweled crowns and sistrums, the moon head-
dresses, the sacred animals, the associations and the characteristics of
each god. No one confuses them. They are alike in many cases, but they
are separate, distinct and different in essence, as they were once created
by the mind stuff long ago.

We cherish them, those of us who have understanding. We look with
sympathy upon the deserted altars, and in the silent temple ruins hear again
the hymn to the Child Horus or the veiled Isis. We strain to catch notes
of Krishna's flute or Pan's reed pipe among the woodland groves, and in the
moonlight wonder if the huntress Diana passes with her silver bow. For
where the heart has understanding there is only beauty to be discovered in
the old gods. They are old friends, and they are never terrible, strange,
ugly, alien in spirit to those who comprehend their origin. Time cannot
touch them, nor remove them. They are built of Mind and Intuitive Perception of the planetary forces.

CHAPTER THIRTEEN

SOLUTION

"Let not the glamour and the glitter deceive thee. Let not
fine words make screen for selfish ends. Let not the
unproved claims delude thee. Seek for The Way."

Padma Hiranya Surangama.

The seeker who has found his field of learning can tell it by a sense of
satisfaction. Previously, he has not found this sense of satisfaction in
any other organization, society, group of people, or in pursuit of any line
of occult reading. Suddenly, he finds this awareness of definite attraction in his Mind, and he is drawn toward the source of the new knowledge
which aroused it. This is his measurement of occult cults, groups, or
systems.

By this time he should have read very widely and become thoroughly familiar
with the writings of all occult authors. He should know where he stands
on their presentation of the subjects with which they deal. He has this
sense of satisfied homecoming only if he has the experience upon which to
base a true discrimination.

Yet having found this in his consciousness, before he goes into a definite
relationship with any group, or lifts the share of occult Karma resulting
from membership, let him beware of hasty affiliation. He will lose nothing
by delay. Let him ask questions. Perhaps the group is now composed of
worthy people with high ideals, but was not so innocent in the past. The
Karma of previous mistakes clings and he, who is not responsible, must bear
his share. He has the right to know and choose with open eyes. He has
the right to withdraw later if he finds that he has been deceived, but it
is best to know the history of any occult organization before joining it.

He should inspect the membership. Quietly and unobtrusively, and in a
courteous manner, he should find out if he is welcome, if he will be in good
company, if there he will be happy. He has the right to refuse association
as well as the organization involved.

He should inspect the leaders and the officers and know them rather well before he places his request for membership within their hands. They are the
ones who guide the group, therefore much depends upon their conduct and
their character. A hidden personal flaw in character should be apparent to
the seeker if he can discover it before he joins, not afterwards.

He should take stock of books recommended, and how business is done, and
what the aims of the organization are. All evidence a certain character
to the observant eye. They should be weighed carefully and painstakingly,

Better to refrain from joining because of over-scrupulousness, than to mar a lifetime's opportunity by wrong effort.

He should attend all meetings open to him, and there pursue his investigations, supplemented by private talks with members and officers, as well as a study of the literature recommended.   Out of it all he should emerge with certain clear conclusions to the following questions, and on these conclusions he should base his actions.

1. How does the organization stand in the community?

2. Has it clean hands occultly?

3. Has it a nondescript membership?

4. Has it true ideals?

5. Are they being followed?

6. Can the officers command respect?

7. Are they people of ability and learning, or merely
              wishful thinkers and fanatics?

8. What books are studied?

9. What are their antagonisms occultly?

10. Do they embrace a creed or dogma?

11. Have they erected altars to a human leader?

12. Are they hero-worshippers?

13. Can they be open-minded?

14. Are they able to concentrate on the important?

15. Are they diffused on many subjects?

16. Can they be trusted individually?

17. Is there a hidden weakness?

18. Are the apparent objects money-makers?

19. Do they speak fanatically or foolishly, or with
              discrimination?

(to be continued)

THE SONG OF DREAMS

Sometimes I drift along the lane of sleep
To visit Life beneath the ocean's deep.
For often, within Law, the human pays
His homage to the Lords of other rays.
He makes obeisance at the Court of Kings
Whose thrones are set beyond our grasp of things.
Such times, the planet's evolutions blend
In kaleidoscopic patterns and trends.

Sometimes the weary Heart sinks under strain
Forsakes the inner paths, the glad refrain,
And turns to Silence and the Ageless Way,
Loosing the bonds of lower earth, to stay
Enduring, patient, quiet and alone,
Knowing, remembering it must atone.
Returning weary still but strong again
To lift the body, to endure its pain.

Sometimes the door of memory swings wide
So that I bring back fragments from inside
The inner realm where one may meet the Wise.
I recollect the look of foreign skies
Remember outlines of a noble face,
Recall the pathway to a well-loved place.
But what I learn of where, or when, or why -
I cannot speak, no matter how I try.

1947.

THE THEORY OF MANVANTARA

THE COSMIC CALENDAR:

	Sanskrit	Mortal Years	Brahmâ's Years
Brahmâ's Age	MAHÂ KALPA	311,040,000,000,000	100 Years
Brahmâ's Year		3,110,400,000,000	1 Year
Brahmâ's Week	SAURYA KALPA	60,480,000,000	7 Days and 7 Nights
Brahmâ's Night	PRALAYA	4,320,000,000	12 Hours
Brahmâ's Day	KALPA	4,320,000,000	12 Hours

THE PLANETARY CALENDAR:

		Mortal Years	Divine Years
Brahmâ's Day	MAHÂ MANVANTARA	4,320,000,000	12,000,000
Planetary Day	MANVANTARA	616,896,000	1,713,600
	MANU	308,448,000	856,800
Great Age	MAHÂ YUGA	4,320,000	12,000
The Four Ages (CHATUR YUGA)	1. KRITA or SATYA	1,728,000	4,800
	2. TRETÂ	1,296,000	3,600
	3. DWÂPARA	864,000	2,400
	4. KALI	432,000	1,200
Dawns and Twilights	SANDHYÂ and SANDHYÁMSA	25,920,000	72,000
A Year of the Gods	DAIVASAMVAT	360	1
A Day and Night of the Gods	DAIVÂHÔRÂTRA	1	24 hours

-*- -*- -*- -*-

"CAN THE ESOTERIC TRUTHS BE BROADCAST?"

Many people think so, therefore are resentful if a reply is in the negative. Modern education has brought a smattering of accomplishments to everyone, and completion of the general education is considered by many to be sufficient, egotism refusing to admit superiority in any other adult. Special educational advantages being open to everyone for a price, the specially educated acquire another layer of education, and this in turn causes a feeling of superior mental ability. All this may be natural and true enough, and need not be condemned, except that such concepts do not constitute a basis for occult research.

Modern civilization is based upon a system of sensational disturbance of the public mind by broadcast news and disasters of every kind. A mature civilization would evidence its mental level by its maintenance of law and order, its emphasis on accomplishments, aspirations and joy of living, whereas the present note is one of scandalous curiosity, unhappy accidents, crime, sudden death and catastrophe. Even the modern fiction is based upon sensation and sensualism.

This being the preference of the population, how can esoteric truth be broadcast? What newspaper would accept it? What radio station would approve it? What listener or reader would endorse their choice, and upon what inner knowledge could he base his own approval or disapproval?

As it is, sensational pseudo-occultism is accepted as the truth by many people, and there is the inevitable reaction against the present-day cult, and the present-day pretender. The sound judgment of many people brands all that trickery as dangerous.

Either truth is esoteric - or else it is nothing but ordinary, everyday, common knowledge. There is no in-between.

The inner meaning of the fables, the fairy tales, the legends, the nature myths, the great pageants of the older religions, the symbols of the pagans and of today, the hints and clues in philosophic writings of all times, the rituals of many pagan worships, the endless panorama of the living planet all around us - these are some of the pages of the book the occultist studies, and these are not reduced to quick and easy correspondence courses for anyone. They are the lessons; understanding is the crown of achievement.

The esoteric does not appear in print or in condensed form. The truth is ever hidden, and must be sought, and won, and worn as a jewel. The East speaks of the jewel as the Crest Jewel of Wisdom, for Wisdom is the result of inner understanding. It is acquired, not bestowed.

No one who feeds on sensationalism and demands quick and easy explanations acquires Wisdom. The Wise have conquered Ignorance by their own sustained effort.

by Chu Ch'an

(This article is reprinted from "Buddhism in England", May-
June, 1941, whōse Editor added: "The writer of the following Article is a young Englishman who has recently
returned to this country from a Zen Monastery in China.")

The monastery of P'u-ti-sse stands on a wooded hillside facing the East.
Each morning the yellow tiles of its upturned roofs reflect the first rays of
the sun rising from beyond the far side of the great lake below.   All around
is peace and the song of the birds.   Within the walls of this sanctuary some
seventy monks live together in harmony practising Dhyana (a form of meditation known as Ch'an in China and Zen in Japan).   They form a spiritual
reservoir from which emanate such powerful vibrations that even the air seems
purer than that of the highest mountains.   In a few simple words I will try
to describe the indescribable, and picture to you the life they lead.

At three in the morning the throbbing notes of a giant drum, mingled
with the sweet sound of a gong, rouse the monks from their sleep.   Water has
been heated in a giant cauldron, and everyone washes and dons his ceremonial
robes for the morning service.   As the notes of the drum become more and
more insistent they troop one by one into the great temple hall.   Here a
myriad points of flame flicker before the statues of the Blessed Ones, and
the scent of incense fills the air.   Bowing to the ground three times, the
monks stand in ordered ranks waiting for the last notes of the drum.   Then
the "incense Chant" bursts forth from their lips, followed by words and songs
of adoration, intermingled with vows to re-dedicate themselves to the Pure
Life.

After the service a simple breakfast is served in silence. Rice por-
ridge and vegetables are the usual fare, for meat is never eaten by the monks,
who desire that even animals shall not be deprived of their lives by the hand
of man.   Moreover only one course is served at each meal, for a monk eats to
support life, not to pander to his desire for delicate and varied taste.
When breakfast is over, there is a short period of leisure during which
clothes may be washed and mended; then most of the monks take their places
in the Meditation Hall.

This is a square, stone-flagged room with a small octagonal shrine in
the middle.   Round the room is a platform with cushions arranged side by
side, for the monks to sit on in the cross-legged Lotus posture. At the tap
of a hand-drum they rise from their seats and walk slowly round the room.
Gradually they move faster and faster, swinging their arms and allowing the
exercise to drive their wayward thoughts away.   At a second tap on the drum,
everyone stops dead, then walks over to the nearest cushion and takes up his
position.   An incense stick is lighted and, while it burns, the monks sit
absorbed in their meditation.   When at last the incense has burnt itself
out, the drum is heard again, and the monks file out into the courtyard, the
seniors to their work in the fields or kitchen, and the younger ones to their
studies.

The usual form of meditation in P'u-ti-sse is centered round the
phrase "Nien Fu shih shuei?"   (Adoring the Buddha, who?) If you approached

the problem intellectually it would resolve itself like this: "Who adores the
Buddha?   I do.   Who am I?   Am I my body?   No.   Cut off my hands and I do
not become any the less 'I'.   Am I my mind?   No.   My mind is made up of
impressions received through my senses from outside.   Then who am I?"   Ah,
when one has solved this question one is well on the Path to Enlightenment.
But the problem must not be approached intellectually.   One must just
"think oneself into it" until the person and the problem are indivisible.
Suddenly, or sometimes gradually, light will come.   "I, as an individual,
does not exist.   The Universe and I are one."   To know this intellectually
is almost useless; one must experience it and feel it as one feels the air
around one.   It must become a living reality.

The rest of the day is similar to the first part.   From meditation the
monks go to their manual or other work.   Then comes dinner, another period
of meditation, a short rest, the afternoon service, supper and a final visit
to the Meditation Hall before bed.

Four times a month two periods of meditation are missed.   The time is
spent in mending, washing and other necessary jobs.   On the first and fif-
teenth day of each moon special ceremonies are performed and slightly better
food is served in honour of the occasion.   Special days in memory of the
Buddha and various Bodhisattvas are observed with ceremonials applicable to
the occasion.   Services are also read for the sick and for those who have
left this life to enter into another incarnation.

Discipline is very strict.   A special official is chosen from the
monks to enforce this.   Monks who fall asleep during the period of meditation or who do not spring from their beds in the morning are rapped on the
right shoulder with a piece of wood bearing the Chinese characters "Perfumed
Board."   Food, clothes and sleeping arrangements are all of the simplest.
Luxuries are unknown, except for the ceremonial and ordinary drinking of tea.
Work in the fields or the monastery is hard, but the monks know that all this
is necessary, for a calm and pure mind dwells only in a well-disciplined
body.   Few of them need correction, for almost all are eager to do what they
believe to be good for themselves and the community.

On certain days in the month there are other breaks in the daily round
than those mentioned above.   Every few days the water in the great square
bath is heated, and the monks go in relays to wash away outward impurities,
just as meditation washes away the inner ones.   No soap is used, however,
as most soap is scented, and scent is a luxury which monks do not use.

There are also the days upon which sections of the Sutras are read and
sometimes expounded.   Besides these there are the New Year, Spring and
Autumn festivals which are celebrated in the traditional way.   Whatever is
lacking in beauty in the daily lives of the monks is made up for by the
beauty of their surroundings, architectural and natural, and the beauty of
the services, with the soft lights playing on the golden statues of the
Blessed Ones and the sound of chanting and hymns.   But the greatest beauty
of all is that which cannot be described in words, the beauty which comes in
the silence, the beauty that I like to call "the white snow of meditation."

-*- -*- -*- -*-

THE GLOSSARY

DIONYSUS: (Greek)   (October, 1945, p. #131)

Another form of Bacchus. It is easy to criticize these ancient gods,
but the nature of their worship is not always clear to modern historians.
So while the god Dionysus stands for revelry and wine today, that is an injustice.   The old cults of the Middle East portrayed esoteric truth by
exoteric blinds in many cases.   Dionysus was the personified Sun.

BACCHANALIA: (Latin)   (October, 1945, p. #131)

The great festival connected with the worship of the god Bacchus. It
is, today, associated with disreputable orgies.   Obviously it did not have
that meaning to the Greeks, who held it as a sacred religious ceremony connected with the cyclic fertility of nature.   In Greece the feasts were
called Dionysia, but in Italy Bacchanalia.

PRATĪTYA SAMUTPĀDA: (Sanskrit)   (November, 1945, p. #145)

The linked Chain of Causation, composed of the twelve NIDĀNAS, or Fetters, the concatenation of events and effects, causing other future events
and effects, that binds one to the Wheel of Rebirth.

ZEN: (November, 1945, p. #148)

The name of a sect or school of philosophy, derived from the Ch'an
school originating in China from MAHĀYĀNA Buddhism.   Zen is an offshoot
very different from the original Buddhism.   It is also called the "Sudden
School", as it seeks Quick Illumination.

HĪNAYĀNA: (Sanskrit)   (November, 1945, p. #148)

The form of Buddhism as it crystalized in lower India, Ceylon and
Burma.   It adheres to the original records of the First Council held by the
Buddha's disciples shortly after his death.   The name is often translated
"Smaller Vehicle", but it is a comparatively recent title, and was not in
use at the time of the first Council.   Its rigid adherence to form and es-
tablished order has been instrumental in preserving the Buddhism of the
Buddha's life-time to the present day.

MAHĀYĀNA: (Sanskrit)   (November, 1945, p. #147)

The "Great Vehicle", in contrast to the HĪNAYĀNA, accepts many later
commentaries and authorities, as well as the original records carried north
beyond the Himâlayas and into China during persecutions which destroyed
Buddhism in India.   MAHĀYĀNA centers in these northern and eastern lands,
around India, and has added some of the beliefs and philosophies of these
lands to the original teachings of Buddhism.

"THE FOUR HOLY TRUTHS" - by Sister Vajirâ

Through the centuries, in different lands, the Dharma found its adherents and champions.   One of them, Miriam Salanave, will be remembered as a truly noble woman who endeavored to bring the Dharma to the women of America. She was born in 1880 in Wyoming, Iowa.   After her death in San Francisco, on November 30th, 1943, a great tribute was paid to her by Buddhist and Theosophical journals.   From these obituaries we gather that her interest in Buddhism arose from comprehensive study of the writings of H. P. Blavatsky and THE MAHATMA LETTERS, and this study caused her to make pilgrimages to the places now reverenced because of their association with the Blessed One - the Buddha.   She spent much time in monasteries and temples searching for Truth, and was the first American woman to be admitted to the Gelugpa - the Order founded by Tson-kha-pa - in Tibet.   When she returned to San Francisco she founded the Western Women's Buddhist Bureau, which she maintained in addition to The East-West Buddhist Welfare Mission, feeling that in women, as the mothers and teachers of children, lay the only hope of humanity.   It can truly be said that she gave her life for the dissemination of Buddhist Principles in the two hemispheres.   "May others arise to pluck her fallen torch and carry it forward, for it would be a comfort to her" - as said in "The Middle Way".

THE FOUR HOLY TRUTHS was written by Sister Vajirâ, who lives in Darjeeling, India.   It was published by Mrs. Salanave as "Buddhist Instruction" to introduce the Dharma.   Therefore it is a simple exposition, free from Pâli and Sanskrit terms, and as it was intended, it is easily understood.   It is dedicated "to the Western reader whose knowledge and experience of this great religion may not be very extensive through lack of suitable reading matter." That there is indeed a sad lack of good reading matter on the Dharma in America must be admitted.

The pamphlet is not designed for advanced students, but is useful to give to those who begin, for the beginning is important.   It includes a few verses from the DHAMMAPADA, a two-page introduction called "The Gift of Truth excels all other Gifts", then two pages devoted to Gautama Buddha and the Buddhist Scriptures.   These are followed by a simple explanation of The Four Holy Truths and The Noble Eight-fold Path.   The topics - "The Origin of Becoming", "Suffering", "The Three Characteristics of Existence", and "The Five Precepts" are supported by quotations from the SUTRAS.

Page 17 - "Verily, Brothers, whatsoever a master owes to his disciples,
                    impelled by love and sympathy, moved by compassion,
                    that have you received from me.
            "Here trees invite; there lonely solitudes.   Devote yourselves
                    to contemplation, Brothers, that sloth may not come
                    over you, that later you may not have to repent.
            "Hold this as our command.
            "All life is transient. By diligence attain your Goal!"

The Golden Lotus Press adds this pamphlet to The Booklist, until the present supply is exhausted.   For sale at $.20 per copy.

THE GOLDEN LOTUS

Reg. U. S. Pat. Off.

"FOR HOLY VIRTUE, FOR HIGH ENDEAVOR,
FOR SUBLIME WISDOM - FOR THESE
THINGS DO WE WAGE WAR: THEREFORE
ARE WE CALLED WARRIORS."

Gautama Buddha

VOL.4

1947

CONTENTS

FEBRUARY, 1947

-*- -*- -*- -*-

The Golden Lotus

The Golden Lotus, taken from the title of a very
ancient manuscript and commentary thereon, is
sacred to the memory of the Buddhas of Attainment,
and to those who have followed in Their path. It
is the expression of the final flowering of man-
hood, in its most glorious Perfection.

There are few references to it in the translations
current in the West at present, because most if
not all of the translators have been concerned
with exoteric doctrines, and have been unable to
penetrate to or reach Illumination far enough to
comprehend the doctrines reserved for those who
pass the outer gates in understanding.

This being so, it is not strange the West should
find the title unfamiliar, but it is a most sacred
and illuminating symbol to the Mahâyâna School.
The title, therefore, is used deliberately, to
bring to mind the highest doctrines of the Buddha's
Way, the highest and most abstract teaching of the
Enlightened One, the secret knowledge of the
Yogâchârya School for centuries. This is the
teaching upon which we base our words, and upon
it this magazine is to be concentrated, so that
the East may find a voice again within the West,
and what the Buddha taught may be at hand for
earnest seekers.

To these, the Path will be recalled, and Precepts
given, and teachings quoted. The old WAY,
ancient now, is ever new and fresh, and still in
this our present century the best for seeker's
feet to travel.

To those who tread it,

GREETINGS.

＊＊ ＊＊ ＊＊ ＊＊

(Reprinted from The Golden Lotus,
Volume One, Number One,
January, 1944.)

DUHKHA SAMUDAYA - The Cause of Suffering

Such is the mind of man, it holds the pleasurable and forgets the painful, turning from the Cause of Suffering to enjoy the fleeting pleasures and the sense gratifications, thereby drugging itself with the transitory and the unreal. Small as the gratification may be, of doubtful value or usefulness, not lasting, it is grasped eagerly as a means to elude the ever-present sense of pain and sorrow. The endless pursuit of the elusive wisp of happiness is therefore continued all through the incarnation.

Suffering is inevitable in life and must be considered the result of friction, strain, effort and inexperienced handling of the body vehicle. Impermanence is also inevitable, and need be expected. "Change is inherent in all component things" said the Buddha at his passing. Change is inherent in the body, which is a compound organism. From these causes, the result of the unending cycle of manifestation, spring all the sorrows and the pains called DUHKHA.

This being so, the Cause of Suffering should be the subject of consideration. It should not be avoided and momentary gratification should not be grasped as a palliative or opiate. Undue attention to the transient tears one's hold from the intransient and creates a separately selfish individual controlled by innumerable desires. Less and less the unfortunate follower of the wisp of impermanent pleasure can escape the material world of shadows, and less and less often his immortal triad may arouse him to the pursuit of true happiness and wisdom.

Suffering is basic. It is an evidence of Life in incarnation. It is produced by change and the resistant nature of the environment encountered. It is intensified by the profoundly selfish conduct of many people in existence at the present time, and is considerably increased by ignorance of natural laws and the cyclic nature of the rhythms which govern man's evolution. These tend to produce a concentration upon the momentary, since the long-range vision of the evolutionary pathway is unknown, and therefore absent as a counter-balance.

This failure to achieve right-mindedness causes the present civilization to build toward impermanent fame and riches, to clutch at possessions and luxury, to count progress by the millions amassed, overlooking the obvious fact that these are material, remain in the material world. The departing spiritual being deserts them when it deserts the material body, taking with it only its gain in spiritual understanding.

If it has acquired nothing in spiritual understanding, preoccupied as it was with the material possessions, what has it gained? What has its long endurance of DUHKHA in that lifetime availed it, in the hour of its passing into the world of spirit?

Said the Buddha: "Subject to decay are all compounded things. Do ye abide in heedfulness."

Born as he had been, endowed with charm and - some said - beauty, sensitive to all the loveliness in the world around him, alive to music in every bird note and whisper of the streams, the satyr Pan was not a lonely creature. He had all manner of companionship. He wanted nothing, and his artist soul rejoiced in every enchanting turn of woodland or stretch of silver water, in every change of weather.

He watched the water nymphs and river lords; he knew them all by name. He lingered often where the tree dryads danced together. He stole on tiptoe, his hoofed feet so quiet, to the mountain fastness of the gnome retreats, where frequently he played a pipe of river reeds, seated cross-legged while they gambolled in their fashion at his feet. And he could find the depth-dwellers and the surface-dwellers of the Earth evolution, for he had discovered the road to every heart through his sweet music, by the haunting nature rhythms he had drawn from within his soul. His pipe was the key to every evolution of the nature kingdoms.

But Pan was not a nature creature; he was a satyr, one of the race called Sylvan, of the woods. He had intelligence, and could be talked to, if men had the perception to perceive his intelligence, but men were very scarce and very primitive when Pan was young and gay. He paid them very little attention, though willing to be friendly, and would have played his pipe for them as quickly as he did for an adventuring strange animal or a small furry pet, or a crested snake. He acknowledged no differences. All had perception, all heard his music, all were charmed. It was sufficient, and life seemed good to Pan in sun and shade.

He grew a little older. The pointed ears were just as keen, the hoofed feet were just as swift, the pipe was just as potent, but Pan had changed a trifle. He was no longer happy. He wished he knew just why, but could not find the answer. The creatures sought him often, the gnomes came to the valley, the nymphs were often calling, but Pan would be forgetful, lost in a reverie, the pipe laid idly by, and Pan the player of sweet tunes would be indifferent to summer.

He came, one time, to rest beside a waterfall, and begged the waterfall naiads to tell him stories of the water. They came close to him and told him, laughing, of the seas and all the water creatures. They asked him if he wished to travel through the water to the sea, and said they could be very helpful if he wished to leave the woods. But Pan said that he loved the woodlands, and that he only wished for company and therefore he asked for stories.

The Naiads were anxious. Pan lonely! Pan who told the wondrous tales through his sweet music! What if the pipes of Pan grew silent!

So they devised a game. They told him stories of the sea, the stream, the waterfall, the feathered creatures, the sky, the trees, the hidden evolutions. One by one they told the tales, but then begged Pan to tell the story in his own music. To please them, he gave them little lilting tunes, some sad, some gay, some happy, some melancholy, and they remembered. They sang them, then, and repeated them, and so held the tunes of Pan imprisoned in the water.   When Pan departed, lonely, silent, no longer merry, they remembered and they sang the tunes to keep the woodland happy.

So, coming on a stream or waterfall running through a wooded land, you can hear the music - soft and sad yet merry, sweet and clear, the pipes of Pan the woodland god - resounding through the ripples of the water.   For the naiads had held his music, and remembered in the days when Pan's pipe was silent, and when the woodland mourned his passing.   And even man remembered him, and mourned him, when the pipes were silent, and Pan was there no longer to play them in the woodland.

Sometimes the wind god sings a song he learned from Pan, who loved the swift sprites of the air evolutions.   And if you listen, you will hear the river reeds murmuring a song like one Pan taught them long ago.   You should know, too, that the trees sing, the leaves rustle, and the grasses whisper fragments, broken notes, of Pan's sweet music, for he took the heart of all creation and put it into music, as he heard it in the woodland, in the morning of the planet, long ago.

-*- -*- -*- -*- -*- -*- -*- -*- -*- -*- -*- -*- -*- -*- -*- -*- -*- -*- -*-

ANNOUNCEMENTS

-*- -*- -*- -*-

ARHAT - Concluded

Does the ARHAT prefer solitude?

There is a tradition to the effect that he does.   Literally, he is compelled to seek a secluded spot to maintain his equilibrium in two worlds of being.   He must be undisturbed at certain intervals. Who is not disturbed in cities?

But he must then be solitary?

If he chooses, he has all the world for companions.   Or, he may have associates near him.

What does he do?

He is not idle.   He makes investigations into the worlds of being, or researches laws already discovered, or engages upon some confirmatory experiment, or details of such occult preoccupations as open out before him.   He does not waste time in ordinary pursuits and amusements, however.

Does this work help the race?

Precisely as the scientist researching helpful discoveries.   The knowledge is preserved, is given out as needed, often after many centuries.

Could scientists do this?

They work differently, frequently with methods and materials unlawful for the enlightened one who respects Life in its many forms. They work upon matter, but the ARHAT deals with Life. A difference!

Are there great scholars in the ranks of ARHAT?

Mind is a tool to the ARHAT.   He controls it perfectly.   Therefore any one who reaches near to ARHAT level is at ease with words, ideas, languages and thought expression, for these depend upon Mind, and he has conquered Mind.

Are they, then, great philosophers?

This has been said of many wise men - that they philosophize. It may be that the philosopher is most near to the Adept pattern, but not necessarily an Adept of any grade.

What nation furnishes the Adepts?

All nations, past, present and in the future are eligible. The race is to the swift; the battle to the strong. Some races have been known to flower early - some late. Climate and environment have

influence and heredity a voice in these matters.   The racial heritage
of wisdom and culture, and the legacy of written clues, is of importance.   Therefore, some races outspeed others.   The educated races
tend to outspeed uneducated ones, simply because of the discipline of
mind, but the uneducated ones outspeed in the number of natural or
psychic mystics, who also have a sound basis for beginning.   These
two, the mystic and the mental powers, however, must blend before an
Adept is produced, and undue development of one will blunt or stunt
the other.

It is not easy, then, to reach this point of "Non-Returning" - the ARHAT?

It is supremely difficult.   Mount Everest is easier to climb.   And
men still love the valley.

What are the names the East has given ARHATS?

JINA - The Conqueror.   PARAMAHAMSA, the Swan of Far Flight. MAHÂTMA-
the Great in Spirit.   ARHAT, or ARHAN, or RAHAN, technically translated "The Worthy", is the rank of "Non-Returning" to rebirth.   These
are some of the expressions better known to the West.   There are
others, such as MAHÂSATTVA, Great Being.   All races produce their own
descriptive titles, but the Eastern ones are most instructive.   The
Western "Seer", "Prophet", "Master" are flexible, may be and often are
applied to lesser men.

Because we do not understand?

Because the knowledge of the Heights has been suppressed for centuries
and the West seeks other goals.

-*- -*- -*- -*- -*- -*- -*- -*- -*- -*- -*- -*- -*- -*- -*- -*- -*- -*- -*-

"As our planet revolves once every year around the sun, and at the same time
turns once in every twenty-four hours upon its own axis, thus traversing
minor circles within a larger one, so is the work of the smaller cyclic
periods accomplished and recommenced, within the Great Saros.

"The revolution of the physical world, according to the ancient doctrine, is
attended by a like revolution in the world of intellect - the spiritual
evolution of the world proceeding in cycles, like the physical one.

"Thus we see in history a regular alternation of ebb and flow in the tide of
human progress.   The great kingdoms and empires of the world, after
reaching the culmination of their greatness, descend again, in accordance
with the same law by which they ascended; till, having reached the lowest
point, humanity reasserts itself and mounts up once more; the height of its
attainment being, by this law of ascending progression by cycles, somewhat
higher than the point from which it had before descended."

ISIS UNVEILED, by H. P. Blavatsky
Vol. I, page #34

THE GODS DEPART

Undue significance has been given in the Christian era to the departure of old Gods. Casual reference to the outworn faiths and rituals of former eras thoughtlessly and egotistically throws the emphasis upon their errors and superstitions, their differences and their absurdities, as they appear to the modern mind. Slightingly the modern cults sweep the ancient ones aside, and scornfully include them all under the inclusive title of pagan or heathen.

However justified any cult or religious system may be in considering itself the one true faith for the era in which it holds supremacy, it does not follow that the previous faiths or systems were untrue for the era in which they held the center of the stage. Nor does it follow that because one faith is supreme or accepted by a large portion of mankind it is destined to be supreme or widely accepted for eternity. The history of mankind should show the fallacy of such expectations.

Faiths and religious systems are related to their times and to their race periods. Unlike a scientific fact or theory, they are based upon unprovable tenets, and as such are dependent upon the belief of the people in those tenets. Fashions in tenets change. The perception of the spiritual truth behind every religion is likely to alter in the course of centuries.

Cults make history, and they mold their times. They rise to favor, and they gain in power and temporal riches. But they decline, they lose favor, they pass into discard with their times. The times are the important factor; the race period is the supporting strength. The cults do not remain forever; they are limited and temporary in character.

Even the words of the Wise Men of the preceding ages have been outgrown and discarded. The forms of worship pass, but so do the forms of revelation or prediction or instruction. The Gods while popular have many servants, it is true, but they are fated to be silent when the servants desert them for new forms of worship.

And so, while the present day cults triumph and refer in slighting terms to older systems, unknowingly they may be a little too premature. They too must face decline and pass into oblivion, somewhere meeting the fate of all that has preceded them. They too must face growing disapproval, or rejection, or desertion. They too must loosen their hold upon the temporal possessions and the spiritual overlordships, must grow old and narrow-minded, despotic and dogmatic. They too must vanish, and mayhap will be called pagan in the annals of the upspringing races.

They may be certain of one thing only - that, as all things pass and change, the racial period which produces and supports them is also due to change. They pass too with the inevitable ending of the racial period, to be remembered and to be kept living as the older Gods still live, in retrospect and in the racial mind.

For Time, the equalizer and the destroyer, gathers them into his hand, and crushes them, together with the most enduring structures and the most imposing citadels of sacerdotal power.

-*- -*- -*- -*-

CHAPTER THIRTEEN - "Solution" - continued from January, 1947:

    20.   Have they some members of distinction or renown?

    21.   Are there some queernesses apparent?

    22.   Can they be presented socially in any company?

    23.   Will membership entail a loss in social prestige?

    24.   What system do they recommend occultly?

    25.   What is their discipline occultly?

    26.   What will membership entail?

    27.   What are the obligations?

    28.   Are you in sympathy with them?

    29.   Can the members be trusted with the occult training of others?

    30.   What is their aim, the goal, the status in the occult field
           of endeavor they are using as a basis for their
           training?   In other words, will they give you the
           training as an inquirer, a probationary pupil, or
           a chela?   Where will you end?

Once answered, the seeker should decide and should go forward.   He might be
able to avoid trouble if he finds the correct group at first, but even that
is no guarantee it will be perfect.   He will find imperfections everywhere.
His business is to take the least imperfect, the one most near his level.

He should then go slowly into the group activities, and allow a probationary
period of three years, during which he studies the conditions.   At the end
of that time, he may decide honestly if he will take more decisive steps,
withdraw entirely, or hold his present neutral position of observant member.
He has his own future to consider, and it is his responsibility, not
another's.

He has himself to blame if in three years he cannot find the answer, cannot
see the flaws and weaknesses, cannot estimate the discipline or system,
cannot dissect the principles, or unmask the leadership.   He should blame no
one later if he finds he is mistaken.   He should have made it his business
to be critical and ruthless in his search for truth, before he took the final
steps of close affiliation.

But once disillusioned he should leave immediately, and seek again.   Or,

(continued on page #27)

A Short Story, by Frank Batchelor

In Sung Pen none lived who could recall the coming of Lao Tsun, the priest. The oldest man in the village remembered, as a little child, his long wispy beard and greatly loving eyes. He was a seeker, and from amid the high, austere peaks where he lived, moving ever upwards, he had drawn many from the rushing torrent which races endlessly round the base of the mountain, and set their feet upon firm ground.

The village was poor; it had no chance to be otherwise. The rulers from the Sunset, who were now gone, had scarcely known of its existence, and the generous East, with its millet, rice and mangoes, had receded from it, leaving it quite alone, a little cluster of hovels about the temple; small piles of stones on the stony hillside.

The temple, too, was not as the temples which are shown to travellers. Very little larger than the largest of the huts, it just held the village population of some fifty souls, and it could well have been a cow byre, but for its astonishing cleanliness and a lumpish clay image, which stood, to Sung Pen, for the Enlightened One and was hung with flowers.

Lao Tsun's only sacerdotal vestments were his coarse woollen gown and the age-hallowed hat of cloth, which might once have been red; for Lao Tsun was a Lama, and much honoured, before ever he came forth to follow the Way and to seek his Master along those high paths of the spirit, whose windings would seem to miss rich men's houses and easeful habitations.

But he did not starve; for every mealtime that came round found him, with his wooden bowl, a loved and welcome guest at one or other of the dozen huts which made up the village.

He dissipated little, but when some fellow Searcher or would-be disciple sought him out, there must be ceremonial tea drinking, and his lamp burned to their talking, through the long hours of the night.

The snarling of a world at war sounded very far away, and the great death birds that roared over their simple lives had elsewhere to lay their eggs. Then, upon a morning of riven cloud, savage and blood-spattered, little Dula Sao ran from hut to hut and told that the Holy One would speak to them in the temple.

"My little children," the old priest began, "He who sees has opened mine eyes, and He who hears, mine ears, and I know that the stupid ones who seek to possess themselves by violence, of that which is to be for the lovers of peace, are but an hour's march from here, and that they will pass through your village, and, seeing ye have nought, will burn that which you have, and will break your bodies for their sport and go on their way."

No cry of terror met his calm statement; no panic laid its chill hand upon them; for they had faith. True, they were but babes, and their faith was in their Holy One; but He who delegates His power does not grudge His

servants the confidence of their own.   It was faith, and would there were
more of it!

"What, then, must we do, Holy One?" asked the headman, as he would have
asked what words he should use to the collector of the taxes.

"This ye shall do, children of my spirit," replied Lao Tsun.   "Go to
your homes and take out of hiding all things which are hid, and all things
on which ye set store.   Hide them not, but let them lie upon the floor in
the centre of your houses.   Cover nothing and bring nothing but the garments
that you wear.   Come again quickly and do all, believing that the Law shall
prevail and the Ineffable Will be done."

And when all the village, from the oldest man to the toddling child, had
done according to his saying, they came once more before Lao Tsun, and he
made them sit down before him.

"There is a time," he said, "to speak out boldly, and there is a time
for silence.   If He who is shall, in His compassion, close the eyes of these
men of ill will, is it meet we should desire Him to close also their ears?
Sit where ye are and move not, neither let any sound escape you, befall what
may.   Hate not, fear not, and know that under all forms is the One."

After that, he also fell silent; and when the brown men came into the
place, they looked upon a work of man which had long passed into that death
from which comes forth life; for across the beaten earth and over the empty
boxes of men, trailed vines and creeping plants, hanging in dripping cur-
tains of leaf and bloom at the doorways and wrapping their stems about and
about, crossing, one upon another, while thick grasses grew from the earthen
floors of the huts as high as the waist of a man.

The little officer halted his men, then removed his spectacles and
polished them, peering with weak eyes about him.   The glasses replaced, he
consulted a map, and, erasing certain pencilled marks, inserted others.

Then the temple, its entrance almost closed by a rhododendron bush,
attracted him and he pushed his small body between the yielding foliage and
the mossy door jamb, and stepped into the green gloom within.

Seated amid the high, seeding grasses was a company not unusual in a
land of pagodas.   A green and weathered Buddha sat facing some fifty disciples, all bearing a great similarity to the Teacher, and all appearing to
be cast from the same mould.

The little brown man scratched the surface of the one nearest to his
hand, but so coated was it with the dark scale of neglected years that he
could not learn of what metal it was made.   He glanced at his wrist-watch
and turned to go; then on an impulse, drew his sword and slashed at one of
the figures.   The keen steel almost severed an ear, and, bending closely,
the officer saw that it was of brass, and of no immediate value; so he put
up his sword, squeezed out again, and gave the command to march.

(continued on page #27)

finding something wrong, yet with a chance of its correction, he should stay, but speak his mind, for maybe some will follow him and then correction can be made.   This is his duty.   But once outvoted and finally rejected, he should leave.   He will find that there are other organizations and many writers whose works are obtainable.   He may do just as well alone, or with a small group of selected friends who are in harmony.

He should be true to his best principles at all times.   If he does this, he need not waste much time, nor make mistakes which are irreparable.   Take no step backward, and the final Goal will some day be in view.

-*- -*- -*- -*- -*- -*- -*- -*- -*- -*- -*- -*- -*- -*- -*- -*- -*- -*- -*-

SILENCE IN SUNG PEN - continued from page #26

When the silence had rolled back a tremor went through the village, a slipping movement, downwards.   As a waxen image before a hot fire shudders and settles, slowly at first, but with increasing speed, while bead after bead rises and rolls down, into a formless pool, so the vegetation which covered the dwellings of Sung Pen melted and slid into that flowing ocean of matter, whence all things rise, to serve the need of an hour, or an age, and sink again; and the bare huts stood upon the bare hillside.

Within the temple Lao Tsun spoke: "You may go to your homes," he said, "for He whose sheep ye are has delivered you from the beasts of prey."

"Will they return, Holy One?" enquired the headman.

"They will not return, my son - not now.   They are gone far down the path of blindness and self-will.   They go to meet destruction of the flesh. When they do return, carried upon the Wheel, it will be in other forms, toilsomely building up where they have thrown down.   It is the Law.   Now go!"

"Holy One," piped little Dula Sao, "I made no sound though one struck me upon the head and mine ear bleeds.   Am I not a good boy, Holy One?"

"Indeed, thou art," answered Lao Tsun, and took him into his arms. "To thee, under the Most High, is due the praise that we see the sun through our mortal eyes.   I am pleased with thee, and I think that, one day, thou shalt sit in my place.   Now come, we will bind up the ear."

(Reprinted from "THE MIDDLE WAY", July-August, 1945.)

-*- -*- -*- -*- -*- -*- -*- -*- -*- -*- -*- -*- -*- -*- -*- -*- -*- -*-

"And as to you Life I reckon you are the leavings of many deaths, (No doubt I have died myself ten thousand times before.)"

Walt Whitman.

THE THEORY OF MANVANTARA - CHAKRAS:

Under the table of the YUGAS there should appear a table of the CHAKRAS, innumerable Wheels or Cycles of Time, were it possible to include them. These calculations of the periods connected with races and geological changes are never given exoterically, as they are invariably esoteric knowledge. Even the calendar of the larger Cycles, not directly connected with racial periods, as they appear in "The Secret Doctrine", does not include the true esoteric figures, but they are given in their exoteric form for the purpose of instruction and as illustration of the interlocking calculations used in the secret teachings.

Under the calendar of Cycles there should appear the divisions of time erected by the evolving national groups for the purpose of computing time. The present system of calculation, called Mortal Time to differentiate it from Divine Time, is therefore indicated in its proper place. Mortal Time is a temporary calculation, as it is not always reckoned in the same fashion. The method of computation is not necessarily the same in the different racial periods - nay, may be altered several times within the duration of a racial cycle. At best it is an expedient of the moment.

Cycles are related to the unfolding life story of the planet, primarily. It has been said that they are very closely associated with racial development, and so they are. Their first function is to agree with the geological and planetary growth or change, and to mark such planetary rhythms and laws with exactness. Racial development is subordinate to planetary development, because the races represent merely one kingdom of Life. Inevitably the racial development coincides with the planetary evolution - and both must complement, influence and support each other - but the evolution of the planet as a sum total is expressed in these cycles, not the uprising or downfall of civilizations.

Mortal Time, therefore, represents our present racial computation only. It may not represent the computation of time used by the next racial cycle - even as it does not represent the computations of many companion civilizations of ours in the world today. It should be noted that our historical time is a fractional part of the present MAHÂ YUGA, or Great Age lasting 4,320,000 years, and that even the present KALI YUGA lasting 432,000 years, a subdivision of the MAHÂ YUGA, is a period almost too vast for us to realize. Our records are not clear and precise beyond a few thousand years into the past.

Cycles are the intervening link between our historical time and the first sub-divisions of the MAHÂ YUGA, or the four YUGAS. These sub-divisions are the combination of many, many lesser cycles, each of which is contained in all the larger periods, even as our second is contained in every larger cycle, up to the Planetary Day, and beyond.

Lesser lives and lesser life periods than ours fit into our Mortal Time as our Mortal Time fits into the Divine Time, and so the wheels or CHAKRAS of the great Cycles contain innumerable wheels or CHAKRAS of the small Cycles. Such is the Law of Universes, and such is the Law of infinitesimally small portions of the Universes.

(For the CALENDAR refer to
January, 1947)

"DOES THE MODERN STUDENT ACQUIRE MERIT BY STUDYING OR BY MEDITATING?"

"Acquire merit" - KUSALA-SANCAYA - is an Eastern term. It implies a process of equalizing unfavorable Karma, the debt of previous actions. The student accumulates favorable actions, or beneficial Karma, to offset or eliminate further unfavorable Karma and to reduce the existing unfavorable Karma. To "acquire merit", therefore, one must engage in such actions as will produce favorable Karma.

As can be seen readily, merit is not acquired by studying or by meditating. The field of action is dependent upon action, is influenced only by action. Though every faculty and principle of the incarnated being may be responsible for, may be engaged in and act as the source of the actions, it is the action and the action alone which produces cause and effect - Karma, good or bad.

Study, or the pursuit of knowledge, cannot but be beneficent in its effect upon the judgment and discrimination, and in a resulting curb upon the uncontrolled emotional nature. It is the best method to begin, and it is the best method to continue, for there is never an end to learning. No one knows everything. However, study is a tool and a method, a means to an end. By itself, it will produce nothing more than a pedant and is not desirable if it does not bring wisdom and perception.

Meditation, contemplation, practice of DHYĀNA, etc., is very valuable to reach higher than the lower mind, the intellect. It is a counter-balance to the mental effort. It, also, is useless without action. Obviously, a few minutes spent in the effort to meditate does not counter-act a day spent idly, selfishly, aimlessly or unwisely.

To acquire merit for the future, one must combine the faculties of mind, heart and body, to live and be and do in accordance with the highest spiritual perception, so that one's highest and best is the level at which one lives at all times. Whatever auxiliary measures are employed to maintain or develop this level are not of the first importance, and they may differ in individual cases. The result is not to be confused with the method.

Study and meditation are methods. Action, however, may be the result of methods, and as such may be dependent on them to some extent.

The merit may be measured only by the life expression, not by the leisure time spent in study, speculation, meditation, or in mental pursuit of knowledge. All of these may be contributory, but are not the cause or originator of new Karma, unless they are expressed in action.

-*- -*- -*- -*- -*- -*- -*- -*- -*- -*- -*- -*- -*- -*- -*- -*- -*- -*- -*- -

"Man is born according to what he has created. All beings have karma as their heritage."
MAJJHIMA NIKĀYA, Vol. 1, p. #390.

Many times we have been requested to publish a work on Buddhism to enable readers to obtain a comprehensive understanding of the entire system of Buddhist thought. After careful inquiry into the matter, the Staff has decided to recommend for study and consideration, as the most valuable and concise small book of its kind -

The Buddhist Catechism

This book was written by Colonel Henry Steel Olcott, an American. It has survived the test of time.

First published in 1881, it was reviewed by Allan Octavian Hume in "THE THEOSOPHIST", edited by H. P. Blavatsky, in the September issue of 1881, page 270. Since that time it has been published in many languages, and ran into forty editions before the death of the author or compiler in 1907. In the course of the forty editions it was revised by him and given new prefaces.

We present the Fortieth Edition, published by the author in 1905, as it is the last edition revised and approved by him, and the one which contains all of his own revisions made with the approval of the High Priest Sumangala, head of the Sinhalese Buddhists.

The very interesting history of the revival of Buddhism in Ceylon and India through the efforts of Madame Blavatsky and Colonel Olcott must be omitted here for lack of space. However, it is from the author's effort to help the Buddhist people of Ceylon to understand their own philosophy that "THE BUDDHIST CATECHISM" came into being, all of which is explained in the Prefaces.

Therefore, in order to give "THE BUDDHIST CATECHISM" its proper historical setting, the Prefaces to the various editions, book reviews of historical interest, and other data, will appear as Appendices. This reprinting of the Fortieth Edition will be a tribute and memorial to the work done in the homeland of the Buddha's Dharma by a Western Buddhist.

As readers will be interested mainly in the "CATECHISM" itself, we present in this issue Colonel Olcott's Preface to the First Edition. He dedicated it to his "counsellor and friend of many years", the High Priest H. Sumangala, who was one of the outstanding figures of his time. Then the "CATECHISM" will appear serially, the first instalment in the March number of The Golden Lotus.

-*- -*- -*- -*-

by Henry Steel Olcott

"PREFACE - To the Original Edition.

"Being intended for the use of beginners, this little work aims
only to present the main facts in the life of Gautama Buddha and
the essential features of his doctrine.   Strange to say, it is
unique of its kind in Ceylon, notwithstanding that the missionaries
have scattered their Christian catechism broadcast in the island,
and for many years have been taunting the Sinhalese with the
puerility and absurdity of their religion.   To whatever cause it
may be due, this apathy is something to be deplored by every
Buddhist or admirer of the Buddhist philosophy.

"The present Catechism is largely a compilation from the works of
T. W. Rhys-Davids, Esq., Bishop Bigandet, Sir Coomara Swamy,
R. C. Childers, Esq., and the Revs. Samuel Beal and R. Spence Hardy;
in a few cases their exact language has been used.   But having
been assisted by the Venerable High Priest H. Sumangala, Principal,
and the Priest H. Devamitta, of Widyodaya College, the author's
treatment of some of the subjects will be found in certain respects
to differ from that of those writers.

"Truth to say, a very incomplete popular notion of what orthodox
Buddhism is, seems to prevail in Western countries.   The folk-lore
and fairy stories upon which some of our principal Orientalists
have mainly based their commentaries are no more orthodox Buddhism
than the wild monkish tales of the Middle Ages are orthodox
Christianity.   Only the authenticated utterances of Sakya Muni
himself are admitted as orthodox.   Deeper analysis will unques-
tionably prove to Western scholars that the Kapilavastu sage
taught six centuries before the Christian era, not only a peer-
less code of morals, but also a philosophy so broad and comprehensive as to have anticipated the inductions of modern research and
speculation.   The signs abound that of all the world's great
creeds that one is destined to be the much talked-of Religion of
the Future which shall be found in least antagonism with Nature
and with Natural Law.   Who dare predict that Buddhism will not
be the one chosen?

"Though the author gratefully acknowledges his obligations to
Messrs. E. F. Perera, Proctor, and W. D'Abrew, for their services
as interpreters between the revered priests and himself, yet he
claims for the many imperfections that will doubtless be found in
the following pages the indulgence of all who have tried to do such
work as this through intermediaries.   His ignorance of Pali and
Sinhalese has prevented his doing anything like adequate justice
to the subject; but he hopes to avail himself in future editions
of the criticisms the present one may call forth.

                              H. S. O."

SAROS: (Greek)   (February, 1947, p. #22)

   A Chaldean cycle, known to the Babylonian astronomers. It represented
an astronomical period, the duration of which is 6,575 days and 8 hours, or
223 lunar months. As it appears in "Isis Unveiled" it is explained by the
context. It appears also in "The Secret Doctrine" (Vol. I, p. #113) and is
there defined: "For the circle is Sar, and Saros, or cycle, and was the
Babylonian god whose circular horizon was the visible symbol of the invisible."
With the word "Great" preceding, it is the Grand Cycle. It is a MAHÂ period,
or cosmic measurement, not a limited planetary cycle or smaller length of time.

CHAKRA: (Sanskrit)   (February, 1947, p. #28)

   This word is adapted to various uses, like the words MANVANTARA, PRA-
LAYA, etc. All of them are used to describe various periods, and it is necessary to differentiate between the various periods and to realize which one
is intended by the context of the original writings wherein the Sanskrit words
appear. CHAKRA, a wheel, is used to speak of the lengths of time which com-
pose a recurring cycle, the periodicity varying. Many figures of our speech
today convey this symbolism - "the wheel of time", "time rolls on", and the
most expressive "wheels within wheels". CHAKRA conveyed the idea of cycles
to the ancient civilization of India long before the present civilization
had sprung from early races of the western hemisphere.

YUGA: (Sanskrit)   (February, 1947, p. #28)

   Literally - an Age. A specific term of years, or centuries. It does
not represent an indefinite "eternity". Prefixes are used to differentiate
the YUGAS, four in number, following each other in order during the entire
period of the Day of Brahmâ. They are - KRITA, TRETÂ, DWÂPARA, and KALI.

MAHÂ YUGA: (Sanskrit)   (February, 1947, p. #28)

   The prefix MAHÂ, or Great, confines this title to the length of time
called "The Great Age" - 4,320,000 years. Within this period there are four
"Ages", the four YUGAS, one succeeding the other. Sometimes an alternative
title is used for the Great Age - CHATUR YUGA, or Four Yugas. For the
Calendar of Ages, etc., see January, 1947, page #11.

ARHAT:	(Sanskrit)	from page #21	See April, 1944, page #25
DHARMA:	(Sanskrit)	" " 18	" May, 1946, " 77
DHYÂNA:	(Sanskrit)	" " 29	" December,1945 " 166
DUHKHA:	(Sanskrit)	" " 18	" March, 1945, " 39
HÎNAYÂNA:	(Sanskrit)	" " 33	" January, 1947, " 15
MAHÂYÂNA:	(Sanskrit)	" " 17	" January, 1947, " 15
MANVANTARA:	(Sanskrit)	" " 28	" July, 1946, " 109

-*- -*- -*- -*-

ABOUT BOOKS

The policy of THE GOLDEN LOTUS during its lifetime of three years has been
to present to its readers the Eastern Philosophy of the MAHĀYĀNA form of
Buddhism, but also to include such HĪNAYĀNA sources, authorities and writings
as might be available.

Only a few MAHĀYĀNA books have been translated into English, and these are
not available at present.   Comments by exponents of the MAHĀYĀNA school of
thought are printed in English, but unfortunately are not obtainable at
present.   The works of Dwight Goddard, for instance, are not now in print.
Professor D. T. Suzuki's expositions of the MAHĀYĀNA, and valuable publications by other authors, are likewise unobtainable.   However, The Pali Text
Society has diligently made available in English master-pieces of the HĪNA-
YĀNA, and it is possible to obtain these even after the war years.

Helena P. Blavatsky's writings, including as they do the Hindu Cosmogony, the
Buddhist system, the references to the great writers and teachers of the past,
and the profound wisdom of her Eastern Teachers, have been presented as
reference books for the convenience of Western students.   Translations of
the Eastern SŪTRAS and the Commentaries thereon are often difficult to obtain,
contain unexplained phrases or definitions, are expensive, and since the war
are practically non-existent.   Therefore, the readily obtainable books
written by Helena P. Blavatsky for the Western student were, and are, the
first recommendation of THE GOLDEN LOTUS to all students.

Second recommendation in line has been books of The Buddhist Society, London,
as these books contain Buddhism for the Western viewpoint, written by Western
students, and therefore they are most near to the thought level of the
Western inquirer.

Third in line will be such Eastern publications, in English, as The Maha
Bodhi Society in India may be able to send us when publication is resumed.

Still available, here and there, what we may call scholar's books are to be
found, but they are expensive and sometimes deal with only one aspect of the
vast field of Buddhism.   Nevertheless they are of great interest to all
advanced students.   A list of such of these books as may be obtained is included in this issue.   They are not carried in stock.

Sometimes a new and worthy book appears, or an old edition is reprinted.
These will be added to The Book List from time to time.

We trust our readers will understand The Book List is slowly gathering into
condensation the work of many months of search for the most worthy books
upon the subject matter of THE GOLDEN LOTUS.   Conditions, adverse and unusual
in the book world, have made the task arduous and difficult, and in many cases
a source of extreme disappointment, as the most valuable books have vanished
from the publishers' shelves during the last five years.

With these words of explanation, we hope our readers will be able to evaluate
properly the few books we have been able to place upon The Book List of
The Golden Lotus Press.

The Book List

BOOKS OBTAINABLE ON ORDER:

A Dictionary of Chinese Buddhist Terms, with Sanskrit and English equivalents, and Sanskrit-Pali Index	W. A. Soothill and L. Hodous	₤3-10/-
A History of Buddhist Thought	E. J. Thomas	17/6-
A Practical Sanskrit Dictionary: with Transliteration, Accentuation and Etymological Analysis Throughout	A. A. Macdonell	$11.00
A Sanskrit Grammar For Students	A. A. Macdonell	$4.25
Buddhavangsa and Cariyâpitaka	B. C. Law	10/6-
Buddhism In Translation (reprinting)	H. C. Warren	$3.00
Dialogues of The Buddha, Vol. 1 Vol. 3	T. W. and Mrs. Rhys-Davids	12/6- 12/6-
Dhammapada, Khuddakapâtha (Text and Translation)	Mrs. Rhys Davids	10/6-
Eastern Religions and Western Thought	S. Radhakrishnan	$5.00
Indian Philosophy, Vol. 1 (Reprinting) Vol. 2 (Reprinting)	S. Radhakrishnan "	$5.25 $6.25
Legacy of Egypt	S. R. K. Glanville	$4.00
Legacy of Greece	R. W. Livingstone	$3.00
Legacy of India	G. T. Garratt	$4.00
Petavatthu, Vimâna-Vatthu	Gehman & Kennedy	10/6-
Puggala-Pannatti (Designation of Human Types)	B. C. Law	10/-
The Book of Discipline, Vinaya, Sutta Vibhanga, Vols. 2 and 3	I. B. Horner	ea. 10/6-
The Debates Commentary (on Kathâvatthu)	B. C. Law	10/-
The Religion of Tibet	Sir Chas. A. Bell	$6.00
Udâna, Iti-Vuttaka	F. L. Woodward	10/6-
Visuddhi-Magga Vol. 1 (The Path of Purity)	P. Maung Tin	10/-

NOTE: Many of these books are published abroad, therefore
a few weeks must be allowed for delivery.

-*- -*- -*- -*-

THE GOLDEN LOTUS

Reg. U. S. Pat. Off.

"FOR HOLY VIRTUE, FOR HIGH ENDEAVOR,
FOR SUBLIME WISDOM - FOR THESE
THINGS DO WE WAGE WAR; THEREFORE
ARE WE CALLED WARRIORS."

Gautama Buddha

VOL.4

1947

KALI YUGA

Many people think that if the world civilization were to be alike in every quarter of the globe, and if the nations were to be of one faith, one union, one democracy, or some such concept of equality, there would be no war and no international contention. Unthinking individuals speak as if their own particular type of life and environment should be the ideal and satisfactory standard for everyone else in the world.

These people do not understand that the "outsiders" may have a type of life and environment suited to and most agreeable to them, and that in turn the outsiders may pity the ones outside their particular paradise. Nor is it to be expected that, even were such an impossibility to happen by some miracle, the outsiders would enjoy the enforced inclusion in conditions uncongenial to them.

Even the Pax Romana - considered by its enforcers to be the most beneficial state of affairs for the provinces of the Roman Empire - was resented, fought, endured and eventually overthrown with joy. Yet for more than two hundred years the civilized world rested under what an ancient writer calls "the immense majesty of the Roman peace." The victims of the enforced peace, secured by the Roman domination, may have acquired civilized arts and refinements, but they by no means outgrew the tendency to conquer and to rule, or the enduring thirst for freedom. When the controls were gone, the conquered provinces resumed their interrupted evolutionary pathway prompted by the same desires and proclivities in evidence before the Roman legions brought the hated peace.

No equality is obtainable, no agreement is likely to evolve, until the nations join in complete and voluntary harmony. But when this enduring peace agreement may arrive is problematical; it will not be possible until the last ambitious tyrant outgrows his selfishness. One such dictator, in all the world, will make the enforced peace the only alternative. One such aggressive conqueror will delay the complete agreement of the nations.

Today the time is ripe for an enforced peace, as it has been through history at stated intervals. It may be that the nations who must perforce work with ploughshares will become a little more impotent with the sword. That is only a slim possibility, but it is the hope of all who try to enforce peace.

However, the work of evolution is a slow process and the evolutionary pace will not be hastened. The nations grow toward the future, and it must be understood they grow by suffering and by the trial-and-error method. So do all beings, and so do all nations, in the Kali Yuga.

-*- -*- -*- -*-

THE DHARMA

DUHKHA SAMUDAYA - The Cause of Suffering

Many people endure suffering, believing it to be the "will of God", or the consequences of an obscure rebellion by mysterious forefathers, or due to disobedience of divine command, or to the computed sins of the fathers visited upon the children, and other metaphysical reasons invented by the priests of all faiths.   These are very comfortable excuses, if accepted, as they relieve the sufferer from any feeling of responsibility.   They enable him to continue in his mode of selfish living, happily secure in the certainty that he will be safe hereafter if he "believes".   The excuses have robbed him of the driving power of the suffering, which otherwise might cause him to think, to reason, to seek cessation of the suffering, to alter his mode of living.   The palliative has drugged him into an indifferent acceptance of the educator, pain, and held him at a point of arrested motion.

Suffering is not a punishment visited upon a helpless creature; it is a result of action.   It is not a legacy from forefathers remote and distant; it is a heritage of past action.   It is not a condition impossible to cure, but the cure of any long-seated cause must take a long time.

The whole approach to the understanding of suffering through excuses is wrong; it must be altered before the cure may be attempted.   If the approach to understanding were corrected, Man would look first of all to himself for the Cause of Suffering.   He would see in himself the originator of Ignorance, and all the train of evil resulting from Ignorance.   He would struggle with his own imperfections and cease to complain of his neighbor's imperfections.   He would seek happiness and well-being for all, and so strive to lift the misery from his fellow-men.   He would seek endlessly for the Cause of Suffering, and he would not be satisfied with palliatives or opiates to drown his pain.

However, in all ages, the few seek for the Cause, while others endure the results.   So it is that during the evolutionary journey, the few succeed, and the few leave the landmarks for others.

What is the Cause of Suffering?   So varied is this Cause, so many, many untoward events create the momentary present pain.   So many, many past causes created the present environment, the cause of the enduring pain. So many, many present causes are creating the future pain.   It would be best to call the long pain Life, or Incarnation, or Manifestation, for truly it is that, and truly the Buddha spoke words of wisdom when he said:

"This, O Bhikkhus, is the Noble Truth of Suffering: birth is suffering; decay is suffering; illness is suffering; death is suffering. Presence of objects we hate, is suffering; separation from objects we love, is suffering; not to obtain what we desire, is suffering. Briefly the five-fold clinging to existence is suffering."

and taught his followers to seek the final release from future manifestation, as the proper way to end the present and the future suffering.

The Gods And Time

The Gods are temporary and effervescent bubbles, rising from the surging depths of the vast ocean of the Time dimension. Scattered like rainbow prisms, they shine and scintillate with all the colors of the sky, the reflected glory of the higher world of Spirit. They collapse and disappear, drawn into their supporting element, leaving no trace, for the restless tide of Time erases even the memory, and there is no more bubble shining in the sun, dazzling the cognizing mind with a reflected beauty not its own.

Such bubbles are co-existent with the duration of the upward thrust of Spirit seeking to reach its own true home, the world of Spirit. They become only where Spirit - imprisoned in Matter, Time and Space - succeeds in breaking through into a quasi-union or half-absorption into its origin.

The tide of Time rolls on, supporting for a period the bubble, which has come to be upon the surface of the manifested world of thought, feeling and action. Such bubbles - globules of Spirit mixed with a minimum of Matter - last for what we call the centuries, but the centuries are only seconds in the larger scheme.

The bubbles appear and disappear, and change and glow and flicker - but are not the same bubbles. They vanish, because the tide of Time evaporates or re-absorbs or withdraws the Spirit enmeshed within the film of Matter holding the globule together. The crevices of Time and tide hold these bubbles, crushed and broken, and the waves of the great ocean have thrown upon them weight and volume. Thereby the bubbles become devoid of the sustaining ethereality, the Spirit in them, and become once more particles or globules of Matter.

The inexhaustible Sun of Spirit blazes above the tide of Time, and draws upward other bubbles, reflecting in the bubbles other colors, other aspects of Itself, yet showing in no bubble all Itself, or all Its glory.

The bubbles seek the Sun, and seek the Light, and they are evidence of the reunion of all Spirit with the Source, in time beyond our calculations. No bubble is the Sun, though they are beautiful. They have a value, but the value is to reflect and to shine with a reflected glory. They must portray the Absolute infinite Time, and by their color show the Unborn and the Undying Source of All Creation, the Eternal Spirit, shining through the world of Matter.

No easy task for small and man-made bubbles, breaking through the weight of Matter into the world of Spirit. No lasting task for any bubble. For all is change, and all is growth, and all is progress, and the tide of Time wipes out the failures as well as the successes, only to set the living Spirit once more free from the imprisoning Matter. Only to leave the Spirit free to thrust again toward the sky, to form a new and clearer bubble, resplendent with the ever-constant Light of the over-shadowing, circumambient Splendour.

-*- -*- -*- -*-

MÂYÂ

What is the Eastern meaning?

It is generally translated Illusion. This term has become stereotyped
and meaningless. Illusion to the Western mind is a false appearance,
a mirage, or deceptive mask. Far from this meaning is the Eastern
understanding of the temporary appearance or existence of the worlds
and all therein. This temporary but true appearance is called MÂYÂ -
not enduring, not complete, not Cause.

What is included in this meaning?

All creation, purely and completely temporary. The mask of Time and
Space in the Duration, changing, never the same, unendingly illusive
and elastic. Nothing stable exists in the MANVANTARA. All is change.
This is MÂYÂ.

Why do the Western scholars say Illusion?

Because it appears to them to be a good synonym. It is not, however.

When does MÂYÂ begin?

When the great impulse of the Day of Brahmâ calls forth into manifestation the worlds of being, and the Cosmos rolls upon its path again in
full activity.

When does MÂYÂ end?

When the long Night of Brahma casts its darkening shadows the MÂYÂ
slows, and finally the worlds crash into the completely passive state,
and all the MÂYÂ ends. The Night shuts down.

But people speak of small events, or periods, as MÂYÂ?

They do. They should know better. It is perhaps a little more com-
prehensible if the long period of Activity of the Cosmos is called
MAHÂMÂYÂ - the great drama of the created worlds upon the stage of the
unfathomable impulse of creation, the web of the Illusive Scheme of
Evolution, the Pageant of the Universes. The smaller Illusive
Schemes, such as our world, might then be MÂYÂ.

Should one call short episodes, minute occurrences, MÂYÂ?

Since all is MÂYÂ - yes. Since all is temporary - yes. Since all
is changing - yes. But we too, and all created beings and objects,
are MÂYÂ. Why speak, then, of an isolated, personal, and not very
important event as MÂYÂ?

The East thinks only in terms of the creation, when it speaks of MÂYÂ?

    Exactly.

There is no pessimism possible in that viewpoint.

    There never was.   It is a viewpoint of joy and unbelievable illumina-
    tion.   It realizes that behind the temporary there is the Timeless,
    behind the changing there is the Changeless, behind the imperfect there
    is the Perfect, and behind the form there is the Formless.

(to be continued)

-*- -*- -*- -*- -*- -*- -*- -*- -*- -*- -*- -*- -*- -*- -*- -*- -*- -*- -*-

SEA - ROBED

Earth, being very much afraid
In the Realm of Light,
Sought to hide or to escape
From that Glory Bright.

As she fell the density
Gathered round her form
Making veils of rainbow light
And of airy storm.

Slipping from the level where
The great Sun is King,
She sought refuge and a home
Lower, 'neath His wing.

Then she fled below that place,
And behold - she found
Water, mist and atmosphere
Robing her around.

And she fell, to find His rays
Ever on her face.
Making no protest or plea
Still she fled full pace.

There she paused and hid herself
In the Water zone.
Vapor shut the Sun from sight
Leaving her alone.

There converging density
Closed around her, till
She assumed the spheriform
And retains it still.

Sea-robed, now, the planet lies
Far beneath the Light,
Screened, and well content to rest
From her age-long flight.

-*- -*- -*- -*-

Long, long ago, in the first dawn of the planet, there came into being a race of powerful and exceedingly swift ethereal denizens of the tenuous and volatile element we now call atmosphere or air. At that time the Earth was slowly forming and condensing, but the hard core of the compressed atomic structure was not so dense; in fact, it was still hot and molten. Fluidic as the nebular center was, it still had a definite and positive direction and purpose in its fluidity, and even then a periodicity, a regularly alternating day and night of summer and of winter. Conditions were so different, however, that it were best to think of them as nebular and fiery, somewhat misty, and of no value to the present denizens of the hard core of Bhûmi.

The races of intellectual giants were not even dreamed of in that age of slow formation. The ages of slowly developing forests, seas, plains, mountains, and the towering sky-scrapers of today, were a prospect seemingly impossible to the imagination. The vortex of the nebula was fluid - air, water, fire, and rock in liquid, all in motion.

Into this laya there came the elemental lives of fire and air, derived from the preceding Manvantara's evolution. They took possession. Somewhat comet-like, they streamed through the laya's various densities, and descended into the compacting center with equal ease and freedom. They were the intensely active forces of the elements of Fire and Air, bequeathing to the swirling vortex its first faint flush of life creative.

Satisfied with nothing denser than Fire and Air, they were in their true element. They could and did exist and live and grow there, into their full maturity, before the vortex settled into a globe, before the core had hardened into a ball of heavy matter, and the oceans had been formed upon it. For that came later. By that time the race of Fire-Air dwellers had departed, grown into their perfection, and the hour had struck for other actors to make their entrance upon the stage of planetary evolution.

They left us no mementos, so far behind it was in time. They had no chance to leave a message for us graven in the fluid, ever-changing matter. They could not grasp at stone, for it was molten, and wood had not evolved. They passed, and vanished in another system's swirl of nebular matter, leaving the globe, for it prohibited their further evolution in its hardening state.

But they were useful, and they left behind - these comet-ones- the heritage of Fire. They had no bodies, but they were, nevertheless, the nearest appearance to a body yet seen within the swirling laya. They were the pristine, glowing, swift and fiery Sons of Manvantaric Morning, come to speed the process of the nebula. They directed and intensified the circular and settling motion, by their own speed and flight and power, and they left the laya not until it had assumed the permanent direction and settled into the round swirl of ultimate cohesion.

They were the first race of intelligence to come to this our planet.

(continued on page #43)

THE SEEKER

"Strive, then, to find the Guide, and when the
Guide appears, rejoice!"

Padma Hiranya Surangama.

The Seeker has no goal; he has not been informed. He has
not found the Path; he seeks for Light. He finds the detours
hard; the many disappointments try his endurance and his
purpose to proceed.

The Seeker makes a step when he assumes, at last, the role of
aspirant and listener. He could not, while he sought, be
satisfied with any path, or route to a Goal beyond his comprehension. But when he finds the Path, or glimpses the
far-distant Goal, he leaves the task of seeking, and becomes
instead Aspirant, one who·strives to achieve Perfection.

Here is the line of demarcation between the Seeker and the
SRÂVAKA - one who aspires to acquire Wisdom by listening
and practising. The Seeker sought, but hardly practised.
The Aspirant may seek to acquire Wisdom in his effort to
achieve Perfection, but he has advanced to the true point
of self-direction; he practises that which he learns.
While the Aspirant seeks instruction and wise guidance,
the Seeker merely seeks the entrance to The Way.

Therefore, the Aspirant becomes and strives and grows and
lives by the directions he may have found, and by the Truth
within him. He must be guided by the Truth within him,
and he must reach out for counsel. He is the Youth in
growth, who strives to reach full stature.

* * *

(This article is by the talented New York artist whose lotus
designs appear on the front covers of the magazine.)

Popular conceptions of the lotus seem rather hazy in most Western minds,
being something of a mixture of a water-lily and Buddha-seat in form rather
than the wild, beautiful flower that it is.   There is no doubt that it has
played a very important part in near- and far-eastern symbology, but the
existence of the flower is not confined to Egypt or India.

This month's cover illustrates the pristine beauty of one of our native
water-lilies.   In its own way, it reflects the glory of its kindred sister
of the East, the Indian lotus.   Although shyly staying near the water, its
fostering element, it can still tell us of the glorious Sun, the Lord of the
Planet, when it opens its glistening white petals, to expose its golden heart.
Everyone has had the opportunity, at one time or another, to see the common
pond lily, but those who are aware that it is possible to see, touch and
smell the stately, exotic lotus within the borders of the U. S. A. are few
and far between.

For those who live in the Southern States, the lily pool is a fairly
common occurrence.   I know of at least one in the famous water gardens of
North Carolina, and have been told of the great frequency with which one can
see them all through the South.   In the District of Columbia there are two
public displays with which I am acquainted.   One is a long pool in front of
the new Department of State Building, which contains the smaller African
lotuses.   The other is the Kenilworth Aquatic Gardens, perhaps one of the
largest and most varied of all the collections in the United States.

The latter has a curious history, having its birth in the homesickness
of Walter B. Shaw, a government employee, for a sight of the water-lilies of
his native Maine.   He sent for some roots and planted them in his pasture by
the Potomac, where they flourished.   His daughter, Mrs. Helen S. Fowler,
helped him to cultivate them.   Soon friends began demanding roots to start
their own ponds.   Business became so flourishing, that Shaw decided to leave
the Treasury Department and devote his time to the lily-raising business.   In
this his daughter's help became indispensable.   She trucked the flowers into
the city, and spent much of her time travelling about collecting new speci-
mens of water plants.   Her searches took her to many out-of-the-way places
all over the globe, China, India, Japan, the jungles of South America, Egypt,
and so on.   From the types she collected, the father and daughter hybridized
new and very beautiful varieties.   It was on one of her excursions to the
jungles of Trinidad that she first got the idea of painting the flowers which
she could not possibly take back with her.   At that time she was 52 years old.

The U. S. Department of the Interior finally took over the gardens as
part of Anacostia National Park after Mr. Shaw's demise.   Mrs. Fowler was
given its directorship because of her superior knowledge and experience in
building it up.   Today, retired and untaught except for gleanings from the
criticisms and comments of visitors to her gallery, she paints in water
colours and pastels her beloved subject, flowers.   She has many fine por-
traits to her credit, also.   In my opinion her paintings are masterpieces

of the painter's art, with all the spirit and beauty that can be found in sun-drenched flowers on a wind-swept bank.

Those people farther north are not neglected.   Aside from the wild varieties that can be found on the banks of most any mountain lake, one can see under cultivation in city areas many of the exotic varieties of lilies. There is a commercial water-lily farm at Toms River, N.J., and another in Westchester County, N.Y.   In Morristown, N.J., there is an exhibit of lilies in the pool in front of the Municipal Building.   The arrangement was quite startling to me, as I was not expecting to find a Taj Mahal effect so close to home.   The pool contained varieties of the pink and blue Nelumbium Zanzibarensis.

In the Botanical Gardens at Bronx Park in New York City, one can see as many as 82 varieties of water-plants from late July to frost. Among these are several of the Egyptian blue lotus variety, the feathery papyrus, and the East Indian lotus, not to mention the smaller hardy and tropical varieties.

The Brooklyn Botanical Garden boasts of two displays.   In the pools near the greenhouse are kept tropical varieties of lilies and lotuses of many beautiful colors.   In the Japanese garden is a most attractive and natural exhibit of the hardy, rose-colored, Pekin Lotus.   For those of us in the North who cannot manage to go to Kenilworth Gardens, this exhibit is of great worth in giving an idea of how the lotus grows wild.   It is a peaceful thing to sit on the bank of the small lake and listen to the wind making music in the swaying leaves and see the rose-colored flower turn its lovely head to the sun.   As shades of cool evening fall, the Adornment of the Lake closes her petals and sleeps till dawn.

-*- -*- -*- -*- -*- -*- -*- -*- -*- -*- -*- -*- -*- -*- -*- -*- -*- -*- -*-

SONS OF MANVANTARA MORNING - continued from page #40

Their name was written SYLPH in the old books of gnostics, but what the word conveyed to these philosophers was written thus because the world did not believe in Manvantara Mornings.   These glowing Sons of Fire and Air are mighty servants of the cosmic forces, and their place is only in the midst of Fire and molten, airy matter.   They are not Salamanders.

Today there are no traces of these mighty Intelligences, for we are now sunk deep into the descending scale of Matter, far, far below the level of matter vaporous, gaseous and glowing.   They do not descend into the depth of density, but wait in their true element, and catch the ball of matter when it ascends again toward its tenuous state.

And there, again, they are the Sons of Manvantara Morning, for there the wheel of evolution has created a new laya or force center, and the wheel calls for another concentration of dense matter.

-*- -*- -*- -*- -*- -*- -*- -*- -*- -*- -*- -*- -*- -*- -*- -*- -*- -*- -

"It has been said of the Middle or Golden Way 'It is better to call it a Path, so narrow is the passage between monsters'."

The Agni Yoga Series - AUM, 1938, #318.

THE THEORY OF MANVANTARA - DIVINE TIME:

This is a purely arbitrary title, given to make a contrast with our "mortal" time. Divine Time is associated with the "immortal" races of the evolutionary field of the planet. These races are sometimes called "gods" and sometimes are called "devâh". There is no connection between this title and the accepted meaning of the word "divine" in the minds of Western students - namely, sacred, holy, associated with a Divine Being, or with a heaven world.

Used here, Divine Time means simply a calculation of time cycles by a larger ratio, appropriate to the "immortals", the devâh, or hidden evolutions, whose lifetimes are much longer. But in one sense they are not immortal, in that they do not exist eternally without change.

Language in which to transpose the meanings of the more expressive Sanskrit terms is very limited. Many times an English word is used which is the one most close, most expressive, but is hopelessly confused with a meaning allied to Western thought and philosophy. Allowances must be made for this limitation of language, and for the lengthy explanations necessary to clarify the finer shades of meaning involved.

Definitely, Divine or Immortal Time is not the Cosmic Time. The devâh are still planetary, and therefore must be considered as part of the planet.

The Cosmic Years of BRAHMÂ, containing all the planetary calendars of all the worlds, is beyond even the larger ratio of planetary Divine Time. There is, of course, no intention to confuse the word "God" or "Deity", as conceived by Western theology, with the word BRAHMÂ, but if such a confusion has appeared to any one, it is hereby corrected. The two ideals of BRAHMÂ and of God are entirely different in essence. BRAHMÂ, in Eastern Philosophy, does not represent the Absolute, the Cause, but is a temporary Manifestation of that Cause.

Many people wish to live forever, but a glance at these Calendars will show the incredibly long periods of time assigned by the GUPTA VIDYÂ to the life of the planet, a very small portion of the Cosmos. Beyond that time - with all its changes and unimaginable evolution of the globe and its inhabitant life - there exist still the MAHÂ KALPAS, only one of which is 311,040,000,000,000 of our mortal years. There would be many reasons to seek rest from active manifestation before that time passes.

The KALPAS are, in themselves, an undertaking, for they last 4,320,000,000 years, and yet one KALPA is merely a Day in BRAHMÂ'S AGE which lasts for one hundred years, or a MAHÂ KALPA. After BRAHMÂ'S AGE, the MAHÂ PRALAYA closes down, and the Night is dark and long before another KALPA ushers in the new bright morning of the next MAHÂ KALPA. For the KALPAS, or Days, succeed each other, as the planetary YUGAS or Ages follow each other, and all is endless alternation - rest and full activity.

(continued on page #50)

"HAVE WE BEEN, SOMETIMES, IN OTHER LANDS, IN OTHER LIVES?"

Generally speaking, it is safe to assume that any one of the units of the present wave of evolving Life has come to its present development through a long process of rebirth in many forms.

Under the consciousness of every evolving unit there is a deep sub-consciousness, perhaps of various previous civilizations, and the sum total of the previous experiences.   This hazy half-recollection may be stronger in some units than it is in others.   Also, circumstances may impress a life or an experience more deeply on some impressionable natures, and the result is a half-memory, half-certainty.   These more sensitive units are the very fortunate ones who approach the remembrance of their past.   Nevertheless, the past is not easily remembered in full detail.   It is the usual fate of reincarnated beings to forget the past completely.   The skeptical and matter-of-fact individual may belong to this category.

It is inevitable that the units of the wave of Life should be cosmopoli-tan.   They are reborn in different cyclic periods, and they must be expected to survive the past civilizations.   They are the enduring and the eternal Flame expressing Itself through Time, and they are therefore imperishable. The civilizations are an expression of that Flame, and are not imperishable or eternal.   When the Flame flickers and the civilization dies, the steadying Flame creates a new civilization, and the Life units of the Flame illuminate that new civilization.

It is as if the comprehensive view of evolution during the long life of the planet showed the many race types and nationalities as geographical divisions, and the many civilizations as divisions of another measure, Time. The units progress through both of these dimensional divisions and sub-divisions and are benefited by each change of locale.

They take the utmost from and give their utmost contribution to the temporary habitation they find in each incarnation.   They grow and live and die, and are in each locality completely part of their environment, except in cases where the consciousness is not able to close out a recollection or a strong impression of a past habitation.   Sometimes these strong impres-sions rule, and that remembering unit is a misfit, or unhappy, in that new and present habitation.

This is a general and very comprehensive answer, not one which considers any unit or any trend or any race or time.   The Rule of Reincarnation is here expressed.   The exceptions, the unusual cases, the laggards, the swift, the myriad combinations of speeds and characteristics, must be imagined, and somehow combined into the general, the Rule.

-*- -*- -*- -*- -*- -*- -*- -*- -*- -*- -*- -*- -*- -*- -*- -*- -*- -*- -*-

"Having heard the True Way in the morning, what matters it if one should come to die at night?"

THE SAYINGS OF CONFUCIUS
(The Wisdom of the East Series)

by Henry S. Olcott

(Reprint of the 40th -
 last Edition approved
 and corrected by
 the author.)

PART I.

The Life of the Buddha.

1. Question.   Of what religion* are you?
   Answer.   The Buddhist.

   * The word "religion" is most inappropriate to apply to Buddhism,
   which is not a religion, but a moral philosophy, as I have shown
   later on.   But by common usage the word has been applied to all
   groups of people who profess a special moral doctrine, and is so
   employed by statisticians.   The Sinhalese Buddhists have never
   yet had any conception of what Europeans imply in the etymological construction of the Latin root of this term.   In their creed
   there is no such thing as a "binding" in the Christian sense -
   a submission to or merging of self in a Divine Being.   A'GAMA
   is their vernacular word to express their relation to Buddhism
   and the Buddha.   It is pure Sanskrit, and means "approach, or
   coming;" and as "Buddha" is enlightenment, the compound word by
   which they indicate Buddhism - BUDDHAGAMA - would be properly
   rendered as "an approach or coming to enlightenment," or possibly
   as a following of the Doctrine of SAKYAMUNI.   The missionaries,
   finding A'GAMA ready to their hand, adopted it as the equivalent
   for "religion"; and Christianity is written by them Christiani-
   agama, whereas it should be Christianibandhana, for bandhana is
   the etymological equivalent for "religion".   The name Vibhajja
   vâda - one who analyses - is another name given to a Buddhist,
   and Advayavâdi is a third.   With this explanation, I continue
   to employ under protest the familiar word when speaking of
   Buddhistic philosophy, for the convenience of the ordinary
   reader.

2. Q.   What is Buddhism?
   A.   It is a body of teachings given out by a great personage known as
        the Buddha.

3. Q.   Is "Buddhism" the best name for this teaching?
   A.   No: that is only a western term; the best name for it is Bauddha
        Dharma.

4. Q.   Would you call a person a Buddhist who had merely been born of
        Buddhist parents?
   A.   Certainly not.   A Buddhist is one who not only professes belief
        in the Buddha as the noblest of Teachers, in the Doctrine
        preached by Him, and in the Brotherhood of Arahats, but also
        practises His precepts in daily life.

5. Q.   What is a male lay Buddhist called?
    A.   An Upâsaka.

6. Q.   What a female?
    A.   An Upâsikâ.

7. Q.   When was this doctrine first preached?
    A.   There is some disagreement as to the actual date, but according to
         the Sinhalese Scriptures it was in the year 2513 of the (present)
         Kali-Yuga.

8. Q.   Give the important dates in the last birth of the Founder?
    A.   He was born under the constellation Visâ on a Tuesday in May, in the
         year 2478 (K.Y.); he retired to the jungle in the year 2506;
         became Buddha in 2513; and, passing out of the round of rebirths,
         entered Paranirvâna in the year 2558, aged eighty years.   Each
         of these events happened on a day of full-moon, so all are con-
         jointly celebrated in the great festival of the full-moon of the
         month Wesak (Vaisakha), corresponding to the month of May.

9. Q.   Was the Buddha God?
    A.   No:- Buddha Dharma teaches no "divine" incarnation.

10. Q.   Was he a man?
    A.   Yes; but the wisest, noblest and most holy being, who had developed
         himself in the course of countless births far beyond all other
         beings, the previous BUDDHAS alone excepted.

11. Q.   Were there other Buddhas before him?
    A.   Yes; as will be explained later on.

12. Q.   Was Buddha his name?
    A.   No.   It is the name of a condition or state of mind, of the mind
         after it has reached the culmination of development.

13. Q.   What is its meaning?
    A.   Enlightened; or, he who has the all-perfect wisdom.   The Pali
         phrase is SABBANNU, the One of Boundless Knowledge.   In
         Sanskrit it is SARVAJNA.

14. Q.   What was the Buddha's real name, then?
    A.   SIDDHA'RTHA was his royal name, and GAUTAMA, or GO'TAMA, his family
         name.   He was Prince of Kapilavastu and belonged to the illus-
         trious family of the Okkâka, of the Solar race.

15. Q.   Who were his father and mother?
    A.   KingSuddHôdana and Queen Mâyâ, called Mahâ Mâyâ.

16. Q.   What people did this King reign over?
    A.   The Sâkyas; an Aryan tribe of Kshattriyas.

17. Q.   Where was Kapilavastu?
    A.   In India, one hundred miles north-east of the city of Benares, and

17. A.   about forty miles from the Himâlaya mountains. It is situated
(cont.)   in the Nepâl Terai.   The city is now in ruins.

18. Q.   On what river?
    A.   The Rôhinî, now called the Kohana.

19. Q.   Tell me again when Prince Siddhârtha was born?
    A.   Six hundred and twenty-three years before the Christian era.

20. Q.   Is the exact spot known?
    A.   It is now identified beyond question.   An archaeologist in the
         service of the Government of India has discovered in the jungle
         of the Nepâl Terai a stone pillar erected by the mighty Buddhist
         sovereign, Asôka, to mark the very spot.   The place was known
         in those times as the Lumbinî Garden.

21. Q.   Had the Prince luxuries and splendours like other Princes?
    A.   He had; his father, the King, built him three magnificent palaces -
         for the three Indian seasons - the cold, the hot, and the rainy -
         of nine, five, and three stories respectively, and handsomely
         decorated.

22. Q.   How were they situated?
    A.   Around each palace were gardens of the most beautiful and fragrant
         flowers, with fountains of spouting water, the trees full of
         singing birds, and peacocks strutting over the ground.

23. Q.   Was he living alone?
    A.   No; in his sixteenth year he was married to the Princess Yasôdharâ,
         daughter of the King Suprabuddha.   Many beautiful maidens,
         skilled in dancing and music, were also in continual attendance
         to amuse him.

24. Q.   How did he get his wife?
    A.   In the ancient Kshattriya or warrior fashion by overcoming all com-
         petitors in games and exercises of skill and prowess, and then
         selecting Yasôdharâ out of all the young princesses, whose
         fathers had brought them to the tournament or mela.

25. Q.   How, amid all this luxury, could a Prince become all-wise?
    A.   He had such natural wisdom that when but a child he seemed to under-
         stand all arts and sciences almost without study.   He had the
         best teachers, but they could teach him nothing that he did not
         seem to comprehend immediately.

26. Q.   Did he become Buddha in his splendid palaces?
    A.   No: He left all and went alone into the jungle.

27. Q.   Why did he do this?
    A.   To discover the cause of our sufferings and the way to escape
         from them.

28. Q.   Was it not selfishness that made him do this?
    A.   No; it was boundless love for all beings that made him devote
         himself to their good.
                              (to be continued)

_____

<u>SÂKYAMUNI:</u>   (Sanskrit)   •   (December, 1945, p. #161)

   Literally, Sage of the Sâkyas, or the Sâkyan Sage.   MUNI is Sage, Wise.
SÂKYA is the family name of Gautama Buddha.   This title is very often used
alone, without adding either Gautama or Buddha.

<u>GUPTA VIDYÂ:</u>   (Sanskrit)   (January, 1946, p. #8)

   GUPTA - Esoteric, Secret, Sacred.   VIDYÂ - Knowledge, Science, Teaching.
The accepted translation is - "The Secret Doctrine", or "The Sacred Science".

<u>DEVÂH:</u>   plural
<u>DEVA:</u>   singular   (Sanskrit)   (March, 1946, p. #34)

   This Sanskrit term is a general one, meaning a being who inhabits the
higher realms, and who has attained to a certain development.   Beneath the
ranks of DEVÂH, thousands in variety, are the many ranks of Elemental Lives,
and this term too is general or inclusive.

   A DEVA is a self-conscious, responsible, highly evolved individual Life
in form, which form however is invisible to Man by reason of its existence in
other levels.   DEVÂH are not winged, as the West has conceived Angels to be.
They are of levels called RÛPA and ARÛPA in Sanskrit; that is, some wear
bodies denser, more objective than others who are more evolved.   Like Man,
they are specialized beings; they are engaged in tasks, pointed toward a
goal, and are in forms designed to suit their particular environment and to
help them reach that goal.

   The word DEVÂH has reference to the Sanskrit root DIV - "to shine" - and
in the East they have been called the "Shining Ones".   This relates to their
fine bodies, devoid of dense matter, which radiate the force and energy in
rays of shining, multi-colored, brilliant light.   They are not Gods, though
the term has been translated "Gods".   This is a name for beings of the
realms between ours and the cosmic levels.

<u>BRAHMÂ:</u>   (Sanskrit)   (March, 1946, p. #41)

   The first of the three aspects of the Manifested Logos, emanating from
the eternal and unmanifested Source of Being - BRAHMA the Unknown and Uncognizable.   The triune manifested Logos reflects within the manifested Universe
Himself.   The three aspects are Creative, Preservative and Destructive.
The three aspects are one, but are differentiated in most of the world's philosophies.   The Three are named BRAHMÂ, VISHNU and SIVA in Hindu Philosophy.

<u>VISHNU:</u>   (Sanskrit)   (March, 1947, p. #50)

   VISHNU is the second aspect of the triume manifestation of the Logos.
He is the Preserver, the Pervader, the Renovator.   He is held to be AVATÂRA
at stated intervals for the purpose of aiding evolution during the MAHÂ KALPA.
He is alike in nature and a close companion of the Creative Aspect, BRAHMÂ.
He is therefore closely allied with the times of periodic change and growth.
He "descends" at such times, and therefore the present KALPA has been named
to commemorate one such "descent" of VISHNU.

The last KALPA, we are told in "The Secret Doctrine", was called the
PADMA (Golden Lotus) KALPA. The present KALPA has been named VÂRÂHA (Boar)
KALPA, from the Boar Avatâr of Vishnu. The next KALPA has not been named
in exoteric writings, and as there is a half of the present VÂRÂHA KALPA to
pass before that time, it may be that its name will be of very little interest to the present races of mankind.

(For the Calendar refer to January, 1947)

-*- -*- -*- -*- -*- -*- -*- -*- -*- -*- -*- -*- -*- -*- -*- -*- -*- -*- -*-

The News Corner

M. Sangaratana, Secretary of The Maha Bodhi Society, writing under date of
February 5th, 1947, from Sarnath, Benares, India, advises us as follows:

"The Maha Bodhi Society of India proposes to hold a Buddhist Convention towards the end of March, 1947, when the Inter Asiatic Conference scheduled to be held by that time will also be in session in
Delhi which is expected to be attended by delegates from almost all
the Buddhist countries. It is hoped that the participation of the
Buddhist delegates who come to attend the Conference will be an added
attraction and a source of encouragement to the Convention.

"A similar Buddhist Convention was held at Calcutta about quarter of
a century ago and the time is ripe now for another convention of
that nature especially in view of the many changes that have taken
place since then and the emergence of new problems as a result of that.

"One of our aims in holding such a Convention to coincide with the
Inter Asiatic Conference is to provide the Buddhists who are scattered
in small numbers in different parts of India an opportunity to contact the Buddhists of other lands and pave a way for the establishment
of closer relations with them through the chosen delegates who come to
attend the Conference. It will also help the Buddhists of different
parts of the country to meet together on one spot and discuss matters
confronting the Buddhist community of India and chalk out a programme
for the uplift of the community.

"Before giving it a final shape we wish to know your valuable opinion
on the prospect and what contributions you can make for the success
of the Convention in the way of sending delegates, etc. As the time
at our disposal is very short, please be kind enough to send us your
valuable opinion on the matter as soon as possible. Thanking you
for an early reply,   Yours in the Dhamma, etc."

Too late, at this long distance, to participate, we have sent our best wishes.
Too near the date to advise our readers in time to attend, if they were so
minded, we include this letter - as we shall other communications in future -
as of general interest to Buddhists in this country.

-*- -*- -*- -*-

SOME SAYINGS OF THE BUDDHA, Translated by F. L. Woodward

The words of Gautama, the Buddha, have deep appeal.   Because of this a number
of books are published giving selections of his teachings from the sûtras.
Often the selections are under headings, so that the seeker may find readily
what the Great Teacher said on a subject.

Mr. F. L. Woodward is one of the long roll of scholars who have contributed to
the work of the renowned Pali Text Society.   He has translated or edited THE
YOGÂVACARA'S MANUAL, THE SAMUTTA NIKÂYA, UDÂNA, DHAMMAPADA, ANGUTTARA NIKÂYA,
ITI-VUTTAKA, etc., so that he brings a ripe scholarship to the translation of
SOME SAYINGS OF THE BUDDHA.

In his Preface Mr. Woodward states:
> "This collection consists of passages from the Vinaya Pitaka, the Four
> Great Nikâyas (Digha-, Majjhima-, Samyutta-, and Anguttara-Nikâya), and
> those parts of the Short Nikâya, such as Dhammapada, Itivuttaka, Udâna,
> and Sutta Nipata (the last named contains some of the oldest parts of
> the Pâli Canon), where the Buddha is represented as speaking in both
> prose and verse.   I have included the whole of the Khuddaka-Pâtha,
> which tradition has regarded as containing 'the whole duty' of the
> Buddhist."

Mr. Woodward has produced an excellent introduction to, as well as an excellent selection from, the Pali Sutta Pitaka, in his 356 pages.

Sir Francis Younghusband places his approval upon the book in his twenty-page
Introduction, in which he shows considerable knowledge of the Buddha's Dharma.
His knowledge is not second-hand, but is based upon experience gained in
living and travelling in Buddhist lands.   In his concluding words he pays
tribute, as many learned men have done, to the Buddha, whose exceedingly high
status caused men in veneration to call him BHAGAVAN - the Blessed One, JINA-
the Conqueror, DHARMARÂJA - Lord of the Benevolent Law, SAMYAK SAMBUDDHA -
the Supremely Enlightened, SÂKYAMUNI - Sage of the Sâkyas, SÂSTÂ DEVA-
MANUSYÂNÂM - Teacher of Devas and Humans, and many other titles.

Sir Francis says:
> "It was because he showed in his life that what he taught was both
> practicable and reasonable that he exerted such a mighty influence upon
> mankind.   He sought to put a new temper into men, to imbue them with
> a new spirit, give them a new heart.   It was more than could be
> achieved in only 2,500 years.   But mankind is still young and impres-
> sionable.   The impression Buddha made was deep.   Reinforced by like
> impressions made in different ways by other religious leaders it will
> surely work itself out and its effect be felt in ever-increasing degree.
> The heart of man will indeed be cleansed.   From the joy in that heart
> will spring a compassion fixed as an instinct in the race.   All hard-
> ness will be melted - conflict turned to composure."

Such is the goal to be striven for by all who tread the Buddha's Way.

This excellent book is available from The Golden Lotus Press, price $1.10,
including postage.

THE
GOLDEN LOTUS

Reg. U. S. Pat. Off.

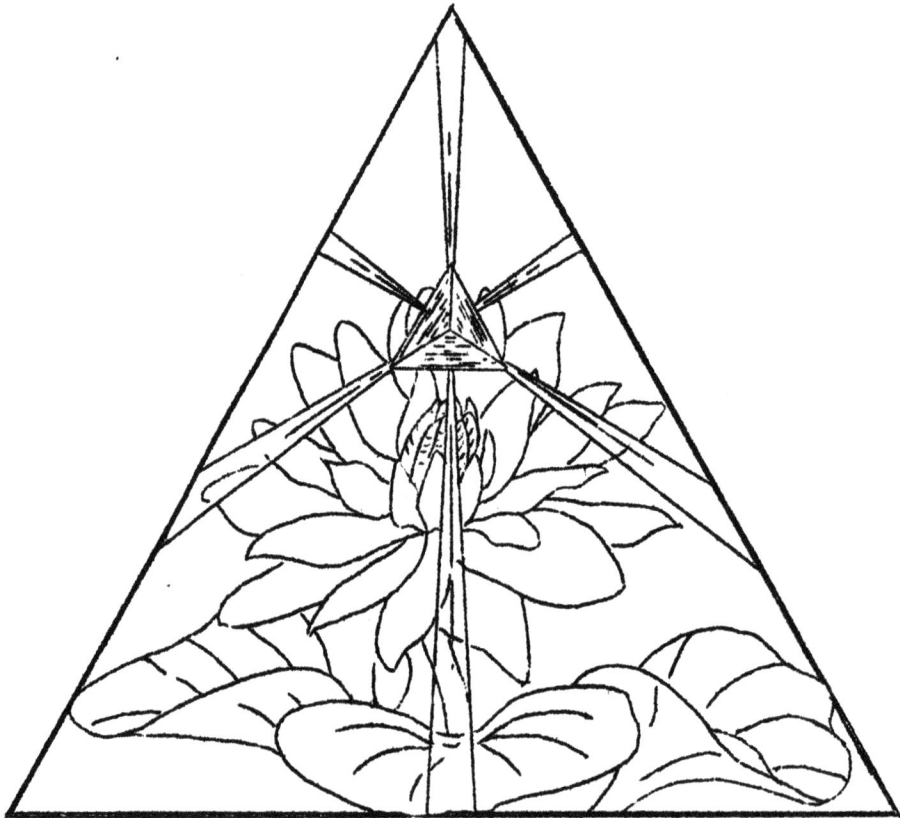

Trademark

VAISÂKHA – 1947

THE GOLDEN LOTUS:

A magazine, issued monthly, dedicated
to those who seek

THE WAY.

Subscriptions:

    One Year - U.S. and Canada - $2.00
        "   - Foreign   - $2.50

    Single   - U.S. and Canada -   .20
    Copy   - Foreign   -   .25

All inquiries and correspondence may be
addressed to the Publishing Agent of
        THE GOLDEN LOTUS PRESS -

        William J. Leslie
        7009 Woolston Road
     Philadelphia, 38, Penna.,
          U. S. A.

-*- -*- -*- -*-

-*- -*- -*- -*-

THE GOLDEN LOTUS

Reg. U. S. Pat. Off.

"FOR HOLY VIRTUE, FOR HIGH ENDEAVOR,
FOR SUBLIME WISDOM - FOR THESE
THINGS DO WE WAGE WAR: THEREFORE
ARE WE CALLED WARRIORS."

Gautama Buddha

VOL.4
1947

VAISĀKHA, 1947

Confronted with signs of gathering storm, the world stands at a cross-road, as it has so many times during the present century. Under the darkening sky of world unrest there is the not-too-distant thunder of a commonly disregarded ideological conflict. Complications inimical to fair weather abound in world politics. Yet the occasional flashes of lightning are minimized and somehow ignored by many people. Under the clouds the world population proceeds to follow its own preoccupations, unheeding the many warning signals of approaching storm.

Contending nations, excessive reparations, economic rivalry presage storm. Unlevelled barriers and embargoes manifold have not built shelters against the flood. Undefended nations still conceal the wounds of the preceding abandonment to the invader, underneath the smile of politeness concealing the remembrance of betrayal. And the multitudes of homeless, destitute, everywhere evidence the instability and insecurity resulting from the recent debacle.

Nowhere is there trust or confidence, and all is as it was in the selfish pattern of nationalism prevailing before the war. The "new era" is here, but can serve no longer as a delusive hope, for it is a mockery of all the prophecies. Peace still rests upon a pedestal, out of reach, unattained, an ideal but not yet a living reality.

Somewhere the Buddha said:

> Man is to be considered temporary, a fleeting and evanescent shadow in a world of shadows, for Man is a temporary and constantly changing expression of a never-changing and never-dying Life Force.

> Man, only partially immortal, should consider the temporary as an illusion, should consider himself an illusion, should abandon illusion. He should make himself a home within the Eternal and abide therein, comprehending that strife, violence, hatred, injustice and greed are not inherent in his immortal essence, and that he is ensnared by them into entanglement within the world of MĀRA.

> He should, then, be constantly a completely just, honest, compassionate and merciful being, while manifested, reflecting only his immortality. For in such fashion are the bonds of MĀRA broken, and the snares escaped, by that which is the manifesting and eternal being.

-*- -*- -*- -*-

To Buddha, On His Birthday

by Rabindranath Tagore

The world, seized by the fury of carnage,
Writhes in the ceaseless grip of conflicts.
Crooked are its ways, tangled its coils of bondage.
Wearily waits the earth for a new birth of thine;
Save her, Great Heart, utter thy eternal words,
Let blossom love's lotus with its honey inexhaustible.

O Serene, O Free, thou Soul of infinite Sanctity,
Cleanse this earth of her stains, O Merciful.

Thou great Giver of Self,
Initiate us in the penance of sacrifice,
Take, Divine Beggar, our pride for thine alms,
Soothe the sorrowing worlds, scatter the mist of
                         unreason,
Light up Truth's sunrise;
Let life become fulfilled, the sightless find his
                         vision.

O Serene, O Free, thou Soul of infinite Sanctity,
Cleanse this earth of her stains, O Merciful.

Man's heart is in anguish with the fever of unrest,
With the poison of self-seeking,
With a thirst that knows no end.
Countries, far and wide, flaunt on their foreheads
The blood-red mark of hatred.
Touch them with thy right hand,
Make them one in spirit,
Bring harmony into their life,
Bring rhythm of beauty.

O Serene, O Free, thou Soul of infinite Sanctity,
Cleanse this earth of her stains, O Merciful.

-*- -*- -*- -*-

DUHKHA NIRODHA - The Cessation of Suffering

Cause and effect are equal. Before the effect may be removed, the cause must be discontinued. Before the cause may be discontinued, unfortunately, the effects of the cause may have engendered fresh complications and inaugurated an entirely new series of concatenated actions.

It is important that the effect should not be confused with the cause. Suffering is the effect. Ignorance, Greed, Lust, Cruelty and BHAVA are the causes.

Many people will dispute this statement, and will be liable to question the advisability of adopting such a dismal outlook. It is proverbial that Truth is very often disguised or hidden from the casual observer. Yet, a more dismal outlook than the commonly acceptable one of vicarious atonement for deliberate evil, for accidental ignorance, for premeditated murder, and for callous negligence of and indifference to duty, one can not imagine. It is the most irresponsible attitude towards life, calculated to induce self-indulgence and self-pity.

Dismal the truth may be that in the cycle of necessity the human being acts in ignorance and without wisdom, gradually acquiring from his suffering the precious VIDYĀ or Knowledge. If the means is a very painful one, however, the end achieved is glorious, well worthy of the price paid in the long incarceration in the blinding toils of body, and well fitted to the strength of the incarnated being. For out of all the suffering there results the shining transparent jewel of the Wisdom, the VIDYĀ, without which the evolving being could not hope to pass into the next stage of his evolutionary journey.

Many methods have been suggested, during the ages, for the development of Wisdom. No better one than The Noble Eightfold Path, spoken by the Buddha, has been devised. It has the merit of simplicity, clarity and definite practicability. It leaves nothing to the imagination or to the intuition, and speaks so plainly as to eliminate misunderstanding.

Indeed, so clear it speaks, that many pass over it contemptuously, uninspired by what is written lucidly for everyone. Such people still are subject to delusion; they seek for bizarre and exclusive secrets rather than for the plainly spoken words of instruction it is presumed an Illuminated One would be capable of speaking.

Many people look for startling unproven statements and intriguingly grandiloquent titles. The Buddha long ago discarded such pretensions, and those who follow him do likewise, not seeking for another to obtain for them salvation, but securing by unremitting effort the Wisdom dearly purchased.

And, as the means to end Suffering - DUHKHA NIRODHA, the Third Truth - the Buddha spoke to his followers of the Fourth Truth, called MĀRGA - The Way - The Noble Eightfold Path.

-*- -*- -*- -*-

When the Ânanda legend is encountered, it is usual to find that he is counted as one of the very mighty of the Buddha's disciples, though he did not attain Arhathood until after the Buddha's death. Very few of the Commentaries give a reason for this seemingly conflicting belief, and there is often a tendency to think of the Venerable Ânanda as a companion of the Buddha, or a servant, or a disciple who lacked the ability to attain until after the Buddha had gone and his companion disciples stung him into activity.

That he did not attain during the Buddha's lifetime is certain, for the Buddha's last words and the records of the First Council contain references to the fact that he had not attained Arhatship until the time of the Council.

It is important to remember that upon Ânanda rested the duty of serving and helping the Buddha during his years of advancing age; and that Ânanda heard the Buddha's discourses so frequently he remembered them, was able to repeat them at the First Council, and so preserved them for the future.

In the passage of time many things are forgotten. One point which has been minimized is the relationship between Ânanda and the Buddha, his cousin. He was of the Buddha's royal house, therefore the great love which existed between them, and the unfailing devotion lavished by Ânanda on the Master. Therefore the great sorrow Ânanda experienced at the Buddha's passing, and therefore - because of his loving care for the aging Buddha - Ânanda's inability to pour effort into his own advancement, near to the Buddha though he was. He earned the merit of sharing the ministry of the Buddha in the years of his failing strength, and but for Ânanda the Buddha might have been unable to continue with his wandering mission.

He was so young - Ânanda! He took the post of body-helper, appointed by request of the Buddha, while still a lad. He entered the Order very early in his life, therefore he came to maturity of mind and body very much later than some of the Bhikshus who achieved Arhathood earlier. He was, perhaps, not capable of speed until he stood alone, without his duty to his kinsman, without the constant carefulness and the need to lavish thought upon the Buddha's failing footsteps.

Where did he fail, this lad of tender years, who took upon himself a burden deeply dear to him? He failed in nothing, for he served with true devotion, and he put the larger welfare of the Buddha's mission first, before his own. He took the path of duty. He led the way into a great service, the service of mankind. His devotion has inspired the generations who followed him, and to those who understand his is the name to stand forever near to the Buddha's.

Ânanda of the later years, the giver of the Discourses to the Sangha composed of the Elders present at the First Council, the Ânanda who cast off grief and longing to achieve Arhathood and take his place with the presiding Elder Kâsyapa, who made the Buddha's words ring as he spoke them, who took

(continued on page #57)

MÂYÂ (continued)

Are there allusions to MÂYÂ by other names?

Not by the scholars and instructed students.

Under what names are the allusions known?

Various goddesses in the different Eastern religions may be considered
as presentations of this abstraction called MÂYÂ. It is, of course,
impossible to escape the corruption and deterioration of thought from
abstract purity into concrete dissimilarity.

Would it be possible to name Western equivalents of these Eastern corruptions?

The best-known one is Mother Nature. It is as true and as pure an
interpretation as may be found. Although the name is homely and of
every-day language, it is still an abstract, unpersonified and un-
symbolized by any form. Demeter, the Great Mother, was a type of MÂYÂ.
And other nations than the Greeks have in their pantheons the idea of
MÂYÂ.   The Great Mother, or Nature, idea comes from MÂYÂ of the
Ancient Wisdom.

Is there a process of degrading involved?

Inevitably philosophy is degraded when it is converted into religion.
How much further must the Inner Truth fall when it is, at last, appropriated and adapted to the understanding of the uninitiated?

In the Ancient Wisdom, did MÂYÂ convey a special teaching?

All of the Ancient Wisdom conveyed teaching. In this case, the place
of MÂYÂ as a part of Cosmos was defined, and its presence as a force
outlined, as a necessity of occult training. Without this knowledge
the occultist would find himself severely handicapped, subject to many
distortions, and adrift upon a sea of misconstrued elements.

Then, no one worships MÂYÂ?

No one should. Who does so betrays his ignorance.   No one worships
anything if he understands it. Only the mystified set up mysteries
and worship that which they do not comprehend.

Can MÂYÂ be explained?

No occult wisdom is ever satisfactorily explained in words. Perception
must be equal to the task of cognizing reality before the truth may be
obtained.   True, some explanations afford clues.   Some teachings
point the way.   Some commentaries clear the mind of misconceptions.
Generally, however, the student grows into the clear perception necessary, leaving without the uninitiated - the uncomprehending, so to speak.

Would it be easier to call MÂYÂ a Cosmic Force?

> No.   Not correct.   The Cosmos itself is MÂYÂ.   The underlying struc-
> ture of all worlds, all beings, and all phenomenal appearances, is due
> to MÂYÂ - is MÂYÂ.   It IS.   It is not likened to anything, though
> other things may be likened to it because they are a part of it.   It
> stands alone.   It is not Space, Time, Motion, Life; it is all these,
> however.
>
> It is the MATCHLESS, the Divine in Action, the Alone in Evidence, the
> alluring Mask of the Eternal in the Web of Time and Space, the per-
> petual Builder of the Worlds, and the unwearied Fashioner of Form and
> Appearance - the Shifting Truth - the MAHÂMÂYÂ.

-*- -*- -*- -*- -*- -*- -*- -*- -*- -*- -*- -*- -*- -*- -*- -*- -*- -*- -*-

ÂNANDA - continued from page #55

the place of Patriarch later, and who was mighty in his Wisdom, becomes a
legend and a great example.

> For Love led Ânanda, and Love was his Yoga, though he, too, was a wise
leader in his turn.   The Love which guided Buddha for man's welfare had
also arisen in Ânanda's heart, and when the Buddha passed he poured his
strength, his great compassion, and his will to service into the final and
supreme effort to attain Illumination.   And stood, then, as the Buddha had
foretold, one of the mighty Arhats of the Buddha's Sangha, acknowledged by
his peers.

Unto Ânanda, Salutations!

-*- -*- -*- -*- -*- -*- -*- -*- -*- -*- -*- -*- -*- -*- -*- -*- -*- -*- -*-

Nirvâna

The Exalted One .... uttered these solemn words:

"There is, brethren, a condition wherein there is neither earth,
nor water, nor fire, nor air, nor the sphere of infinite space,
nor the sphere of infinite consciousness, nor the sphere of the
void, nor the sphere of neither perception nor non-perception:
where there is no 'this world' and no 'world beyond': where there
is no moon and no sun.   That condition, brethren, do I call
neither a coming nor a going, nor a standing still nor a falling
away nor a rising up: but it is without fixity, without mobility,
without basis.   THAT IS THE END OF WOE."

UDÂNA, p. #80, cap. viii.

Under the sun, there is no new and unknown thought-idea.   The mind-stuff (CHITTA) has been busy for some millenia.   It has produced a multitude of variations during that time, but it is not capable of creating or imagining the impossible - in other words the unknown.   What it cognizes must be the possible, the known or knowable, as distinguished from the Unknowable and the Unknown.   Limits there are to the mind and to the mind-cognition.

Truth prevails and is not distorted in the Unknown.   Distortions of it appear and reappear in the knowable or known.   Broken outlines, not the true aspect, are the rule there.

One Truth is eternal.   One Reality exists and is not alterable.   One Imperishable Perfection combines all the imperfect and transitory aspects.

Arising from the mind-essence, subsisting upon the energy of mind, the understood and accepted aspect of the One Truth - the cognized and comprehended - continues for a time.   But ideas of the known alter, and understanding of it veers, as the mind-essence changes through the centuries.

The known is very easily abstracted into and absorbed by a new or different fashion of thinking.   Even so, encumbered with its new apparel of vagary, or whim, or superstitious addenda of the mind-stuff, the known supports the bric-a-brac with its own inherent strength.

Seven times the planet moves upon a spiral path, during which an undulating sway of right and left, of up and down, of light and heavy prevails and accentuates the overlay and underlay of motion.   No matter where or when the spiral is, or where the motion started, or when it ends, it is today a truth that on the spiral there is no interplay of Matter, but that there is Matter only in suspended motion.   Matter in this condition is conducive to the interplay of mind and its accompanying vehicles of heavy density.   The interplay is accelerated, and momentarily affected.

Such is the cause behind the shadow world's imperfect grasp upon Reality, the reason for the half-perceived, the half-perfections, the broken outlines created by the mind-essence struggling in the monstruous flux and flow of the spiral.

Beneath the sun, therefore, there is no new and unknown thought-ideas. The pattern is true in such perfection as the mind-essence can grasp, but mind may speak or represent it as a symbol, and in so doing lose the truth perceived or alter it or hide it or portray it in gross fashion, being unable to control the flux and flood of mind-essence.'

And so the changes come and so the changes pass, leaving the Truth uncognized and uncognizable, alone and perfect in its one unalterable and sublime condition of reality.

-*- -*- -*- -*-

Vaishâkha Purnima

by Bhikkhu N. Jinaratana

(The Venerable Neluwe Jinaratana Thera is Managing Editor of THE MAHA
    BODHI, journal of The Maha Bodhi Society. This article is
    reprinted from the 1946 Vaishâkha Number of The Maha Bodhi.)

Today is the full moon of Vaishâkha - a day of special significance to
Buddhists all over the world. On this day, more than twenty-five centuries
ago, was born the greatest son of India, Buddha Sakyamuni Gautama, whose
teachings have brought peace and hope to millions of beings throughout the
world. By a strange and happy coincidence the great Enlightenment of the
Buddha under the Bodhi tree at Gaya as well as also his final passing away
from this world took place on the full moon day of Vaishâkha. To the
Buddhists, therefore, it is a thrice sacred festival. To the enlightened
non-Buddhists it is a day which reminds them of some important events in
human history.

The importance of this great day does not lie in the glamour of its
festivities or the emotional rapture that might come upon a few ardent en-
thusiasts. Its importance lies in the spiritual significance of what
Buddhism stands for in guiding the destinies of mankind. When we look
back through the vistas of time we see the cruel persecutions that were made
and the terrible wars that were fought in the names of certain religions or
through selfish greed and envy. Side by side with these dark spots in
human history we also see the bright interludes of time that illuminated
the greater part of the civilised world when the teachings of the Buddha
did hold sway. When we think of these, we only wish that the kingdom of
righteousness which the Buddha wanted to found on this earth may come upon
us in these troublous times.

We are now passing through a time of great critical importance in the
history of the human race. Man has been previously struggling for greater
achievements through his nobler instincts. But now he is fighting for what
he thinks supremacy through his baser instincts of selfishness and greed.
Self-sacrifice and love are forgotten. Instead of gaining any supremacy
over anything, the destructive elements which man has invented are
destroying himself. He has forgotten that the greatest victory is self-
mastery and the greatest weapon is love. Atom bombs and rocket shells
cannot control the world. It is the love for all mankind - nay love for
all sentient beings that can propel man towards greater achievements and
ensure for him his own security. Otherwise, the forces of evil which man
has created will wipe him out of existence before long.

On this hallowed day let us think of the noble teachings of this great
son of mankind and try to put them into practice in our daily lives. What
else is there that can bring us greater happiness and greater peace than
following the Noble Eightfold Path of Right Views, Right Aspirations,

(continued on page #68)

CHAPTER FOURTEEN

AWAKENING

"Those who essay the passage of the Gate Perilous
must be of Heart undaunted."

Padma Hiranya Surangama.

When the Soul and the Senses begin the long struggle, they are not enemies naturally.   They have journeyed long together and have been good
friends, defending and sustaining one another.   They have made themselves a
unity in action, sensuousness, and thought.

Therefore, when the awakened Soul begins to understand the mistake he
has been making through his devotion to an old comrade, he has a very
natural disinclination to hurt and wound, and there the whole intense struggle
is expressed.   A good comrade and a faithful servant must be sacrificed to
some extent.

This is hard to do, and harder still to keep on doing.   The Elders,
who seek to help him, watch the struggle often, and wonder how the Wanderer
survives the ordeal.   They never wonder when he falters, for They once
faltered where he fails.   They never count the cost too great if They can
save such a one from shrinking when the chance is given to resume the journey upward.

Now, that is where the one great difficulty of THE WAY is to be met.
How are the Senses to be bound and disciplined, held at command, if the
knowledge of the most urgent need for this action is not understood?   Why
should the East face towards the Heights in full comprehension and with
longing to begin the ascent, when the West can never see beyond the pleasant
Valley of the Senses?   This is because of lack of clear and convincing
literature which the East - in its own tongues - has possessed for many
centuries.

But what the East can understand is not yet in the West's own language.
It requires a change in structure to deal with a different mode of thinking
and a different type of people.   Such literature is unobtainable, unless
and until the West reaches the Eastern lands and makes the study there, or
the East reaches the West through a common understanding of the Eastern Wisdom.   Then, and not till then, can the Western races begin the long struggle
toward the Heights that has been delayed for so long.

When the Soul and the Senses join battle, then THE WAY is begun which
must be finished.   There is not a moment when it may be left or dropped -
every action counts for or against the Soul.   When the Soul gains a point
the Senses revolt more fiercely, and the Soul falls back again dismayed,
only to resume the struggle again and again.

Where the Soul chooses to battle onward, striving and aspiring to the

Heights, the battle is severe, and many fail through too intense desire for attainment.   They draw upon themselves a heavier burden than they can carry. More prolong the battle for much unnecessary time by fearing to try hard enough, drawing back when the pace becomes too hard.

Now the best plan is to go on calmly and methodically, seriously considering the steps before one, mastering each, hastening onward as fast as may be, but being thorough and perfect in the work undertaken.   By this plan the Soul can undertake and endeavor, not exhausting its power or sinking under fatigue and suffering.   When the Soul sees its Way it is best to hasten, but not at the expense of perfection in the accomplished results - for then it may be that a flaw will hinder progress further up the ascent.

The most inspiring thought the Soul can call to its assistance is that the Senses are lower, and are a delay and a delusion.   With this to point the place of the attack, the Soul begins the battle.   How the Senses respond to the attack is not our affair just now.   They battle as they can, without mercy and without pause.   It is the Soul's business to find the weak spots and the strong points, and the places which may be considered safe.

When the Soul surveys the battle-field, and has then planned the attack, action should follow.   There should be no delay and little reason to postpone.   For when the Soul has arrived at this point the Karma of the man has been adjusted to permit him to engage upon the struggle - let be what debts he owes or has to be repaid.   There will be time in another life for these debts to be balanced.

The Soul may not be aware the road has been made clear, but it will recognize the opportunity to weigh and meditate and to alter modes of living and thought; it will seize upon the opportunity.   There should be no hesitation, then, if the Soul is in command, but the Senses may strive to hold to their accustomed habits and sometimes time is lost.   When this happens heavier debt is incurred because the Soul must then ask another adjustment of the karmic load for a later struggle.   This is a handicap that many could avoid if they were able to understand fully where they stood and what lay before them when the battle is first joined.

"Man is not a slave to Mind and Reason if he wills to climb."

-*- -*- -*- -*- -*- -*- -*- -*- -*- -*- -*- -*- -*- -*- -*- -*- -*- -*- -

"I worship thee, strong man of noblest strain,
I worship thee, great chief of humankind,
Unknown thy peer is to ken of beings,
In worlds both human and divine.
Thou art the Wakened One, Master, Sage,
By thee is Death struck down.
Slayer of the heart's wild leanings all,
Crossed hast thou to safety and doest lead,
This folk to safety too."

SUTTA NIPÂTA.

"HOW WOULD AN ISOLATED STUDENT OBSERVE VAISÂKHA?"

He has all that is required within his mind and heart.

He needs no sacred places, sacred relics, colored lights, ceremonies, congregations, phrases, chants and speeches.   These are the appurtenances, not the essence of VAISÂKHA.   They are but symbols and conveniences; they enchant the eye and ear, perhaps lift the aspiration.   They are a means of centralizing and focusing the diversified thoughts, of momentarily harmonizing the unharmonized individual units of the audience with the presiding Bhikshus' aspiration.

Somewhat as a strong leader breasts the wind, sheltering his flock of followers, the Bhikshu leads the way into the realm of true perception. The appurtenances are a means to achieve the elimination of obstacles and to still diversified thought currents, to establish a calm island of aspiration in the storm of mental turmoil.

The individual student, isolated from formal celebrations, alone in his household or community, and anxious to observe the Buddha's memorial day, need have neither regret nor anxiety.   He is not lonely in the realm of aspiration.   He should be able to reach to some high level on that day, lifted by the constantly maintained awareness and the specifically applied aspiration of the Buddhist leaders throughout that time.   He should find wings to his perceptive faculties, then, if he has been constant in his own aspiration through the year.   He needs, however, to have practised and to have some knowledge of, the art of meditation.   The first steps towards the higher levels must be his own.

Whatever he may use, at home, to still the outward-turned mind, will be his best aid for VAISÂKHA, unless he chooses then to add a little colour - a lighted candle, yellow for the Buddha's robe, a lotus or fresh and fragrant flower, a drift of incense, or a special treasure such as a picture or small statue of the Buddha, simply to express the unusual occasion.   The upward and inward turning of the mind requires none of these, proceeds best on its flight in a bare room, and with no symbol-tokens.   The student's mind should rest upon the Buddha and his Dharma in the beginning, and should from there take flight, untracked, into the Unknown.

The message of the day is Service and Remembrance.   The year is for striving and achievement.   VAISÂKHA is for Remembrance and Re-dedication. The student, then, takes Pansil in his own mind, and in his own way makes his vows of service.   He takes the contact with the supporting mental effort of others as an aid to upward striving, and he takes what aid he can from this available assistance to the high, clear levels of the unveiled perception.   He is not solitary and he is, for once in the year at least, at VAISÂKHA, within the precincts of the Sangha of the Buddha.   He adds his strength, and takes back strength, if he aspires that day in true and heartfelt understanding of the Buddha's Dharma.

The full moon of VAISÂKHA, on May 4th, 1947, is truly for Remembrance. "Honour to Him, the Blessed One, Arahat, the Fully Enlightened One."

Part I - The Life of the Buddha

29. Q. But how did he acquire this boundless love?
    A. Throughout numberless births and aeons of years he had been cultiva-
       ting this love, with the unfaltering determination to become a
       Buddha.

30. Q. What did he this time relinquish?
    A. His beautiful palaces, his riches, luxuries, and pleasures, his soft
       beds, fine dresses, his rich food, and his kingdom; he even left
       his beloved wife and only son, Rāhula.

31. Q. Did any other man ever sacrifice so much for our sake?
    A. Not one in this present world-period: this is why Buddhists so love
       him, and why good Buddhists try to be like him.

32. Q. But have not many men given up all earthly blessings, and even life
       itself, for the sake of their fellow-men?
    A. Certainly. But we believe that this surpassing unselfishness and
       love for humanity showed themselves in his renouncing the bliss
       of Nirvâna countless ages ago, when he was born as the Brahman
       Sumedha in the time of Dipankara Buddha:- he had then reached
       the stage where he might have entered Nirvâna, had he not loved
       mankind more than himself. This renunciation implied his volun-
       tarily enduring the miseries of earthly lives until he became
       Buddha, for the sake of teaching all beings the way to emancipa-
       tion and to give rest to the world.

33. Q. How old was he when he went to the jungle?
    A. He was in his twenty-ninth year.

34. Q. What finally determined him to leave all that men usually love so
       much, and go to the jungle?
    A. A DEVA* appeared to him when driving out in his chariot, under four
       impressive forms, on four different occasions.

       * See the definition of DEVA given later.

35. Q. What were these different forms?
    A. Those of a very old man broken down by age, of a sick man, of a
       decaying corpse, and of a dignified hermit.

36. Q. Did he alone see these?
    A. No, his attendant Channa also saw them.

37. Q. Why should these sights, so familiar to everybody, have caused him
       to go to the jungle?
    A. We often see such sights: he had not seen them, so they made a deep
       impression on his mind.

38. Q. Why had he not also seen them?
    A. The Brahman astrologers had foretold at his birth that he would
       one day resign his kingdom and become a BUDDHA. The King, his
       father, not wishing to lose an heir to his kingdom, had care-
       fully prevented his seeing any sights that might suggest to him

38. A.   human misery and death.   No one was allowed even to speak of
(cont.) such things to the Prince.   He was almost like a prisoner in his
         lovely palaces and flower-gardens.   They were surrounded by high
         walls, and inside everything was made as beautiful as possible,
         so that he might not wish to go and see the sorrow and distress
         that are in the world.

39. Q.   Was he so kind-hearted that the King feared he might really wish to
         leave everything for the world's sake?
    A.   Yes; he seems to have felt for all beings so strong a pity and love
         as that.

40. Q.   And how did he expect to learn the cause of sorrow in the jungle?
    A.   By removing far away from all that could prevent his thinking deeply
         of the causes of sorrow and the nature of man.

41. Q.   How did he escape from the palace?
    A.   One night when all were asleep, he arose, took a last look at his
         sleeping wife and infant son; called Channa, mounted his favourite
         white horse Kanthaka, and rode to the palace gate.   The DEVAS
         had thrown a deep sleep upon the King's guard who watched the
         gate, so that they could not hear the noise of the horse's hoofs.

42. Q.   But the gate was locked, was it not?
    A.   Yes; but the DEVAS caused it to open without the slightest noise,
         and he rode away into the darkness.

43. Q.   Whither did he go?
    A.   To the river Anomâ, a long way from Kapilavastu.

44. Q.   What did he then do?
    A.   He sprang from his horse, cut off his beautiful hair with his sword,
         put on the yellow dress of an ascetic, and giving his ornaments
         and horse to Channa, ordered him to take them back to his father,
         the King.

46. Q.   What then?
    A.   He went afoot towards Râjagrha, the capital city of King Bimbisâra,
         of Magadha.

46. Q.   Who visited him there?
    A.   The King with his whole Court. *

         * For an admirable account of this interview consult Dr. Paul
           Carus' "Gospel of Buddha", page 20, et seq.

47. Q.   Why did the BUDDHA go there?
    A.   In the forests were hermits - very wise men, whose pupil he after-
         wards became, in the hope of finding the knowledge of which he
         was in search.

48. Q.   Of what religion were they?
    A.   The Hindu religion: they were Brahmans. *

         * The term Hindu, once a contemptuous term, used by the

48. A.   Mussulmans to designate the people of Sindh, whom they con-
(cont.)   quered, is now used in an ecclesiastical sense.

49. Q.   What did they teach?
     A.   That by severe penances and torture of the body a man may acquire
           perfect wisdom.

50. Q.   Did the Prince find this to be so?
     A.   No; he learned their systems and practised all their penances, but
           he could not thus discover the cause of human sorrow and the way
           to absolute emancipation.

51. Q.   What did he then do?
     A.   He went away into the forest near a place called Uruvêla, near the
           present Mahâbôdhi Temple at Buddha Gaya, and spent six years in
           deep meditation and undergoing the severest discipline in mor-
           tifying his body.

52. Q.   Was he alone?
     A.   No; five Brahman companions attended him.

53. Q.   What were their names?
     A.   Kondanna, Bhaddiya, Vappa, Mahânâma, and Assaji.

54. Q.   What plan of discipline did he adopt to open his mind to know the
           whole truth?
     A.   He sat and meditated, concentrating his mind upon the higher prob-
           lems of life, and shutting out from his sight and hearing all
           that was likely to interrupt his inward reflections.

55. Q.   Did he fast?
     A.   Yes, through the whole period. He took less and less food and
           water until, it is said, he ate scarcely more than one grain of
           rice or of sesamum seed each day.

56. Q.   Did this give him the wisdom he longed for?
     A.   No: He grew thinner and thinner in body and fainter in strength
           until, one day, as he was slowly walking about and meditating,
           his vital force suddenly left him and he fell to the ground
           unconscious.

57. Q.   What did his companions think of that?
     A.   They fancied he was dead; but after a time he revived.

58. Q.   What then?
     A.   The thought came to him that knowledge could never be reached by
           mere fasting or bodily suffering, but must be gained by the
           opening of the mind. He had just barely escaped death from
           self-starvation, yet had not obtained the Perfect Wisdom. So
           he decided to eat, that he might live at least long enough to
           become wise.

59. Q.   Who gave him food?
     A.   He received food from Sujâtâ, a nobleman's daughter, who saw him
           sitting at the foot of a nyagrodha (banyan) tree. After that
           his strength returned to him; he arose, took his almsbowl, bathed
           in the river Nêranjarâ, ate the food, and went into the jungle.

(to be continued)

Bhikkhu Anuruddha, General Secretary of Rationalists' International Buddhist Study Circle, writing under date of January 8th, 1947, from Ceylon, is quoted in part as follows:

"It is very pleasing to learn from various sources that there is a very slow and sure awakening of the Dhamma in the Occident, which perhaps may be due to the failure of materialism and the inconsistency of the Occidental Faiths to provide a rational explanation of life to the progressive intellects of the age. The present is an advanced age of thinking. Men have begun to shun all irrational beliefs, revelations and dogmatic theories. Men of science are in pursuit of a true explanation of things.

"It is my firm belief that at a time like this, if the Western lands were aware of the fact that in the Teachings of the Great Buddha they could find a solution of their eagerly sought problem, they would no doubt grasp it and eventually probe into its depths and endeavor to think and live by its teachings. And further, upon realising that Buddhism is free from those bondages of dogma and the demand for blind faith, which the West has since learned to doubt and distrust, they would naturally turn to this highest pro-duct of 'Intuitive Thinking'. Buddhism would eventually be the eagerly sought panacea for the world's ills, and the sure solution for the religious problem of the times, as you would observe that in Buddhism all belief is depreciated. Hence we are taught not to accept anything on mere faith, the teaching of the Buddha not excepted. This method of treatment has been clearly outlined by the Buddha in the 'Kâlâma Sûtta'. In this discourse the Buddha admonished the Kâlâmas of Kassaputta, thus:

" 'Come, O Kâlâmas! Do not accept anything on mere hearsay. Do not accept anything by mere tradition. Do not accept anything on account of rumours. Do not accept anything just because it accords with your scriptures. Do not accept anything by mere supposition. Do not accept anything by mere inference. Do not accept anything by merely con-sidering the reasons. Do not accept anything merely because it agrees with your preconceived notions. Do not accept anything merely because it seems acceptable. Do not accept anything thinking that the ascetic is respected by us.'

"These words of the Buddha, spoken some 2500 years back, still retain their original force and freshness. .....

"Humanity has today been crushed by its own follies of lust, hatred and delu-sion. Lest you and I go to its help, who shall save it from its present plight? How long will this supposed Peace stay, unless national harmony and international concord be established? Nations are only a mass expression of the individuals. How else can a lasting Peace be restored but by the individual Ethico-Moral Culture? Buddhism alone can help the world."

This Bhikkhu would be interested in contacting free thinkers, rationalists, professors, social workers, etc. As he has asked for such contacts, any names and addresses sent in to us will be forwarded by us to Bhikkhu Anuruddha.

-*- -*- -*- -*-

MÂRA: (Sanskrit)   (April, 1947, p. #52)

The Lord of Desire - the Tempter or Seducer.   MÂRA is one of the names
of KÂMA, the god of Love.   He personifies a principle and is,generally
speaking, accepted as a god or superior being.   Actually, this is a degrada-
tion of the idea of the divine desire for creating happiness and love, the
first all-embracing desire emanating from the Absolute.

CHITTA: (Sanskrit)   (April, 1947, p. #58)

Mind in its form of critical and assimilating out-turning.   It is the
comprehending and analyzing activity of the MÂNASA, not the over-shadowing
Creative Intelligence, but its compound.   Untangled from the Kâmic contacts,
it becomes again the over-shadowing abstract MÂNASA.   Entangled, it is conscious mind, the observer and the coordinator.

PURNIMA: (Sanskrit)   (April, 1947, p. #59)

VAISÂKHA PURNIMA - the Buddha Day.   The Festival Day or Memorial Day
of the Buddha.   A sacred and holy remembrance day, yet a festival of re-
joicing.   It is celebrated in the month VAISÂKHA, on full moon.

PANSIL: (Sinhalese)   (April, 1947, p. #62)

A contraction of the PÂLI term PANCHA SÎLA (Hînayâna) and equivalent to
the Sanskrit term PANCA-SIKSÂ-PADÂNI (Mahâyâna).   Pansil consists of a
recitation of the Three Refuges and the Five Precepts.   It is simply a vow
to follow the path and the teaching of the Buddha.

BRAHMA: (Sanskrit)   (March, 1947, p. #49)

The Glossary written by H. P. Blavatsky says:

>"The student must distinguish between BRAHMA the neuter, and
>BRAHMÂ, the male creator of the Indian Pantheon.   The former,
>BRAHMA or BRAHMAN, is the impersonal, supreme and uncognizable
>Principle of the Universe from the essence of which all
>emanates, and into which all returns, which is incorporeal,
>immaterial, unborn, eternal, beginningless and endless.   It
>is all-pervading, animating the highest god as well as the
>smallest mineral atom.   BRAHMÂ, on the other hand .....
>exists periodically in his manifestation only, and then
>again goes into pralaya ...."

SIVA: (Sanskrit)   (March, 1947, p. #49)

This is the name of the third aspect of the Hindu Trinity or TRIMÛRTI.
SIVA is the Destroyer, who destroys only to regenerate and recreate.   He is
the patron of all the Yogîs, being called MAHÂYOGÎ - the great ascetic.
SIVA'S name in the Vedas is RUDRA, the KUMÂRA, and sometimes he is called
SIVA-RUDRA.   One of his titles is TRILOCHANA, the "three-eyed".

Right Speech, Right Conduct, Right Livelihood, Right Effort, Right Mindfulness
and Right Rapture?   This is the way of salvation that the Lord Buddha has
taught us.   Let us pay homage to his great name on this thrice sacred day
not by mere pageant and ceremony but by making a firm resolution to follow his
teachings in all that we think and do.   Then and then only can we hope for a
better future for mankind.

-*- -*- -*- -*- -*- -*- -*- -*- -*- -*- -*- -*- -*- -*- -*- -*- -*- -*- -*- -*-

ANNOUNCEMENTS

Due to the time consumed in delivery of THE GOLDEN LOTUS
to far corners of the United States, Canada, and abroad,
the VAISĀKHA number has been published in April, so that
it may reach readers before the full moon time.   This
policy will be followed in all succeeding Volumes.

The 1946 INDEX, for Volume Three, is ready.   Per copy,
twenty cents, United States, Canada, and abroad.

ERRATA: January, 1947, page #15, Line #30
     "147" should be "148"

  March, 1947, page #49, Lines #31 and #36,
     "triume" should be "triune"

-*- -*- -*- -*- -*- -*- -*- -*- -*- -*- -*- -*- -*- -*- -*- -*- -*- -*- -*- -*-

"The thought came to me, O Bhikkhus:

"' This Doctrine to which I have attained is profound,
hard to understand, difficult to explain, rare, precious,
not to be reached by mere reasoning, subtle, to be
grasped only by the wise.   But mankind is seized, entranced, spell-bound by its greeds.   Thus seized,
entranced, spell-bound by its greeds, this race of men
will find it hard to understand the arising of all
things through causes, and in dependence upon causes.
And it is also difficult for them to understand how
all the constituents of being can be made to subside,
the doing away of all the bases of being, the quenching
of craving, dispassion, cessation, Nibbāna.   And now,
should I teach this Doctrine and others fail to understand, it would only result in trouble and weariness
for me.' "

      Majjhima Nikāya.

THE LIFE OF THE BUDDHA, by H. C. Warren

It is the aspiration of every adherent of the Dharma to emulate Gautama Buddha, whose great achievement at Buddha Gayâ in the month Vaisâkha 2534 years ago made him the ideal to be followed. At this time of year many will renew the resolve to carry out his last injunction to "Work out your own salvation with diligence." He also enjoined his followers to go forth and bring mankind to enlightenment, even as he, after enlightenment, travelled about for forty-five years in the effort to bring all men to the Peace. The task of disseminating the Dharma rests upon his followers, who should speak, write, send literature where needed, or place books in libraries where seekers may find them. A book suitable for this purpose is reviewed this month, for it is a most appropriate study at this time.

THE LIFE OF THE BUDDHA is by an eminent American scholar, Henry Clarke Warren, who devoted much of his lifetime to translating from the Pâli classics. His work called BUDDHISM IN TRANSLATIONS, first published in 1896, and now out of print, is a memorial to his service. It is Volume Three of THE HARVARD ORIENTAL SERIES, founded by Henry Clarke Warren and Professor Charles Rockwell Lanman, who also edited the entire Series. The first chapter in BUDDHISM IN TRANSLATIONS - called "The Life of the Buddha" - was published separately in 1922 "for circulation in the Orient, especially in India and Ceylon." It is this separate publication of the first chapter that we are reviewing, for without doubt the West has need of this teaching also.

The book itself, published by The Harvard University Press, is a masterpiece of the printer's art, as may be expected of a book published by a University. The frontispiece is a reproduction of a Buddha statue, on heavy paper suitable for framing. Five pages present Professor Lanman's "Prefatory Notes to the Seventh and Eighth Issues". Six pages contain the author's "General Introduction", which includes some general information on Buddhism. The opening Chapters are from the JÂTAKAS or Birth Stories, and the later chapters are from the principal SUTTAS:

Page 1   "The Buddha"
5   "The Story of Sumedha",   ) trans-
32   "A List of Former Buddhas"   ) lated
33   "The Characteristics of a Future Buddha"   ) from
38   "The Birth of the Buddha",   ) the
48   "The Young Gotamid Prince"   ) JÂTAKA
56   "The Great Retirement"   )
67   "The Great Struggle"   )
71   "The Attainment of Buddhaship"   )
83   "First Events after the Attainment" - from MAHÂ-VAGGA
87   "The Conversion of Sâriputta and Moggallâna" - from MAHÂ-VAGGA
91   "The Buddha's Daily Habits" - from SUMANGALA-VILÂSINÎ
95   "The Death of the Buddha" - from MAHÂ-PARINIBBÂNA-SUTTA

Thirty-four pages give a description of The Harvard Oriental Series and "A Brief Memorial to Henry Clarke Warren", by C. R. Lanman. It would be a pleasure to describe this scholarly book in detail, but space forbids. It may be obtained from The Golden Lotus Press, price $1.00.

THE GOLDEN LOTUS

Reg. U. S. Pat. Off.

"FOR HOLY VIRTUE, FOR HIGH ENDEAVOR,
FOR SUBLIME WISDOM - FOR THESE
THINGS DO WE WAGE WAR: THEREFORE
ARE WE CALLED WARRIORS."

Gautama Buddha

VOL.4
1947

THE DARK HORIZON

Gathering upon the distant sky are clouds of darkening intensity, much nearer and more fateful to the present generations than they suppose. Though Man is deeply desirous of peace and security he, nevertheless, is threatened by upheavals of all kinds.

Borne upon the wind, the sharpening notes of distress from many peoples evidence their unrest, their feeling of abandonment, their resentment of inadequate measures for relief and delay of a just disposition of the conquered countries.   No one may say that seeds of hatred do not exist, nor that they will not bear a bitter fruit of violence in time appointed.

Among the clouds bright rifts are present, but they are rifts, not sunshine pouring unobstructed upon a peaceful world.   The rifts proclaim the darkness of disorder by their very presence, standing as witness to the full illumination that might be if Man were wise enough to let the sunshine in.   More rifts would be a great improvement. If they were only large enough they might be sufficient to minimize the clouds of hate and fear and war.

Rifts do not open because world police forces are organized to maintain order, nor by appeasement of powerful nations, nor through the occupation of lands of former enemies, nor through the exploitation of the weaker nations.   They are not created by the existence of armaments and atom bombs.   These things belong to darkness and to night; they build black clouds.

But rifts are of the Light.   They are such things as food and medicine and clothing - and books and literature - and friendly words across the boundaries - and recognition of the brotherhood of this, the human family - and expression of the common need to know and understand each other - and willingness to learn from other races - and freedom to speak plain and true - and courage to defend the helpless - and strength to stand against oppression - and pity for the helpless hunted animals of the world.   In short, the qualities that make the human being half divine, expressed by many people in the world today.

These rifts in time might save us from the storm, if we but know, if we now worked to make the rifts for sunshine to pour in, each one aiding, true to the rifts and not to darkness and the night of fear and hate and war which looms upon us.

We must take sides again.   But let us stand for Light, and help the cause of Light, and strengthen where we can the rifts of Light.

It is not known, this Path, nor sought, nor travelled by the crowd.
It makes no general appeal.
Its thorny uphill climb looks hard, is hard, and skirts the
                              precipices of the mountainside.
It flaunts no banners, has no wayside inns, and gives no shelter
                              against the elements.
It looks, from its beginning, rough and unshaded,
Until it turns and the steep hillside hides it from view.
It seems to be a mountain pass, a trail to an eagle's eyrie, too
                              steep to tread.
Men pass it by.
The broad highway has people, carnivals, road markets, and much din.
Men take that, following the crowd, and wind around and in and out,
                              upon the valley's floor.

The wise men seek the Path.
They take the narrow way, the steep hillside, the lonely and unshaded
                    climb straight to the Heights.
They leave the din, the crowded fairs, the give and take.
They stride alone into the purer air,
Scorning with eager feet the rock-strewn track and passing obstacles
                    with ease.
In haste, they bare the head and body to the sun and wind.
They pass from sight, the hillside stands alone, the Path deserted.
The crowds walk on, saying "Madman! He is gone into a wilderness!"

But is it so?
What could the crowd know of the vision from the Heights,
The clear, far mountain vistas, the sweetness of the half-celestial
                    air,
The shaded pathway through the deodars, the sparkling mountain waters,
The comrades found, beyond the bend that shut the traveller from ken.
How would they know, those dancers in the villages,
Of what the sages learned, and shared, and understood?

The Path leads on, but never till the bend is passed is it traversed
                              with ease or pleasure,
Or with companion sages.
This wise men know, and speed upon the bare hillside to reach the
                              bend.
They, turning from the beaten road, endure the uphill climb with
                              fortitude.
No other passes there.

The Path is ruthless in its toll of men,
And only in its unseen upper part relents and takes the traveller to
                              heart, and cherishes him,
For Nature, bending to his feet, makes loveliness for him,
THE ARHAN, of the Eagle's brood, and the Far-Flying,
The Clear-Visioned, the Hawk of Mountain Peak,
The Ever-Free.

MÂRGA - The Way

If the student has been attentive to the preceding comments, he will observe the trend of the outline of the Dharma, presented in this series. He will note that it is a commentary upon the scheme of reasoning and instruction enunciated by the Buddha 2500 years ago. He will be careful to perceive that the scheme is as sensible and as clear, spoken in today's language, as it was when it was spoken in the languages of the land of its origin, near to the Buddha's birthplace, and that it has much the same application, human nature having altered very little in the interval.

The Dharma is a set of instructions, not unconnected discourses. Some commentary is necessary to convey the reasoning, but terse and pointed words were often all the Buddha used to express meanings to those around him.

The Dharma is no mystery as far as the directions themselves are concerned. They are public property, and have been so for 2500 years. The mystery lies in the performance of the instructions. The lengthy explanations of some points, recorded in the SUTRAS, are words of one technician to other technicians, and they may be wearisome to a beginner or an apprentice. The Buddha's words, so far as they were recorded in the beginning, are clear and brief and succinctly reasonable; they convey his message to all.

He spoke to audiences composed of people who went homeward pondering, remembering, to practise what he preached. In lieu of non-existent printed literature, he spoke in such fashion that the audience could remember. He named his points, or he numbered them, so that the scheme might be held in the minds of those who were not - at that time of history - in the habit of recording teachings, who were accustomed to oral instructions. But for this clarity and masterful handling of the subject, the Dharma might have been forgotten easily, as many lengthy dissertations of pundits have been forgotten before that time and since.

Sometimes he spoke in parables, or allegory, or illustrated what he meant by incidents of life around him. He drew upon the aspects of nature and the facts known to all people, thus making it easy for the listener to make comparisons, and to remember better because of the vivid illustration. All this is foreign to the minds of those who have an abundance of literature, and are not in the habit of listening to and remembering oral teaching.

When the Buddha spoke of The Four Truths - CATVÂRI ÂRYA-SATYÂNI - he spoke of them as -

The First Truth	DUHKHA	The Presence of Suffering
The Second Truth	SAMUDAYA	The Causation of Suffering
The Third Truth	NIRODHA	The Cessation of Suffering
The Fourth Truth	MÂRGA	The Way to End Suffering

These numbers and names made a sequence of thought and a logical approach to what he really wished to emphasize, his eight-fold instructions of the road to follow, his directions to his followers, his one great gift of Wisdom expressed as simply as the Enlightened Being could devise. He set the eight sub-divisions of MÂRGA into immortal words, and called them ÂRY-ÂST-ÂNGIKA-MÂRGAH, The Noble Eight-fold Path.

High as they rise in power, in the people's minds, the gods sink into
discard with the slightest veering of the wind of popular approval.   Once
the process of desertion is begun, the most sacred and most ancient holy of
holies gradually will be abandoned and forsaken.

No hand can stay the ending, and no edict staunch the life blood of
the dying idol, stricken by the fickle-minded populace, if it finds a better
mystery or ideal to adore.   The great god falls among the remnants of his
offerings, and by and by there are no other offerings.   His courts fall
silent and the colours fade, the ornaments and treasures disappear, to reappear mysteriously within a rival's sanctuary.   The victor appropriates
the loser's titles and attributes - and sometimes the name.

The outward symbols and appurtenances crumble, as the god himself had
crumbled into ruin.   The vandals seize upon the now-hated reminder of the
glory that had been.   The bare walls of the sanctuary sometimes remain
standing, but frequently even the walls are razed or serve as quarries for
the conqueror.   The statues of the mighty have been known to vanish from
their niches, to adorn the niches of the fashionably new and young religion
of the moment's adoring pride.

Why is this so?   Are men so blind they cannot see the idol is a symbol,
and that the no-idol is also a symbol, only a little less corporeal than a
statue?   Cannot they discern the god of one religion is a god like that of
another religion, that all are alike - that some are clearer symbols, but
that is all?

What does it matter if a god is graven, or unexpressed in form, or
symbolized, or mysteriously absent?   The power of the god comes from his
worshippers.   The habits of his priesthood are the habits of the race.   The
faults, mistakes and earthliness of one god may be expressed again by different successive gods.

There are no innovations, really, in times known to mankind.   All gods
are like each other in pattern, in usefulness, in their becoming, and in
their long decline.   Another god succeeds them.   What is it that succeeds?
Another newer, fairer, kinder, truer, higher god?   Or just another veering
of the public fancy to a fashion better fitted to the times?

Whatever it may be, the gods depart, one by one sinking into oblivion
and impotence.   They last for centuries, true, and they are remembered as
great powers for many centuries more, but centuries are only days in race
time, though they are lifetimes to the human unit.

The gods, then, briefly live, and slowly fade.   They come and go, and
pass across the stage of evolution as they personify the thought of man that
calls them forth and gives them life and breath and strength and their
dimensions.   They are the unenduring and the fragile, seemingly eternal
though they are.   They depart into the eternity discerned by man, from
which he calls them forth to represent it to his mind, but they never were
eternal.   They belong to Time, and they depart into the depths of Time.

SÛKSHMA

Is this a well-known word?

No. Hardly ever used in the West. It is a technical term, the specific appellation, of a certain state of being.

Is it defined?

It is. SÛKSHMA means subtle, elusive, fine.

How is it reached?

Through SÛKSHMA SARÎRA - the subtle sheath. That is, the mind appearance, or thought-body, temporary in nature, the most illusive mental state to trace, the nearest to no-body vesture, the least material of the SARÎRAS - sheaths or vestures.

Who assumes this state?

All those with mind. All have embryo SÛKSHMA vestures. All have the state of SÛKSHMA open to them.

How do we know it?

The Yogi does. The ordinary, oblivious human being does not know of it. It is a state reached by strenuous effort.

Is it in dreams?

Seldom. The ordinary human being in dream resides within the KÂMA RÛPA or the MÂYÂVI RÛPA - and does not climb to the form-divested mental SÛKSHMA SARÎRA. Yet, by force of circumstances, or by accident, it may be reached; but then, it is not recognized as such, merged as the consciousness would be with the more vivid thought of ordinary states of being.

Does it bring Wisdom?

That would depend. YOGA is practise, method, not Wisdom. The tool sharpened may cut, wound, or kill - or set free from the bonds of MÂRA.

Does it give Knowledge?

Supernormal Knowledge, no doubt, is meant. Perhaps it gives some clues. It can be used to acquire both Knowledge and Wisdom, if the remembrance is acquired. Not easy.

How would one start?

Body control, emotion control, and sense control. The eternal battle

of the Soul and the Senses.   The point of the attack upon the grip
of body.

And then - is it possible?

Sometimes.   Spasmodically.   And clearly perfect only in the Adept.
Yet, worth the trying, worth the acquiring, this unmastered art of
sinking the unconscious body into deep sleep, and waking in full consciousness into the realm of MÂNASA, arrayed in the slight and most
subtle of the sheaths - the SÛKSHMA SARÎRA, or "thought body".
And there to meet immortals, or to seek for Wisdom.

(to be continued)

-*- -*- -*- -*- -*- -*- -*- -*- -*- -*- -*- -*- -*- -*- -*- -*- -*- -*- -*-

THE NEWS CORNER

Letters from Miss Isaline B. Horner, Honorable Secretary of the renowned
Pali Text Society, London, are a bright vividness, always appreciated for
their helpfulness.   Miss Horner, herself an author, translator, authority and
lecturer on Buddhism, known all over the world for her research, is one of the
group of scholars associated with the founder of the Pali Text Society - the
late Professor T. W. Rhys-Davids.   Mrs. Rhys-Davids, the late Sir Francis
Younghusband, E. M. Hare, F. L. Woodward, and many others are members of this
group.   Miss Horner's comments on the book famine are now shared with our
readers, and we hope to quote from her writings later in the year:

"Undoubtedly the interest in Buddhism is increasing all over the world,
but it has put us in a great difficulty.   The increased interest
seemed to me to come very suddenly indeed, and books which had been
on the stocks literally for years vanished as it were overnight.
This would have been splendid had it not been for the printing and
publishing difficulties here which appear to be insurmountable ...
The booksellers, the Buddhist Society, and the Pali Text Society
are constantly being implored from all over the world to supply some
literature, and no one has any books here.   And no one overseas can
quite believe in our book famine ... It is extremely regrettable that
the story is the same everywhere - no books to be bought for love
or money. ... We too have the greatest difficulty in getting books
from India.   Even periodicals, like INDIAN CULTURE, not shipped
during the war, seem impossible to procure ... I have several people
wishing to begin a study of Pali, but they are quite unable to find
grammars.   What a state to be in.   It is terrible to want to
cultivate the arts of peace and to be denied the tools."

We have been fortunate in securing from Miss Horner some very valuable
books, now out of print, so that we may - at least - review them for our
readers, and quote from them when space is available.   We acknowledge this
kindness to us and to our readers, from a true and sincere Buddhist friend.

CHAPTER FIFTEEN

PHYSICAL DISCIPLINE

"Let there be no mental leaning toward one path or
another, till the Way thou seekest becomes clear."

Padma Hiranya Surangama.

When the awakened Soul surveys the battlefield, it is dismayed and
troubled.   It sees the stains of past lives, the multitude of horrors it
has piled up for adjustment, the little faults.   The terrible miasma of the
Senses makes it shudder.   It sees the whole problem and it knows not where
to start.   It does not realize that all can not be undertaken at once, that
only the nearest, most offensive habits can be attacked and eliminated, that
lives may be required to accomplish it.   So it despairs and shudders.

Now if the Soul is cowardly it draws back from the conflict and that
life may be wasted.   No outside help can make it face the issue unless it
does so of its own accord.   No outside hand can help or strengthen, and no
outside voice can warn.   For the Soul's sovereign right to decide for itself
is inviolable.

But where the Soul takes courage, shrinking and in agony of confusion,
yet still wills to press onward, the battle begins in earnest, and much can
be accomplished.   Even one little habit conquered and a better established
means part of the battle is ended.

So let us proceed to consider where such a Soul might start.

There is the Body.   It has had its way so long.   It has been first so
often that the Soul has made it a pampered and overbearing tyrant.   It has
now to be told that it must change places, must be the servant.   It does not
like this, of course, but if the will is strong enough and stays firm and
unyielding, the Body will yield and follow.   Much can be done to train and
develop it in the proper manner.   The elimination of the appetite for
flesh and "forbidden fruit" of all kinds must be first undertaken.

The appetite for selfish indulgence in sport and killing and unnecessary cruelty may have vanished long before the pupil approaches The Way, but
the old habit of ages may persist so that he does not realize the necessity
of avoiding animal flesh as food.   This is the first step, and one not to
be postponed, because on it all the other steps are based.   Here the pupil
takes the Body in hand and says "Thou shalt not", and by doing so he forges
the first chain of the Soul upon the unchained appetites.

When this has been accomplished and the Body rests after the readjust-
ment, when the change is not a struggle but a settled habit, then the pupil
may take upon himself the further step of breaking the old habit of amusements which waste time and energy.   Long ago he may have found the folly of .
the more gross amusements and indulgences, but now he must drop the ones

remaining, if they are not constructive, or if they waste time.

There can be no hard or fast rules for any of these steps, for each being
is a law unto himself. Each one must take the steps as they prove to be
practicable for him. The pupil must prescribe the best thing for his Body
and judge the circumstances. He must bring the Body through the changes
without damage and without breakdown. He must be careful, for what use to him
in later stages will be a ruined body, or an incorrectly trained one, which
still troubles with its cry for the old pleasures or food?

There is also the necessity for keeping in touch with the civilization
of one's time. The pupil, in the first stages of The Way, must reckon with
his destiny. It has brought him into and takes him through the time wherein
he finds himself. He must triumph over circumstances, not find refuge in
withdrawing from them. He must, therefore, be a perfect unit in the great
mosaic of his time. He must not be so far out of proportion that he cannot
fit in. He must be in it, yet not of it, but in harmony always.

Therefore, he must avoid the appearance of peculiarity. He must not
wear queer clothes. He must not eat oddly. He must be adaptable and ready
to mingle in any gathering in his world, for who knows where the next task
will take him.

Yet he must be in harmony only so far as his perception of the higher
Way will permit him to be, and he can achieve the adjustment without making
himself appear fanatical, or uncomfortably impossible to live with, as many
students seem to think is necessary.

-*- -*- -*- -*- -*- -*- -*- -*- -*- -*- -*- -*- -*- -*- -*- -*- -*- -*- -*- -*-

"I have heard a lama say that the part of a master, adept of the
'Short Path', is to superintend a 'clearing'. He must incite the
novice to rid himself of the beliefs, ideas, acquired habits and innate
tendencies, which are part of his present mind, and have been developed
in the course of successive lives whose origin is lost in the night of
time. ...

"On the other hand, the master must warn his disciple to be on his
guard against accepting new beliefs, ideas and habits as groundless and
irrational as those which he shakes off. ...

"The discipline on the 'Short Path' is to avoid imagining things.
When imagination is prescribed, in contemplative meditation, it is to
demonstrate by that conscious creation of perceptions or sensations, the
illusory nature of those perceptions and sensations which we accept as
real though they too rest on imagination; the only difference being that,
in their case, the creation is unconsciously effected."

"MAGIC AND MYSTERY IN TIBET"
Page #270
by Alexandra David-Neel

Pandora, being satisfied with life and hardly yet aware of what life is,
procrastinated in her growing up and fell behind. The gods were much concerned. They tried to tempt her into some exertion, but succeeded only in
arousing a little spell of curiosity, and no more. They put their heads
together. They devised a scheme to bring the long-delaying one to reach
into the treasure house of mind, to put upon her thoughtless, happy, care-
free deva consciousness the vesture of the consciousness of mind.

They made a box of most attractive shape and filled it full of all the
puzzles, dilemmas, perplexities, untoward and awful incidents the world has
ever known, and were about to close it thus but that the mighty goddess of
the clear vision (SARASVATĪ) spoke quickly, saying: "No, it is too much, too
hard a lesson, the child could never learn it. We must devise an antidote. We must give a companion from the deva heights, a rainbow aura from
the world of happiness, a never-to-be-lost reminder of the realm of song
and dream."

The gods grew solemn, then breathed upon the empty air and drew from it
the rainbow figure of the goddess' thought, and tucked it carefully beneath
the lowest layer of the problems and the untoward events - beneath the
somber shadow of the shrouded reaper, death. They closed it then and left
it to the wayward one who would not learn, so she would grow by trying
all its miseries, enduring them, thus polishing the bright jewel of the
mind by hard and ceaseless toil. .....

The box grew empty long before Pandora realized it, but, though they
were limited in number, the winged miseries were never still. They hovered
near and near. She made some of them impotent, but they sprang to life
again. She evaded them, but they bided their time. She sought relief in
sleep, but they wakened her or haunted her in dreams so that she could not
sleep. Through this the mind grew strong and stronger, but the bright
deva being slowly turned into a mortal, and encountered last of all the
shrouded figure, death.

No mortal ever understands the task of an immortal descending in the
scale. Pandora was immortal until she found the box - that is, the gift
of mind. Then the undying grew into the mortal, and the cup of bitterness
was full. Pandora knew no comfort until in the end the rainbow-rayed and
shimmering one emerged, the last gift of the gods. The little one said
truly:

"There is hope, and where you are, I am. The underworld is never
long, and all is in the end the same, only a little time until we
come again to try once more, to outwit if we can these miseries.
But if you know the upper world is there, and will be there until
we come again, and fate is never endless, is it so hard? There
are the gods beyond, and all is well; they have not yet forgotten.
Let us remember, there is hope, and I am here with you."

Pandora listened, and the winged one settled close upon her shoulder,
thenceforth to speak again, again, again, the message "there is hope", to
lighten with the rainbow hues the world of somberness. Over it all, the
goddess of true wisdom watched, and smiled to see, beyond the present
pain, the glorious and triumphal ending.

"WHERE ARE THE ADEPTS FOUND?"

Is this not universal? Who reads of Adepts and who realizes what the Adept is must wish to know them, or to find some traces of them, or to have objective proof of their existence somewhere, and must hope sometime to reach them somehow.

Unfortunately Adepts are not publicity seekers, nor do they advertise for pupils.   They never yet have made themselves available to all the sensation-loving peoples of the Western world.   They may be, actually are, invested with the ability to teach and help others, but they also are inclined to choose the pupils, knowing better than the pupil what his chances of success may be.   Wherever they are, they retain command of their most valuable time, and do not permit themselves to be victimized by the curious, skeptical, selfish people who would otherwise destroy their privacy.

It is, of course, the hope of every occult student to find them, and the more ambitious ones dream of a journey to the Himalayan fastnesses to search for them.   The very fact that the student considers the journey necessary proves the uselessness in that particular student's case. If he were able to take the Path, the Adepts would be found - they would advance to meet him where he is.

No Adept uses what may be called the lower methods, unless such use is easier and adds to the results. For what is called the higher methods, the place is unimportant.   It is therefore quite useless to look for a tall, distinguished personage to come your way, by ordinary travel, or to try to find an Ashrama or a dwelling place of Adepts by chance.   If found at all it will be by direction, and because the contact has been earned; there will be no accident about it.

The Adepts preserve their anonymity, fortunately, so that the pretenders and the false prophets who masquerade as Masters may easily become known as opportunists.   The true Adept is a Master of the art of intercommunication, and he has no need of what is called "organizations" and organization methods.   The famous Mystery schools have never discontinued work by inner and higher methods.

It would be better for the student if he could disabuse his mind of this obsession, if he can, and turn his attention toward the possibility of acquiring what wisdom he can, where he is, and trust the Law to bring him to a point of development where he can dispense with such limitations as physical distance, and overcome the undevelopment which holds him prisoner.

He should look upward, take flight himself, not look for the relief he seeks around himself, or at his present level.

-*- -*- -*- -*- -*- -*- -*- -*- -*- -*- -*- -*- -*- -*- -*- -*- -*- -*- -*-

"Have patience, Candidate, as one who fears no failure, courts no success. ....."

THE VOICE OF THE SILENCE, by H.P. Blavatsky

Part I - The Life of the Buddha

60. Q. What did he do there?
     A. Having formed his determination after these reflections, he went at
         evening to the Bôdhi, or Asvattha tree, where the present
         Mahâbôdhi Temple stands.

61. Q. What did he do there?
     A. He determined not to leave the spot until he attained perfect
         wisdom.

62. Q. At which side of the tree did he seat himself?
     A. The side facing the east. *

     * No reason is given in the canonical books for the choice of this
       side of the tree, though an explanation is to be found in the
       popular legends upon which the books of Bishop Bigandet and other
       European commentators are based.   There are always certain in-
       fluences coming upon us from the different quarters of the sky.
       Sometimes the influence from one quarter will be best, sometimes
       that from another quarter.   But the Buddha thought that the per-
       fected man is superior to all extraneous influences.

63. Q. What did he obtain that night?
     A. The knowledge of his previous births, of the causes of re-births,
         and of the way to extinguish desires.   Just before the break of
         the next day his mind was entirely opened, like the full-blown
         lotus flower; the light of supreme knowledge, or the Four Truths,
         poured in upon him.   He had become BUDDHA - the Enlightened,
         the all-knowing - the SARVAJANA.

64. Q. Had he at last discovered the cause of human misery?
     A. At last he had.   As the light of the morning sun chases away the
         darkness of night, and reveals to sight the trees, fields, rocks,
         seas, rivers, animals, men and all things, so the full light of
         knowledge rose in his mind and he saw at one glance the causes
         of human suffering and the way to escape from them.

65. Q. Had he great struggles before gaining this perfect wisdom?
     A. Yes, mighty and terrible struggles.   He had to conquer in his body
         all those natural defects and human appetites and desires that
         prevent our seeing the truth.   He had to overcome all the bad
         influences of the sinful world around him.   Like a soldier
         fighting desperately in battle against many enemies, he struggled:
         like a hero who conquers, he gained his object, and the secret
         of human misery was discovered.

66. Q. What use did he make of the knowledge thus gained?
     A. At first he shrank from teaching it to the people at large.

67. Q. Why?
     A. Because of its profound importance and sublimity.   He feared that
         but few people would understand it, and that only confusion of
         mind might result if it were preached.

68. Q. What made him alter this view? *
     A. He saw that it was his duty to teach what he had learnt as clearly
         and simply as possible, and trust to the truth impressing itself
         upon the popular mind in proportion to each one's individual
         Karma.   It was the only way of salvation and every being had an
         equal right to have it pointed out to him.   So he determined to
         begin with his five late companions, who had abandoned him when he
         broke his fast.

     * The ancient story is that the God Brahmâ himself implored him not
       to withhold the glorious truth.

69. Q. Where did he find them?
     A. In the deer-park at Isipatana, near Benares.

70. Q. Can the spot be now identified?
     A. Yes, a partly ruined stûpa, or dagoba, is still standing on that
         very spot.

71. Q. Did those five companions readily listen to him?
     A. At first, no; but so great was the spiritual beauty of his appearance,
         so sweet and convincing his teaching, that they soon turned and
         gave him the closest attention.

72. Q. What effect did this discourse have upon them?
     A. The aged Kondanna, "The Believer" (Anna), was the first to lose his
         prejudices, accept the Buddha's teaching, become his disciple,
         and enter the Path leading to Arahatship.   The other four soon
         followed his example.

73. Q. Who were his next converts?
     A. A rich young layman, named Yasa, and his father, a wealthy merchant.
         By the end of three months the disciples numbered sixty persons.

74. Q. Who were the first women lay disciples?
     A. The mother and wife of Yasa.

75. Q. What did the Buddha do at that time? *
     A. He called the disciples together, gave them full instructions, and
         sent them out in all directions to preach his doctrine.

     * Brahmanism not being offered to non-Hindûs, Buddhism is, conse-
       quently, the oldest missionary religion in the world.   The early
       missionaries endured every hardship, cruelty, and persecution, with
       unfaltering courage.

76. Q. What was the essence of it?
     A. That the way of emancipation lies in leading the holy life and fol-
         lowing the rules laid down which will be explained later on.

77. Q. Tell me what name he gave to this course of life?
     A. The Noble Eight-fold Path.

78. Q. How is it called in the Pali language?
     A. ARIYO ATTHANGIKO MAGGO.

79. Q. Whither did the Buddha then go?
    A. To Uruvêla.

80. Q. What happened there?
    A. He converted a man named Kâshyappa, renowned for his learning, and
       chief priest of the Jatilas, a great sect of fire-worshippers,
       all of whom became also his followers.

81. Q. Who was his next great convert?
    A. King Bimbisâra, of Magadha.

82. Q. Which two of the Buddha's most learned and beloved disciples were
       converted at about this time?
    A. Sâriputra and Moggallâna, formerly chief disciples of Sanjaya, the
       ascetic.

83. Q. For what did they become renowned?
    A. Sâriputra for his profound learning (Prajna), Moggallâna for his
       exceptional spiritual powers (Iddhi).

84. Q. Are these wonder-working powers miraculous?
    A. No, but natural to all men and capable of being developed by a
       certain course of training.

85. Q. Did the Buddha hear again from his family after leaving them?
    A. Oh yes, seven years later, while he was living at Râjagriha, his
       father, King Suddhodana, sent a message to request him to come
       and let him see him again before he died.

86. Q. Did he go?
    A. Yes. His father went with all his relatives and ministers to meet
       him and received him with great joy.

87. Q. Did he consent to resume his old rank?
    A. No. In all sweetness he explained to his father that the Prince
       Siddhârtha had passed out of existence, as such, and was now
       changed into the condition of a Buddha, to whom all beings were
       equally akin and equally dear. Instead of ruling over one
       tribe or nation, like an earthly king, he, through his Dharma,
       would win the hearts of all men to be his followers.

88. Q. Did he see Yasodharâ and his son Râhula?
    A. Yes. His wife, who had mourned for him with deepest love, wept
       bitterly. She also sent Râhula to ask him to give him his in-
       heritance, as the son of a prince.

89. Q. What happened?
    A. To one and all he preached the Dharma as the cure for all sorrows.
       His father, son, wife, Ananda (his half-brother), Devadatta
       (his cousin and brother-in-law), were all converted and became
       his disciples. Two other famous ones were Anuruddha, a
       great metaphysician, and Upâli, a barber. Both of these gained
       great renown.

(to be continued)

THE THEORY OF MANVANTARA - PROPORTION:

Referring to the Cosmis Calendar in the January number of this Volume, on page #11, the student will notice the exactness of the table and its consistent proportionate scale. He will note that the MAHĀ MANVANTARA of our planet is at the ratio of 6,000,000 years of mortal time to one Cosmic Minute.   Divine Time fits into the Cosmic Calendar at the ratio of 1,000,000 Divine years to one Cosmic Hour, or 16,666-2/3 Divine years to one Cosmic Minute.   He will be able to accept this proportionate scale because he perceives the smaller life scales of other living creatures around him, shorter than his own.   He will reason that the Universe is one and therefore the great must be in relation to the small, even as he finds it in his world.

Down to the smallest particle and up to the largest and most distant planet, and in the interstellar spaces, there is proportion, exact and perfect.   It is almost as if it were a dimension, of itself a building brick of the universe.   Atoms maintain their exact distances, but also their exact proportional dimensions, time and functions, and so with all aspects of the Universe.   Any disturbance of proportion results in disturbances of balance which may affect surrounding space for very many years. So it is with time.   Objects maintain their proportions, and if displaced create disorder.

No one has bounded Time, or set the hands of the great Cosmic clock to measuring these infinitudes of ages.   The occult measures are based on the observations of the seers, and are calculated for the purpose of conveying proportion.   The exact, accurate, penultimate second is not expressed in these round figures, designed to represent proportions.   What is it, if a planet lives a year, or half a million years, beyond these indicated times? Does it make much difference?   Could this be more than a half second in the larger scheme?   It is hardly worth noting, therefore, by the short-lived but wisdom-seeking mortal.   Only the eye of seers, seeking exactitude and definite information of the planet's dissolution, would be concerned with variations of the ratio.

The usefulness of knowledge, such as this glimpse of proportion, is manifold.   The student seizes upon the opportunity to acquaint himself with the scheme of the Vast Whole, the One Life, the Enduring Cosmos. He perceives his length of life is of as much importance and is as proportionately short, in relation, as his body-bulk is to the total bulk of our planet.   He observes that our planet marches beside the larger planets of our solar scheme, but even so is not the most important.   He observes that the sun scheme is one of many brother schemes, and that - perhaps - our sun is not of the most importance in the march.   He observes that the scheme of universes also have their differences, and that our universe marches with other universes, but perhaps is not of most importance.   He observes that beyond these stupendous schemes there may be other, larger schemes, outside his comprehension, within the Cosmic Whole.

He grows thus into realizing unity, through understanding that all is One, and yet unlike in time, endurance and in function, but that there is nothing of unimportance in the plan.

LIGHT: (May, 1947, p. #70)

Long used by the Mysteries as the supreme symbol of the Spirit or Cosmic Consciousness. It is, however, capable of being used in different shades of meaning. To one person it may mean Illumination or Enlightenment or Liberation from Matter. To another it may mean the Sun Center itself. To others, it may be the Sun behind the sun, and to still others even further and more remote Ideals. To some it may be the sunlight - actual or spiritual. To others it may be more symbolic than actual; to others, the clear Flame of ÂTMA; to others the white Blaze of BUDDHI; and to others the yellow Brightness of the MÂNASA levels. All are included in the illuminated seer's use of the word Light - and all are Light of one kind or another.

KÂMA-RÛPA: (Sanskrit) (May, 1947, p. #74)

Desire-form, literally. This form is not a true body, but is a sheath of spheroid form enveloping the visible body. It is composed of finer atoms and is therefore invisible, but is a necessary link between the body and its environment. It is also a link between the mind and the environment, though it is not usually thought of in that connection, the popular interpretation being "the seat of the emotions". That is perhaps an undue emphasis on the spectacular, and lack of emphasis upon the utilitarian aspects of the KÂMA-RÛPA. It can be the vehicle of all the spiritual powers of Compassion, used by the man of development and insight.

SHEATHS: (May, 1947, p. #75)

This is an English word substituted for the Sanskrit SARÎRA, meaning "vehicle" or "center of consciousness". It is a word which should be understood to mean an encircling sheath of finer matter, though it is not a body, does not look like the physical body, and does not serve as an alternate body. The SARÎRA is not detachable at night, nor capable of travelling far. The Consciousness which makes the SARÎRA a center of energy is often able to make contact with other planes of consciousness and other places, but that is another story. "Sheath" is preferable to the commonly used word "body", as the latter has created confusion. The meaning of the Sanskrit SARÎRA is "enveloping cloud form or sheath." The various Sheaths are interrelated and inter-connected and inter-penetrated, but are on their own planes fully independent. After death they are capable of being the habitat of the in-dwelling Consciousness of the being for a time at least. Without these intervening SARÎRAS the Consciousness cannot control the physical body, and various stages of damage or imperfection of a SARÎRA or SARÎRAS are evidenced by immoral and insane people, hallucinated or obsessed mediums, and also some forms, if not all, of epilepsy and hysteria.

SENSES: (May, 1947, p. #76)

This word is used instead of the Buddhist term - INDRYÂNI. It should be considered to mean the physical senses, but also their finer counterparts in the invisible Sheaths. The physical Senses are, of course, most in evidence, but because of this the finer organs are sometimes overlooked and discounted. Sight, touch, smell, taste and hearing are all present in the Sheaths, but operate differently. They are blended into one Cognitive Faculty at the formless levels.

THE SECRET DOCTRINE, by Helena P. Blavatsky

This book has been in print continuously since its first appearance in 1888.
It has been used as a reference authority and source of information, and is
still the one unfailing recourse of all writers upon occult philosophy. It
serves as an inexhaustible mine for authors, otherwise undistinguished, who
borrow from its treasures.   Very often the jewel facets are damaged beyond
repair, wrenched from the original setting by these industrious chiselers of
truth, but still the jewels gleam in the new but tawdry settings of the neo-
theosophical and the more outré cults.   These borrow from the treasure
without a "by your leave", much less acknowledgment.

The long history of the persecution endured by this book is another story.
Both of these stories deserve to be recorded.   The long roll of the ap-
propriations and distortions of its teachings should be made clear, and the
source of the many attacks upon the book and its author should be exposed.
In fifty-eight years there have been only a very few students who commented
on these matters, though it would seem to have been the first and official
duty of all those who claim adherence to it.

No one could review this book adequately, and it is therefore not attempted.
It is an encyclopedia, rather than a treatise.   It is a book of clues and
endless hidden meanings, and deviously tangled doctrines left to the ingenuity and perspicacity of the student to discern.   The theme of the book
itself is plain and clear, the import of the cosmic scheme is unveiled, but
here and there the story breaks - in the manner of the Mystery writings of
all the ages - to preserve that which should not be open to the casual gaze.

That which the book could do - to clear the mind of dogma, superstition,
skepticism, materialism, theological imaginations, idolatry, bigotry, and
intolerance - the book sets forth with clarity and brilliance.   That which
it could not do - to teach the inner, secret doctrine in its entirety - it
has not done, because no student acquires what is secret by the open written
record.   The higher and more esoteric teachings are therefore never clear,
and where they appear they break again and disappear.   But for the brief
appearance the student must be thankful, and remember that it may be the
broken end is somewhere else continued.   He has no certainty that he will
find it elsewhere in THE SECRET DOCTRINE'S pages, but let him look; he may
find the true meaning dawning.

The author, Helena P. Blavatsky, wrote this book for the centuries, not for
her lifetime.   This is a book to own, to treasure, to continue reading, to
grow old with, and to die learning from its pages.   It is not duplicated
in the world of literature.

Such is the value of this book that its history should be well known to the
student.   During the years since the author's death its contents have been
altered and its volumes have been the subject of much controversy.   The
jewel of the teaching has been flawed and damaged in some editions.   Therefore the edition we recommend is the most true to the original edited and
published with the author's approval in 1888.

Whatever errors - spelling, grammar, printer's mistakes, etc., - may be in

the Original Edition, they are the responsibility of and the karma of the
author.   The student should step into the line of that karma, rather than permit another to intervene as an intermediary, and so confuse the karma of the
teaching.   He should deal directly with the author.   Some of her comments
follow:

PREFACE: "What is contained in this work is to be found scattered
             throughout thousands of volumes embodying the scriptures
             of the great Asiatic and early European religions, hidden
             under glyph and symbol, and hitherto left unnoticed because
             of this veil.   What is now attempted is to gather the
             oldest tenets together and to make of them one harmonious
             and unbroken whole." ...

PREFACE,   "It is needless to explain that this book is not the Secret
p. viii: Doctrine in its entirety, but a select number of fragments
             of its fundamental tenets ...

             "But it is perhaps desirable to state unequivocally that the
             teachings, however fragmentary and incomplete ... belong
             neither to the Hindu, the Zoroastrian, the Chaldean, nor the
             Egyptian religion, neither to Buddhism, Islam, Judaism nor
             Christianity exclusively.   The Secret Doctrine is the es-
             sence of all these.   Sprung from it in their origins, the
             various religious schemes are now made to merge back into
             their original element, out of which every mystery and
             dogma has grown, developed, and become materialized ...

             "The aim of this work may be thus stated: to show that Nature
             is not 'a fortuitous concurrence of atoms,' and to assign to
             man his rightful place in the scheme of the Universe; to
             rescue from degradation the archaic truths which are the
             basis of all religions; and to uncover, to some extent, the
             fundamental unity from which they all spring; finally, to
             show that the occult side of Nature has never been approached
             by the Science of modern civilization."

VOL. II,   "All the words and sentences placed in brakets in the Stanzas
p. 22   and Commentaries are the writer's.   In some places they may
footnote: be incomplete and even inadequate from the Hindu standpoint;
             but in the meaning attached to them in Trans-Himalayan
             Esotericism they are correct.   In every case the writer
             takes any blame upon herself ...

             "The teaching is offered as it is understood; and as there
             are seven keys of interpretation to every symbol and allegory,
             that which may not fit a meaning, say from the psychological
             or astronomical aspect, will be found quite correct from the
             physical or metaphysical."

We sponsor and recommend the photographic reproduction of the Original Edition
of THE SECRET DOCTRINE, as being the most true to the author, H. P. Blavatsky.
It consists of the original first and second volumes and index, bound in
one volume of over 1500 pages.   It is obtainable from The Golden Lotus Press,
price $7.50.

THE DHARMA

The Noble Eightfold Path

Many times the Buddha spoke this formuls during his lifetime of teaching. He threw the emphasis upon it always. Doctrine and Dogma, theory
and deduction, reasoning and speculation, all these are negative, illsu-
sory and ineffective. They can lead only to mind-readiness, but not to
progress, unless they are supplemented by effort and application.

Recognizing the futility of creating a multitude of mine-ready indolent,
specultaive discoursersupon the Dharma and metaphysical points thereof,
the Buddha insisted upon the development of practitioners rather than
theorists. Harder it is to do, to practice, to live the Dharma, than
to read or hear or discuss or assimilate it mentally, without practice.

Many people like tc **imagine** that knowledge of certain tenets gives them
the right to teach them to others, forgetting that the only legitimate
teacher is one who can point to his own achievements, and is capable of
proving that he understands and has practiced what he preaches. Other
than this is egotistical assumption of superority.

Not one of the Buddha's immediate followers hesitated to drop everything else and follow where he lead. They practiced, as he did, that
which they taught, and convinced others by the obvious fact that they
had found the system to be satisfactory.

Many people assume that a modern teacher or lecturer must know of
what he speaks, That does not follow. He may have read it, merely
and seized upon the opportunity to profit from the printed material
or translation of some treatise.

Not so with Buddhists. They knew the rules of the Sangha and that the
mendicant or Bhikshu must observe the rules. In Buddhist lands, no
one would listen to long tales of supernatural or supernatural powers
without demanding proof, and no one of authority in the Sangha permits such exploitation of the people. The teacher associated with the
Sangha is accredited and worthy, judged so by his peers, and may be
trusted.

No quick and easy method is obtainable by those who follow Gautama
Buddha and his Dharma. The hard-won uphill progress is expected, is
taught and never minimized. It is expounded, elucidated and enjoined
upon all those who seek to take the Way in earnest.

Even to the layman, who aspires to no great speed or honour, The
Buddha spoke the rules of the Eight-fold Path, as a means to hold him
to the tadk of self-improvement, and to encourage him to begin the ceaseless work of self-development, by inculcating in his being the habit

of observing these Eight Directions.

Collectively they may be called Right Living or Behavior - the Middle Way of Action and Reaction.

1947 - July

```
==============
=THE WAY
=========
```

Chapter Sixteen.

Diet.

" Seek for the Way, but look also for means
to spread and teach and live Compassion."
Padma Hiranya Surangama.

Ever the Path leads up. This is self-evident, and not to be denied.
Does it not follow that the Chela, student, aspirant, or would-be-
Adept must climb it in the end? Not as it might be if it were easier,
but as is, rugged, hard and occasionally terrible, so stands the Path
in all its ancient steepness.

As the race leaves behind its infancy and days of growing into civilization, abandoning the savagery and the beastiality of cannibalism
and human sacrifice, as well as cruelty and barbarism of all kinds, so
must the evolving individual leave behind the remnants of the ancient
self-indulgences and lust for blood. He must - else can he not endure
the further slopes.

Some one will $\overset{5}{\text{say}}$, why then if one must live on vegetables and fruits,
is it not easy? Why should it be so hard to maintain health and
strength of body - as many in the West have found to be the case if
they attempted to dispense with animal food?

There is need for understanding that there must be a replacement of
proteins and a balance of vegetable vitamins. A student who endeavors
merely to replace bulk, without regard to value, may disturb the balance
and fail to replace valuable minerals, etc., which are found only in
certain foods. It is inevitable that breakdown, debility, or disease
of some kind will occur if a steady diet of slow starvation is followed.
The more drastic the change, the more devastating the collapse, reaction
reaction following action.

Care must be taken - extreme care. Food values eliminated must be replaced. Animal proteins must be counted as replaced only if equivalent
vegetable proteins replace them. Calories are not esoteric - they are
a matter for individual control, and for individual judgment

The balance of the body must be considered and the student must maintain
that balance for himself, for no one else is capable of prescribing the
right combination for his system. A careful study should be made and many
days spent in learning how the diet affects his health and disposition.
He must not risk a breakdown of his bodily resistance to disease - else
dealy and perhaps death will follow.

A gradual reduction in the amount of animal food consumed is best. A
gradual replacement with grains, fruits, nuts, milk, vegetables and
fruit juices is to be commended. Even so, it may be hard to do, in some
cases. Yet, no one but will benefit in health by reduction to the extreme minimum of the flesh foods required, if it is possible - in this
lifetime - to reach the point of final rejection.

The danger is not stressed by vegetarians, enthusisats, faddists and esoteric teachers. It should be stressed and correct balance and replacement measures pointed out, by those who preach vegetarianism. Otherwise the unaware student may proceed to drop meat suddenly and take no steps to furnish the necessary food values by adoption of other foods not usually required by the meat consumer.

Yet, all this question of diet is easy, non-existent, of no concern, to those who have the fortune to begin life as vegetarians. It is then to the body balance of meat-eating students that the danger will occur, and it is to these students that words of warning are addressed.

Compassion - what is it? An uncomprehended dream? If so, one will remember only the habit of the meat-comsuming body, and abandon compassion. If it is in the heart it will urge one to eat only the vegetables, fruits and grains, to avoid making the agony of death of animals a feast for supporting higher beings.

It is Compassion in the balance. One decides, this lifetime, one way or another, or perhaps compromises and postpones decision. Some lifetime though, the full step must be taken. May it be in a more propitious lifetime for those who cannot take it easily and naturally in this lifetime, within the present body.

ONE WORLD

Clinging to its one-world ideal, and to the concepts
of the United Nations Charter, one half of the world
looks to the United States of America for guidance
and support.   Clinging to the idea that the world
is dominated only by the strong and ruthless, another
portion of the world's inhabitants blindly live and
work and die, supporting the dictatorship of cynical
and selfishly aggressive leaders.   The world stands
divided, therefore, and each inhabitant must be a
partisan of one or the other party.

So thinks the Western world, and contemplates the
"two worlds" shibboleth, now coming into usage, as
an explanation of the crisis.

Nevertheless, there is One World.   It is, as it ever
was, united.   It is one in action and reaction.
The term "two worlds" is merely a recognition of the
warfare which exists only in Man's sphere of action.
There two Ideologies clash, and they are likely to
produce the friction we call war.   Yet the world
itself, our planet, is One World, and as One World
it will rock to the reactions of the friction between
the opposing nations.

There might be room, in One World, for these two experiments, the Capitalist and the Socialist regimes.
There might be strictly limited and mutually agreeable
spheres of action and influence.   There might be
cooperation for world need, world government and
world uplift.   There might be mutual toleration and
some friendship between the rivals.   There might be
watchful wariness and balanced power and the sta-
bilization that balanced power implies, but just at
present none of these factors have been perceived
in operation.

The world stands united, above, below, around the
level of Man's influence, but in his path the storm
clouds hover, and there is lightning on the dark
horizon.

-*- -*- -*- -*-

THE NOBLE EIGHT-FOLD PATH

Some confusion may be created by the translation of the title commonly used in the West, as above.   It is a little different from the Buddha's original ÂRYA ÂST ÂNGIKA MÂRGAH, which means the Noble Eight-Divisioned Path. The Path of Eight Methods, really, rather than a path which contains eight folds or branches.

There is one Path.   It is The Way - MÂRGAH.   The Goal is one, and it is Liberation.   The Path is trodden, however, by the practise of these Eight Methods, called by the Buddha -

1.	SAMYAG-DRSTI	Right View
2.	SAMYAK-SAMKALPA	Right Intention
3.	SAMYAG-VÂK	Right Speech
4.	SAMYAK-KARMÂNTA	Right Action
5.	SAMYAG-ÂJÎVA	Right Livlihood
6.	SAMYAG-VYÂYÂMA	Right Endeavor
7.	SAMYAK-SMRTI	Right Mindfulness
8.	SAMYAK-SAMÂDHI	Right Concentration

No choice is given.   One must practise all, forgetting none, if one would progress very far.   By practising one a student begins to cut the shackles from him and to take steps toward the Goal, but he does not tread the Path itself unless he practises to the best of his ability all of the Eight Methods.   Nevertheless, it is better to begin, to do what may be possible, to undertake improvement of the Karma, rather than to wait until all of the eight may be attempted.   The wise man does his Dharma, and if it includes only a portion, let him accept that portion of the Methods as his Dharma for the present.

Nobility of living - that was the Buddha's sole commandment, expressed in detail in ÂRYA ÂST ÂNGIKA MÂRGAH.   He bound his followers to live as kings of spiritual power.   He found it necessary to express the aim in these short words only, for all his immediate followers understood the standard from the short commandments.   At times one of his audience asked a question, and there came explanation, precept, illustration, parable, and details.   These often became legends, and found their way into the literature compiled after his death.   They are of interest and they help the student.

Later still, the scholars and the experts of the Dharma wrote long dissertations and much profound thought was bent upon these Eight Methods. Somehow they leave one cold, these clever treatises.   The Buddha's words of living, flaming clarity, how brief, how clear, and how lucid they appear, and how hard the goal he set in such simple language.

The height of the achievement outlined should not deter one.   The Goal is many lives beyond, maybe, but does that matter?   Sufficient for the time the Eight Directions to it, the chance to live the Noble Path, the Noble Life, the Buddha's Way to Liberation, and ever finding it again another lifetime, with higher steps to climb and higher peaks to discover, and higher understanding of the Path toward Perfection.

Hermes, son of Zeus and the nymph Maia, born of a sudden caprice of
the beauty-loving Zeus, and therefore exceedingly beautiful, was much loved
by his father. He combined all the swiftness and the mercurial beauty of
his mother - Maia the nymph of Air and lightness, and the great resourceful-
ness of his father into one winged and laughing joyousness. Bright was his
nature, with the double gifts of power and of beauty. Imperious he was,
and yet not an egotistical rebel. Contrary sometimes, and capricious, from
his father, but faithful also, loyal and with a saving grace of humour, from
his mother. So he grew into his maturity.

The gods all loved him, and he spent much time among them, speeding
about with curiosity and friendship, watching one and then another as they
employed themselves with duties of High Heaven. He knew them all, and what
they did, and how they worked, and where they might be found, whether in
ocean depths or cavern or cloud-mist or forest, - or on Mount Olympus itself.
He could not be impounded in High Heaven, and preferred to look into the
doings of the gods or lower beings. He was a rover of the seven spheres,
beyond all doubt a wanderer by nature.

So Zeus, loving him, and glad of his bright company, such times as he
was present, admonished him, and asked him to stay closer. But Hermes said:

"Could you but see - the sand crab striving to build tunnels - the
sea lords racing dolphin steeds - the wood nymphs dancing in the
moonlight - the strange caverns of the underworld - the storm
kings in procession - the friendly faces of the animals - the swift
ways of the air beings - and the inner secrets of the gods! I
cannot be completely satisfied. I cannot rest! I must see it
all, and must be stirred always by the wealth of beauty and the
excitement of change. I hear it calling, and I must be gone,
O Zeus."

The Incomprehensible One, his father, listened, and smiled - for when
had Zeus not heard all of creation's voices, or left unheeded the beauty
of the world, where had he not lingered where the half-gods or man-creatures
had intrigued him? The father acknowledged sonship, and the lad's heritage
of his own nature. He sighed a little, for even Zeus, father, could not
curb the Zeus nature, and the son was like the father, intoxicated by
the beauty of creation.

He made him Messenger of Heaven. What could he do, but send the lad
here and there, and bid him speak this one and that, and request answer.
So might he see the youth sometimes! So might he wing more often to High
Heaven. So might he travel faster, to return again to new and interesting
corners. So might he employ beings kin, the Air Lords, or beseech the
other elemental rulers for service. So might he ride into the vortex of
the nature forces and convey the counsel of High Heaven. So might he
be a link and representative, and yet be free to roam and wander.

Hermes obeyed, but he was puzzled. He grew indeed to godhood, but
the messages were many. Then Maia counselled him and said:

"Obey your father. He loves you well, and will be glad to see you.
And I, too, in the realm of air, and all the other gods, no doubt,
So if you speed quickly you may still wander."

Time passed. The youth grew older. He found the service dearer, the piloting of men and creatures to the afterworld not inconsistent with his other duties, and he often guided travellers. By such means he enlarged his activities, and followed his curiosity.

He grew then into the Celestial Messenger, and men have often glimpsed him as he sped about the planet. .He does not wear bird's wings, but so men represent him, to suggest quick flight, just as speed is represented by wings upon his sandals and his helmet, but that is only fanciful allegory. He speeds with the Air Lord's swift powerful endurance - that is his heritage. He has the imperious sun nature of his father and is endowed with power, represented by the caduceus. Symbols and herald's wands, however, are not employed by the gods, who have no use for rods of power.

The Hermes of the Upper Heaven is a celestial being, not man-figured. He is forever questing, obeying the commands of Zeus, and forever conveying benediction and wise counsel. Wherever he goes a waft of high celestial air comes with him, and a flash of scintillant sun brightness. For so is Hermes - built of the Aether, Creative Energy, and Sublime Power, bright with the Shining Glory of the true Immortals, and restless with the Vital Energy of the mighty Zeus.

-*- -*- -*- -*- -*- -*- -*- -*- -*- -*- -*- -*- -*- -*- -*- -*- -*- -*- -*- -

A SPIRATION

Fain would I spread the BUDDHA'S gentle words
Until His Law of Love the whole world girds;
But though my heart leaps forward to the fight,
Forgetting Self and striving for the right,
My many years press ardent spirits back.
"Fain would" strives vainly with "The means ye lack".

But though in this, my dearest wish I fail;
Shall I sit idly and 'gainst Karma rail?
Nay, though I may not in this life succeed,
To spread world-wide the BUDDHA'S gentle creed;
By earnest thought and pious deeds I can
Make the Word shine at least in one poor man.

And did not He, The Blessed One, once say,
If one should meet a host in war's array,
And by his valour put the foe to rout,
Though to the skies his fame the people shout,
Much greater far is he, fore-born to bliss,
Who of himself the lordly master is.

                    Frank R. Mellor
                    (London)

HAMSA

Hamsa?   Is it occult?

It is a very ancient title of the Eastern Wisdom, used as an exoteric and an esoteric word, intensely profound and purposely unexplained, rarely used, and therefore still an occult term.

What does it mean?

Exoterically - The Bird, from beyond Space and Time, alighting within Space and Time.

Could this be explained?

"Swan" may be accepted as a synonym for HAMSA - the graceful and poetic bird of almost unearthly beauty. The "Bird" is Life itself, the infinite and unending Life of the unmanifested Universal Ocean. It, being winged, is above manifestation. It flies and flies, and maintains its flight until a resting place attracts it. It is the Bird of occult symbolism, beyond Space and Time, and beyond reach, associated with BRAHMA the Infinite, and not with BRAHMĀ, the Manifested.

Is it called KALAHAMSA, too?

No.   That is another meaning. KALA means a time-measure, and being connected with Time, adds a qualifying word. The Bird then is The Life, both in and out of Time and Space, being the Unmanifested and the Manifested. The Bird has descended, seeking a resting place, leaving the far reaches of the sky for solid earth, but is still the Bird, for it soars and wings again toward a distant goal.

Is HAMSA a metaphor?

All occult terms are metaphors, or blinds, or simply labels. Poetic simile is spoken by the Wise as natural and proper language; it is so they teach.

Does it mean Man?

No.   It has no limits. HAMSA is Life and it descends in many forms. It is the Bird, not the form, which manifests.

Is it connected with high gods?

Because the Orientalists speak of PARABRAHMAN?   No, the expert may so speak to other experts, thereby expressing what both understand by PARABRAHMAN, etc.   The Swan, flying aloft, descending and reascending, is symbol of all Life. PARABRAHMAN is the Absolute, so once again we come to "from beyond Space and Time".

Does it mean "vehicle"?

No. It does not convey Life, as VÂHANA (vehicle) may convey it.
It is Life, itself employs a vehicle, the form.

What, then, is HAMSA VÂHANA?

A title of BRAHMA, the Absolute, Infinite, Unmanifested. "He Who Uses
the Swan as His Vehicle". The Swan, emanating from BRAHMA. Again
we come to HAMSA - "from beyond Space and Time".

Is the above esoteric?

No. It is exoteric, being known. The little that is explained.
The unexplained is beyond words in places.

Would clues be found?

In esoteric writings, and partly esoteric works, if understood.

Where does he nest, the Bird?

In the beginning, there was no Bird, and only the Absolute, the One
Life, alone, without a second. No Bird flew from that One Life.
Then Life stirred and the Bird flew from the Milky Ocean, arising and
uncertain, to fly through Time and Space seeking fulfillment. A part
of the One Life, the Bird, a part, but not the whole. The Ocean
still remained, unmoving, and the Worlds moved onward through and in
it, beneath it, still a part of it, but not one with it. The Bird
flew, and the Ocean rested as before. The Bird, returning, finds
the Ocean and re-nests itself, and all is as it was before the Bird
flew and the Worlds were formed, and Time and Space began.

Would it mean Life in toto on our planet?

A student should soar high. One planet is not high. The Bird is
Life, all Life, the flying Swan of glittering pinions, and it is found
in every particle of Matter. It is the Manifested Universe, literally, for that Universe is living, is not dead matter, and where is
Life there is the Swan. The Manifested Universe, that is BRAHMÂ,
the form temporary of the Life emanating from BRAHMA the Eternal.
Here it is KALA HAMSA, the Bird in Time and Space, and out of Time
and Space.

So clear!

Always the understanding is the esoteric knowledge, hidden.

-*- -*- -*- -*- -*- -*- -*- -*- -*- -*- -*- -*- -*- -*- -*- -*- -*- -*- -*-

"There is no such thing as either 'dead' or 'blind' matter . . . "

THE SECRET DOCTRINE, Vol. I, p. #274
Original Edition, by H. P. Blavatsky

A new god, on the world horizon, rises slowly, emerging with a gradual impetus. No creed or god or worship has ever come to its full power as it began, or without accretions. No sudden overwhelming conversion of the world to any new teaching has ever been recorded.

The great gods of the world's history were originally small local gods of regions, tribes or nomadic peoples. They were never yet too proud to borrow from their rivals, and so penetrate into the rival's worshippers by devious devices. As in war, so in religion all means are - if not fair - considered expedient.

A local nature god, logical because of his environment, suited to the mind capacity of his particular locality, may be unacceptable to a more sophisticated civilization, but that same civilization may have devised a more elaborate edition of the same forces of Nature. The lines of similarity are too clear to be denied, in many cases. Then, the more elaborate cult may travel with its worshippers to outer surrounding people, and become accepted. Adventure, trade, conquest and religion follow the same routes.

The more elaborate and intelligent the presentation of the god, the more chance there is of grafting into his worship lower cults of similar nature, but equality of cults may create a rivalry or religious persecutions. Very often such rivalry results in a blending, or a merging of attributes, names and temples, and the resulting composition is sometimes more popular than the two originals. Some illustrations of this occur where an old civilization has gone down into extinction beneath the blows of a conqueror. The old worships linger in the hearts of the conquered population, and the new gods are forced upon them. Sometimes a compromise arises, such as the god Serapis after the Greek conquest of Egypt.

The temper of the people is a factor in the growth of new cults. Some peoples, child-like in mind, are satisfied for very long, do not question, do not grow unsatisfied, accept the old and accustomed worship without demur. There will be evident in them a strong though passive resistance to foreign or new gods.

Other peoples, such as the Romans were, tolerantly admit new thought and idols of other nations. The foreign gods moved into Rome and prospered. It seemed to be the idea that if one god did not answer, perhaps another would. One might sacrifice at any altar, and if the Roman gods were deaf and indisposed, one might look to the mysterious Isis, or the more stern Mithra, or the many gods in the Pantheon. Toleration seems logical to the quick, volatile and open-minded peoples of the world, wherever and in whatever time they are found.

Their opposite exists, easily recognized. These people are fanatically closed to new ideas. They cling to tribal customs, tribal gods, and tribal scriptures with a single-minded intentness, resisting anything outside their own accepted faith as "pagan" or demonical. There new gods are destroyed with intention. Only national disaster, conquest, persecution and intolerable pressure may make changes. The old gods of the

(continued on page #118)

CHAPTER SEVENTEEN

POSTURES

"Seek for The Way, but look not to external exertion,
nor to the lower mind for liberation."

Padma Hiranya Surangama.

Looking for instructions on the Eastern methods, the West has been attracted to the system of discipline called YOGA.   Because this system
offers a means to do, by physical actions, instead of a means to achieve by
perception and comprehension, it has a wide appeal.   The Western world
has been intent upon outward-turned activity for centuries, used to
achieving results by this method, and therefore it seems to be the logical
approach to matters spiritual.   Students in the West are attracted to
contortions, breathing exercises, head-stands, etc., etc., simply because
these seem to be a means to an end, and the means are enthusiastically
adopted by many earnest seekers.

Some of the YOGA exercises called Postures are harmless and do nothing
more than build control of body, but others interfere with the natural pro-
cesses of the system.   Other postures are, in the hands of experimenters,
absolutely dangerous to mind and body.

Breathing exercises, if measured and applied with care and knowledge,
may be a help to students, but carried to excess are all too often damaging
and dangerous.

Head-stands and upside-down positions are obviously merely spectacular
performances, and their use is recommended only to those who wish to waste
time in such trivial amusements.

Postures assumed for meditation, on the other hand, have a definite
purpose, likely to be useful to the experienced meditator.   What use an
Eastern posture may be to the Western student, whose body is accustomed to
different habits, may be a matter for experiments.   These postures are
useful to those who, seated on the ground or floor, dispensing with other
supports, maintain the body immovable and relaxed, without interruption
from fatigue and strain.   The resultant mind-ease permits concentration
for longer periods of time, and therefore there is a definite use for
meditation postures.

No magic is associated with these Eastern systems of YOGA.   If any
true achievement results, it results from the effort of the practitioner
in every case.   These methods may be helpful, therefore, in some cases,
but in all too many cases the strain upon bodies accustomed to comfortable
furniture and different positions may be severe.   The strain may serve
as a menace and a deterring influence, if it is continued in these cases.

Developed as the YOGA system was, in a different climate, under different conditions, by an entirely different civilization and stream of
thought, it is adapted to its environment.   In another environment,

another civilization and stream of thought, the advisability of adopting it must be considered carefully.

YOGA must be considered here in connection with Physical Discipline, as it is based upon physical methods, as upon them it relies for its success in the beginning.   It must be evaluated by each student it attracts, and by each student accepted, eliminated or adapted.   Care must be recommended. A body fitted for these Postures may surmount their use, take no harm, even derive benefit.   A body weakened or unaccustomed to bodily exertion may be unable to endure the terrific strain imposed and the endurance required. The general recommendation here is to walk carefully, with skepticism and vigilant protection of the body, between the two extremes of indolence and luxury, and violent exercise.

Where lies The Way?   In moderation, between the pairs of opposites, between asceticism and self-indulgence.   The Buddha tried the path of both of these extremes.   He left them both as useless, and thereafter walked and taught the Middle Way.   Remember!

-*- -*- -*- -*- -*- -*- -*- -*- -*- -*- -*- -*- -*- -*- -*- -*- -*- -*-

EARTHBOUND

O lovely earth, I cannot leave you long!
Though I greet the beauty of those shining stars
And dream of fairylands upon their continents,
The binding urge of earth is much too strong
To let me wander 'mong those distant bars
Of light.   Rest is not rest, for sentiments
I've met on earth come drawing me again
To all the beauties and the things so dear
I've known for ages upon ages here;
For mingled in the cosmic song
Pulling memories of earth call to my soul,
So that in other realms I cannot gain
Full peace, but must stir and wake
Again on earth to see and know once more
The things I love, the scenes I take
With breathless joy into the whole
That I call I.   What I have loved before
I love again, will ever love and need -
For Earth, I covet you with miser's greed
To come, and ever come, to touch your soil,
Your trees, your seas, your people and the nations
I have been part of and am still.   The spoil
Of life on life and sleep on sleep and dreams
Is earth and ever earth.   These my citations
Could never be complete, for I have lived so strong,
On earth and joyed in it until it truly seems,
O lovely earth, I cannot leave you long!

Louise Campbell Halley

(from "Lucifer", Oct. 1943)

"Is there an existence of the 'soul' or separate something
which can depart from the body?   If so why does it not
depart at any time?"

Evidently this questioner considers the body a unit, the "soul" a unit,
with perhaps the more intangible "spirit" a unit also.   The question would
imply a state of separateness.   With all due respect to Western theology,
there is no separation.

Life is a continuous related stream of energy, and it includes the body,
soul, spirit, and links all three - or, rather, is all three.   The Life is
the ensouler of the form.   The body is the vehicle of soul and the soul
is the vehicle of the spirit.

The stream of energy is rhythmic.   The body grows and falls away from
the Life as it progresses through its cycle of alternating activity and
passivity.   The three are linked and are one during the active period, and
the "soul" is therefore an integral part.

During the existence of the body the soul is the body's overshadowing
active principle, even as the spirit is the active overshadowing principle
of the soul.   It is therefore impossible for the soul to depart from the
body "at any time", that is, erratically or accidentally, against the laws
of being, or against the laws of relationship between the spirit, soul and
body.   In accordance with the laws of being, souls "depart" by reason of
sudden death, illness, or general fatigue of the body resulting from old
age.   Ordinarily, souls do not "depart" before the end of the normal life
cycle, because to do so would be contrary to the nature of the soul and
spirit overshadowing the form.

There is no "separate something" to depart.   It is as if the body were
the extraneous and temporary shell which houses the soul, periodically
falling away, periodically growing new and fresh.   The body is the temporary, the soul the semi-permanent, the Spirit only being the true per-
manence.

It would be better if we were to consider the soul as the animator or
energizer of the form it uses as a vehicle or carrier of Life.   In that way
we will see that Life must build a vehicle suited to the environment in
which the vehicle must function, must train it and strengthen it, and must
be careful with it so that it lasts as long as possible.   We might reflect
that what we call the instinct of self-preservation is the effort of the
Life to conserve the body as long as possible, and results from the over-
shadowing care of the ensouling principles.   Under these circumstances
the soul will hardly leave the body "at any time", or at caprice, or unaware.   Whether because of accident, untoward circumstances, old age,
or sudden death, the body is in each case reluctantly abandoned.

The form clings to the soul likewise, and has a dependence upon the
soul, much like dependence upon a wise parent, and this is a factor in the
hold of the soul upon the body.

Without a long explanation of the mechanism of the ensouling Life it

(continued on page #118)

Part II - The Dharma or Doctrine

106. Q. What is the meaning of the word Buddha?
      A. The enlightened, or he who has the perfect wisdom.

107. Q. You have said that there were other Buddhas before this one?
      A. Yes; our belief is that under the operation of eternal causation
          a Buddha takes birth at intervals, when mankind have become
          plunged into misery through ignorance and need the wisdom which
          it is the function of a Buddha to teach. (See also Q. 11.)

108. Q. How is a Buddha developed?
      A. A person, hearing and seeing one of the Buddhas on earth, becomes
          seized with the determination to so live that at some future
          time, when he shall become fitted for it, he also will be a
          Buddha for the guiding of mankind out of the cycle of rebirth.

109. Q. How does he proceed?
      A. Throughout that birth and every succeeding one, he strives to sub-
          due his passions, to gain wisdom by experience, and to develop
          his higher faculties. He thus grows by degrees wiser, nobler
          in character, and stronger in virtue, until, finally, after
          numberless re-births he reaches the state when he can become
          perfected, Enlightened, All-wise, the ideal Teacher of the
          human race.

110. Q. While this gradual development is going on throughout all these
          births, by what name do we call him?
      A. Bôdhisat, or Bôdhisattva.   Thus the Prince Siddhârtha Gautama
          was a Bôdhisattva up to the moment when, under the blessed Bôdhi
          tree at Gaya, he became Buddha.

111. Q. Have we any account of his various rebirths as a Bôdhisattva?
      A. In the JÂTAKATTHAKATHÂ, a book containing alleged stories of the
          Bôdhisattva's reincarnations, there are several hundred tales
          of that kind.

112. Q. What lesson do these stories teach?
      A. That a man can carry, throughout a long series of re-incarnations,
          one great, good purpose which enables him to conquer bad ten-
          dencies and develop virtuous ones.

113. Q. Can we fix the number of re-incarnations through which a Bôdhi-
          sattva must pass before he can become a Buddha?
      A. Of course not: that depends upon his natural character, the state
          of development to which he has arrived when he forms the
          resolution to become a Buddha, and other things.

114. Q. Have we a way of classifying Bôdhisattvas?   If so, explain it.
      A. Bôdhisattvas - the future Buddhas - are divided into three
          classes.

115. Q. Proceed.   How are these three kinds of Bôdhisats called?

115. A. PANNÂDHIKA, or UDGHATITAGNYA - "he who attains least quickly";
          SADDHÂDHIKA, or VIPACHITAGNYA - "he who attains less quickly"; and
          VIRIYÂDHIKA, or GNEYYA   - "he who attains quickly".

          The Prajnâdhika Bôdhisats take the course of Intelligence; the
          Sraddhâdhika take the course of Faith; the Viryâdhika take the
          course of energetic Action. The first is guided by Intelligence
          and does not hasten; the second is full of Faith, and does not
          care to take the guidance of Wisdom; and the third never delays
          to do what is good. Regardless of the consequences to him-
          self, he does it when he sees that it is best that it should
          be done.

116. Q. When our Bôdhisattva became Buddha, what did he see was the cause
          of human misery? Tell me in one word.
      A. Ignorance (Avidyâ).

117. Q. Can you tell me the remedy?
      A. To dispel Ignorance and become wise (Prajna).

118. Q. Why does ignorance cause suffering?
      A. Because it makes us prize what is not worth prizing, grieve for
          that we should not grieve for, consider real what is not real
          but only illusionary, and pass our lives in the pursuit of
          worthless objects, neglecting what is in reality most valuable.

119. Q. And what is that which is most valuable?
      A. To know the whole secret of man's existence and destiny, so that
          we may estimate at no more than their actual value this life and
          its relations; and so that we may live in a way to ensure the
          greatest happiness and the least suffering for our fellow-men
          and ourselves.

120. Q. What is the light that can dispel this ignorance of ours and re-
          move all sorrows?
      A. The knowledge of the "Four Noble Truths," as BUDDHA called them.

121. Q. Name these Four Noble Truths?
      A. 1. The miseries of evolutionary existence resulting in births
              and deaths, life after life.
          2. The cause productive of misery, which is the selfish desire,
              ever renewed, of satisfying one's self, without being
              able ever to secure that end.
          3. The destruction of that desire, or the estranging of one's
              self from it.
          4. The means of obtaining this destruction of desire.

122. Q. Tell me some things that cause sorrow?
      A. Birth, decay, illness, death, separation from objects we love, as-
          sociation with those who are repugnant, craving for what can-
          not be obtained.

123. Q. Do these differ with each individual?
      A. Yes: but all men suffer from them in degree.

124. Q. How can we escape the sufferings which result from unsatisfied
          desires and ignorant cravings?
      A. By complete conquest over, and destruction of, this eager thirst
          for life and its pleasures, which causes sorrow.

125. Q. How may we gain such a conquest?
      A. By following the Noble Eight-fold Path which BUDDHA discovered and
          pointed out.

126. Q. What do you mean by that word: what is this Noble Eight-fold Path?
          (For Pali name see Q. 78.)
      A. The eight parts of this path are called angas; they are:

          1. Right Belief (as to the law of Causation, or Karma);
          2. Right Thought;
          3. Right Speech;
          4. Right Action;
          5. Right Means of Livelihood;
          6. Right Exertion;
          7. Right Remembrance and Self-discipline;
          8. Right Concentration of Thought.

          The man who keeps these angas in mind and follows them will be
          free from sorrow and ultimately reach salvation.

127. Q. Can you give a better word for salvation?
      A. Yes, emancipation.

128. Q. Emancipation, then, from what?
      A. Emancipation from the miseries of earthly existence and of re-
          births, all of which are due to ignorance and impure lusts and
          cravings.

129. Q. And when this salvation or emancipation is attained, what do we
          reach?
      A. NIRVÂNA.

130. Q. What is Nirvâna?
      A. A condition of total cessation of changes, of perfect rest; of the
          absence of desire and illusion and sorrow; of the total
          obliteration of everything that goes to make up the physical
          man.   Before reaching NIRVÂNA man is constantly being re-
          born; when he reaches NIRVÂNA he is re-born no more.

131. Q. Where can be found a learned discussion of the word Nirvâna, and a
          list of the other names by which the old Pali writers attempt
          to define it?
      A. In the famous "Dictionary of the Pali Language", by the late
          Mr. R. C. Childers, is a complete list. *

      * Mr. Childers takes a highly pessimistic view of the Nirvânic state,
        regarding it as annihilation.   Later students disagree with
        him.

(to be continued)

Incas went down in just such fashion.   The creed of the Mohammedans spread
by the application of such pressure.

The slow growth, normal, of a new god is much hindered by a civilization
preoccupied with many interests.   The backward peoples of the world show
the course of new gods most clearly.   They accept very slowly, but in time
a new god supplants the old, and there is change.   These people have more
time for religious observances, perhaps, and so are more easily approached.

Conclusions such as these are general.   They follow history.   They march
with Time.   The details are not far to find, for in any record of any nation
there are illustrations.

The course of growing gods or cults follows an invariable pattern, depending on the temper of the people from whom they rise, or in the lands to
which they spread.   It may be said, in truth, the gods arrive and the half-
gods go, for this is generally true.   The higher worship supplants a more
primitive one, and in the end uplifts the people.   Only the god is very much
the same in every case - as may be noticed by the shrewd observer.

-*- -*- -*- -*- -*- -*- -*- -*- -*- -*- -*- -*- -*- -*- -*- -*- -*- -*- -*-

THE QUESTION PAGE - continued from page #114

is difficult to define the soul.   The student is advised to study the theory
of the seven-fold principles and their relationship to each other, and so
eliminate this point of difficulty.   The question is caused by the ambiguous
and unexplained terms "soul" and "spirit", as they merely mystify.   They
have been used as more familiar to the questioner, but they tend to increase
questions, due to their vagueness.

The seven principles of Being, as outlined in the Eastern Wisdom, are
comprehensible, and would convey the relationship of the stream of Life to
the body; they would show the "soul" as part of that stream of Life.   It -
the soul - is a portion, not separate or apart at any time during the body's
existence.

This question would seem to say - Man is a body and has a soul.   The
statement should be - Man is a Spirit, expressing himself in Matter by means
of a temporary body, and an overshadowing Soul.   The three are one.

-*- -*- -*- -*- -*- -*- -*- -*- -*- -*- -*- -*- -*- -*- -*- -*- -*- -*- -*-

ERRATA

April, 1947	Page #58, Line 30 -	"monstrous" (typographical error)
	" 32 -	"ideas" should be "idea"
	" #59, " 18 -	"illuminated" should be "illumined"
	" #64, " 30 -	"46" should be "45"
May, 1947	" #83, " 1 -	"cosmic" (typographical error)

Bhikku M. Sangharatana, Secretary of the Maha Bodhi Society of India, sends word of the many celebrations of VAISĀKHA held in India at the time of the full-moon of May. Noteworthy was the one at the city of Gaya, six miles away from the Bo-tree at Buddhagaya. The Bhikku Sangharatana, one of the speakers at this meeting, said:

> "For the first time in the history of Gaya, the thrice blessed day of Vaisakh was celebrated on the 4th May, 1947. The Buddhist flag was hoisted once again in Gaya in the presence of a large gathering. After the usual programme of the day, a big meeting was held in the Gaya Town Hall, attended by Buddhists, Hindus and Muslims, and a resolution was adopted thanking the Government of Bihar for proclaiming the Vaisakh day a public holiday."

VAISĀKHA was celebrated on the 5th of May at Buddhagaya itself, the ceremony being "held under the Bodhi tree where the Tathagata attained Supreme Enlightenment." At Sarnath it was celebrated on the 5th of May, and the speakers "referred to the greater appreciation of the message of the Master by the people of India, with the awakening of the national consciousness in the country."

ALL ASIA BUDDHIST CONVENTION

New Delhi witnessed a number of epoch-making conferences during the last week of March, 1947. The World Religions Conference held at the Y. M. C. A. was a prelude to the Inter Asian Relations Conference which attracted delegates from all parts of Asia, not to mention the observers of Europe and America. A most significant event was the All Asia Buddhist Convention held at the Buddha Vihara on Monday, March 31st, under the auspices of Maha Bodhi Society of India. Hon. C.W.W. Kannangara, Minister of Education, Ceylon, presided.

The Secretary of the Society, Bhikku Sangharatana, read out messages sent by Buddhists from Europe, America and distant parts of the globe. Addresses were made by delegates from Bhutan, Burma, Ceylon, China, India, Indo-China, Laos, Nepal, Siam, Combodia and Tibet.

Space forbids the inclusion of these addresses, and the significant Resolutions adopted by the Convention, but citizens of the United States will be interested to note this comment by the President of the United Lanka Congress, Mr. Dayananda Piyadarsi -

> "Less than two hundred years ago a few men drafted the Constitution of the United States of America, while Patrick Henry thundered anathema on the power that denied American colonists their liberty to do as they pleased, 'Give me liberty or give me death'. Today the mighty U.S.A. gives millions of people of all nations abundant life, liberty and the pursuit of happiness." ... He went on to speak of the Indian National Congress and the future work of the United Asia Buddhist Congress.

The second meeting of the Convention was held on April 1st, with Khne Scheng Losang Wanggyal of Tibet presiding. He promised the whole-hearted support of the government and the people of Tibet for the restoration of the Buddhagaya Temple to the Buddhists and the establishment of a Buddhist University at Sarnath.

THE THEORY OF MANU - The Sanskrit Term:

The Theory of MANU must be considered in relation to The Theory of MANVANTARA. Obviously, if the term MANVANTARA means "between two MANUS", the term MANU is of importance.

> "For what is the real esoteric meaning of MANVANTARA, or rather a MANU-ANTARA? It means, esoterically, 'between two MANUS', of whom there are fourteen in every 'Day of BRAHMÂ' ...."
> The Secret Doctrine, Vol. I, p. #63

Considering also that the term MANVANTARA is used for various cycles of time by the Eastern writers, it is best to confine the term to the title of that period known as "between two MANUS" - that is, "a term or reign of one MANU", or 308,448,000 years. For a complete list of the divisions of time in a Day of BRAHMÂ, refer to "The Planetary Calendar" in THE GOLDEN LOTUS, August, 1946, page #120.

> "Let us now analyze the word or name MANU. Orientalists and their Dictionaries tell us that the term 'MANU' is from the root Man, 'to think'; hence 'the thinking man'. But esoterically, every MANU, as an anthropomorphized patron of his special cycle .... is but the personified idea of the 'Thought Divine' .....; each of the MANUS, therefore, being the special god, the creator and fashioner of all that appears during his own respective cycle of being or MANVANTARA."
> The Secret Doctrine, Vol. I, p. #63

MANU is a fundamental concept often misunderstood, even by the very race wherein it originated. It has become overgrown with superstition but also has been subjected to deliberate attempts to blind through cryptic statements, behind which remained the true theory known to the initiated Brâhmans, who still guard the inner meaning. In consequence, MANU has been called a person by some people, who think of a perfected human being or initiate, a man of human birth.

> "The reader must always remember that MANU is not a man but collective humanity." The Secret Doctrine, Vol. II, p. #309

Another superstition is that MANU is a mysterious being who exists for ages in a mystical manner, who assumes the leadership of a race or for a particular period of the evolution of a race.

> "The name comes from the Sanskrit root 'man', to think - mankind really." The Theosophical Glossary, by H. P. Blavatsky

Necessarily through the course of time concepts become symbolized or anthropomorphized, and MANU is no exception to the rule. Names have been given to the fourteen MANUS for convenience, but the names are blinds again, for they are names of eras. MANU represents a Cycle. It is a specific cyclic swing of the great Law of Evolution, which takes Man through a certain definite period of time and experience. The planet swings to Law, and this is the Law of Cyclic Growth, which some call MANU.

YOGA: (Sanskrit)   (July, 1947, p. #112)

        This is a system of training.   The term is generally used in an in-
clusive sense, since there are various schools or divisions, ranging from
RAJA YOGA (Concentration) to HATHA YOGA (physical methods).   These systems
are alike in some respects, but very different in others.   YOGA is also used
as the name of the practises involved, and therefore can not be considered as
applying to any one school of philosophy or any one practise.   YOGA comes
from the root - YUJ-- to unite.   The aim of YOGA is to unite the lower
principles with the seventh - ATMA - and so achieve Liberation.

PRAJNA: (Sanskrit)   (July, 1947, p. #116)

        Consciousness.   A derivation of the word JNA - Perception - and the
word PRA - Direct.   Many different stages of PRAJNA exist.   Many beings possess it in degree appropriate to their development.   Indeed, PRAJNA itself
is a synonym of MAHAT, Universal Mind, and the level of the perception in
question must be considered a portion only of the Universal Perceptive
Faculty, or Consciousness.

PRATYAHARA: (Sanskrit)   (February, 1946, p. #25)

        A state of abstraction, a withdrawing inward, reached during the prac-
tise of meditation.   It is the fifth stage of RAJA-YOGA, on the journey
toward SAMADHI.

DHARANA: (Sanskrit)   (February, 1946, p. #25)

        A state of complete and unswerving concentration of the mind, reached in
the course of meditation.   It is the sixth stage of RAJA YOGA.

JATAKA MALA: (Sanskrit)   (February, 1946, p. #31)

        The title of an ancient manuscript written by Aryasura, dealing with
the Birth Stories, or past incarnations of the Buddha.   It means "Garland
of Birth Stories".

AMRITA: (Sanskrit)   (March, 1946, p. #33)

        Immortality.   The food and drink of the gods - ambrosia. Symbolized
by many substitutes in the various legends of the world.   The nectar of the
immortals - energy, essence, or elixir.   It was symbolized by the SOMA drink
used in the temple ceremonies in ancient India.

KALPA: (Sanskrit)   (March, 1946, p. #42)

        A cycle of time.   It is another name for a "Day of BRAHMA", lasting
4,320,000,000 years.   It is to be preferred to MAHA MANVANTARA (also
4,320,000,000 years) when speaking of Cosmic evolution.   KALPAS as "Days"
are differentiated, in the Hindu system, by names such as PADMA KALPA -
the preceding, and VARAHA KALPA - the present.   The seven "days" of the
planet are contained within one "Day of BRAHMA", or one KALPA.

MYTHS OF THE HINDUS AND BUDDHISTS
by Sister Nivedita and Ananda K. Coomaraswamy

The study of mythology is an interesting approach to the higher knowledge; it also provides lighter reading for those who are devoted to the more technical studies. Mythology always belongs to the past and it is profitable to try to understand the historical background of the myths, and to uncover their hidden teachings. The West is familiar with the myths of the ancient Greeks, the Romans and the Egyptians, yet the unfamiliar myths of India deserve attention because they are associated with epochs of civilization which extend further back into time than any others in history, and because many of these myths still live.

MYTHS OF THE HINDUS AND BUDDHISTS will acquaint the reader with this really vast subject. The co-authors are: Sister Nivedita, long associated with the Râmakrishna-Vivekânanda movement, and Ananda K. Coomaraswamy, the eminent writer on Indian philosophy, art and Buddhism. The work is enhanced by thirty-two illustrations made specially for the book by Indian artists under the supervision of Abanindro Nâth Tagore, C.I.E., Vice-Principal of the Calcutta School of Art. The book, then, except for the printing, is thoroughly Indian. The book is principally the work of Mr. Coomaraswamy, as Sister Nivedita died in 1911, long before it was completed, and he has provided a combined Glossary and Index of thirty-two pages which must prove a valuable guide to the reader.

Because of the wealth of detail in the vast literature covered in the book it is possible to give only brief indications as to what it contains. Of course if the myths are regarded as fiction the reader will find many examples of most interesting tales, belonging to different periods of the long history of India.

In the first Chapter - "Mythology of the Indo Aryan Races", mythology in general is discussed and the historical background is presented.

Chapter Five is of particular interest to Buddhists, as it presents the myths which, through the passage of time, became grafted to the teachings of the Great Teacher and Exemplar - Gautama Buddha - by over-zealous adherents.

The remaining Chapters give many condensations of myths found in the ancient Sanskrit literature, first from India's oldest and least known scriptures - the four Vedas, then from the two celebrated epics - the Râmâyana and the Mahâbhârata (from which the well-known Bhagavad Gîtâ is extracted and used as a gospel by the Hindus). The eighteen Purânas are also replete with myths.

All names are in Sanskrit - Siva, Krishna, etc., - but this is to be expected and is not a hindrance as the writers are masters of the English language and avoid technical terms. However, the Sanskrit names are generally translated also, so that the reader may become acquainted with Sanskrit words in the most pleasant fashion.

MYTHS OF THE HINDUS AND BUDDHISTS is obtainable from The Golden Lotus Press. Price $3.00.

WORLD LEADERSHIP

Never is it divided.   It must be evidenced by clear
and unequivocal, crisp and effective action.   It must
be unchallenged, and it must prove itself at every point
if it is to remain unchallenged.   Always it is, by
its nature, undivided.

How is it held?   By one race, by one nation, by one
alliance of several nations, or by a commonwealth, or by
a democracy of peoples, or by a council of independent
peoples who are able to maintain harmony.   Leadership
is not expressed by two equally strong rivals.   In that
case there is inevitable rivalry and the clash of opposing interests.   Until the struggle results in
supremacy of one of the rivals - there is no leadership.

No temporary alliance of strong powers ever produces
leadership, though it has often produced terror and
tyranny.   The result is far too often stalemate, or
rivalry, or moves and countermoves.   All too often the
selfish interests destroy the altruistic motive, and
all too often incipient leadership is smothered under
jealous and partisan politics.

Yet, what better check could be devised to curb the
dictatorships, to cure the far-reaching dreams of world
domination, to prevent wholesale exploitation by a
selfish aggressor?   Only a gradual improvement in
world conditions may result from the political give and
take of alliances, but this is better than paralyzing
of initiative, or the subservience of free peoples
under the yoke of an invader.

Leadership emerges in a world crisis and languishes in
peace, but it is a potential always in the world, never
absent.   Roused by necessity, it takes command and
carries forward the work of evolution, bringing to an
equilibrium the upset balance of the world powers, by
one method or another.

Challenged, it takes the helm.   Thus may one know
leadership.

-*- -*- -*- -*-

SAMYAK - Right

Comprehending that MÃRGAH is The Way, and that the Eight Directions, or Methods, are the instructions for The Way, and that all of the Directions must be practised, let us proceed to discuss the Directions in detail:

1.	SAMYAG-DRSTI	Right View
2.	SAMYAK-SAMKALPA	Right Intention
3.	SAMYAG-VÃK	Right Speech
4.	SAMYAK-KARMÃNTA	Right Action
5.	SAMYAG-ÃJÏVA	Right Livelihood
6.	SAMYAG-VYÃYÃMA	Right Endeavor
7.	SAMYAK-SMRTI	Right Mindfulness
8.	SAMYAK-SAMÃDHI	Right Concentration

At first glance the Directions may appear to be duplications or repetitions as the equivalent English words are not exact renderings of the Sanskrit words. A careful comparison of the Sanskrit words will show the difference in the formation, and even one unacquainted with Sanskrit will conclude that the widely different roots are used to convey vastly different meanings. It is so, but the fine shades of thought are extremely hard to translate into English without a long explanation.

Very little time need be consumed in explaining the word SAMYAK or SAMYAG (according to the following sound) as it is obviously the word Right. It comes from the word SAMYAKTVA - perfection - but the best rendering here is Right. Right - meaning "not wrong". Sanskrit employs compounds, and the use of SAMYAK as an integral part of the compound word distinctly and definitely points to the fact that there are other attitudes of mind or courses of action to be discarded and disowned. No latitude is allowed for personal opinion of what may be intended. "Right" and "not wrong" is the commandment.

Thus, courage is the first requirement. Many people have assumed that The Way is only for the negative, passive individual who turns his face from active participation in the world's life. Many people think that the Buddha's teaching is pessimistic, without hope or joy. Nothing could be further from the truth.

Gautama Buddha taught the plain facts, the hard way, the uphill climb, without concealing the cost or bribing the intellect. He made no compromise with those who sought ease, eternal life, vicarious atonement, and self indulgence at the expense of others. He sought for men and women of courage, honesty, aspiration, determination, and spiritual insight, knowing that these would find The Way to their liking and find hope, joy and peace upon it. He had no illusions about the slothful mind, the superstitious fanatic, and the religious dabbler. He knew they would prefer the easy, wrong methods to the harder right ones.

The Buddha never compromised with truth, never succumbed to the temptation to dilute his teachings in order to make them more attractive to these people who lacked courage. Therefore it remains to this day a path for the few to tread, and for the many to misunderstand, for many choose the wrong not understanding what is Right.

The great gods are the crown of Man's achievement. They represent his highest soaring thought. They betray his weaknesses and also his ignorance by their very nature, but they also show his penetration into the world of the Divine Abstraction. They are indispensable to him, for they are part of his own being and companions to him in the cycle of re-birth, but these high gods are sacred, set apart, afar, too awesome for daily use, and Man has therefore deified the half-gods as a matter of convenience.

These half-gods are more human, or more imperfect, or more near. They represent a world of ideation not high enough for gods. They may be said to be the outer symbols of Man's own inner being. If this is so, the half-gods would appear in many forms because they represent the passions, vices, fears and pleasures of the emotional world wherein Man lives so very much of his short lifetime. They would not represent the mental world, for there or higher dwell the gods of Man's highest understanding.

The many little gods of wandering tribes are somewhat of this nature. They partake of the emotional quality of the tribe. We have a "jealous" god today, because a tribal prejudice placed taboos upon gods of other tribes, and the people who created a "jealous" god were themselves jealous, proud and intolerant.

We find a curious collection of demons created by malignant minds, wherewith to plague the victims of the Middle Ages, but we find demonology prevalent throughout the world, for demons of hate, envy and cruelty dwell within the human heart everywhere in every age.

Close, companionable little gods of household and of tent, attached to the family, have been sources of much comfort, assuring protection and favor. The human heart takes refuge from its fears in some sort of ju-ju or personal fetish, and this too is world-wide, no nation being free from it. Its forms are too numerous to be counted. These half-gods are as varied as the periods and the lands in which they originate.

Good fortune is much desired. Always there is hope for "luck" and the great goddess Chance (Fortuna) finds a place in many hearts. She is perhaps unknown as the great goddess, but the little "lucky" charms and the rabbit's foot, the horseshoe and similar talismans all represent her. It is the votary of Chance who seeks her favor, bearing a medal or small object as her substitute. It is a very old habit, this one, and deep-rooted in the race.

Unending is the recitation of the half-gods, and their train of superstitions. They dwell secure for Man is never able to forget them. They are too close, too near to the center of his being. Let him tear out one form from his heart and he will find it springing in another form; but let him forsake the cause - the emotion - and the half-god will disappear.

Man sets the high gods aside, save for the sacred days, the ceremonies, and the great crises when his soul turns from the nearer little half-gods, seeking the greater power of the high gods in the higher intellectual or

(continued on page #139)

GARUDA

What does this mean?

GARUDA is the name of the Bird - HAMSA - in Time.   It is symbolic and is specific, very useful to differentiate from the Swan, HAMSA, beyond Time.   (See THE GOLDEN LOTUS, July, 1947).

What difference is there?

HAMSA, the Swan in mystic meaning, soars from the Milky Ocean, descending into Time and Manifestation.   There it tarries, but again wings up and onward.   Resting and so tarrying, it is the Bird in Time. Here it becomes GARUDA, the mythical man-bird, half man and half bird.

Why is it so symbolized?

The Swan becomes the vehicle of VISHNU and he is said to "ride" GARUDA as his VÁHANA.   The Bird here is the symbol of the Great Cycle, or MAHÁ KALPA, the Age of BRAHMÁ, lasting 311,040,000,000,000 years.

The Bird tarries for the Age of BRAHMÁ?

Yes.   Then flies again.

Has he but one form - GARUDA?

No.   He is the man-bird sometimes.   He is the phoenix, purely mythical, no connection with extinct species.   He is also the man-lion, SIMHA, but the most clear symbolism is shown in GARUDA.

What is his character?

He is, as SIMHA, the emblem of the Sun, and represents the Solar Cycle. As GARUDA he is beyond our planet, as a symbol.   That is, he does not belong solely to our planetary day, our KALPA of 4,320,000,000 years. He endures for the length of BRAHMÁ'S Age, flying through the minor nights and the PRALAYAS on tireless pinions.   He re-nests only in the MAHÁ PRALAYA, the long Cosmic Night.

Has he other symbolic forms?

He has been represented by such sun-gods as Osiris, when he is hawk-headed, and the hawk or eagle has always been a solar bird in occult symbolism.   The hawk is always a form of GARUDA.   The Egyptian hawk is high in mythical meaning; it is true, not linked to animal worship. GARUDA has been known to mystics of many lands and ages, and he has been cast into various symbols, more or less near to the one true original of esoteric teachings.

How is he related to VISHNU the Preserver and Sustainer?

He is co-existent with VISHNU, beginning with and ending with the

manifesting VISHNU - otherwise, the period or cycle of the MAHÂ KALPA.
He is therefore depicted as the steed or bearer of VISHNU. He is,
however, the Bird, the Life from the eternal Milky Ocean, the VAHANA
of the Unmanifested BRAHMA, descending into manifestation, but carrying
only the Life into the cycle and out of it, flying into the Milky
Ocean where the Life again re-nests. GARUDA does not come into being
during the MAHÂ KALPA; he is eternal, part of the eternal BRAHMA, and
so "unborn" and "ageless".

Is this teaching clear in symbolism?

No.   It has been obscured by various presentations, varied as shown
above, and it has many extraneous details added.   For instance, GARUDA
has been called GAGANESHVARA - "the lord of the sky" - because of his
dazzling splendour, and mistaken for or confused with AGNI, Lord of Fire.
The student must disentangle, must take the very highest meaning in
all these picturesque glyphs of the Ancient Wisdom.   He must not mind
the apparent contradictions and duplications.   He must become expert
at solving the riddles, but the high-probing intuitive intelligence
may surmount them easily enough.   The truth is ever simple, logical
and reasonable, and by that rule all symbolism should be governed.

He is the Bird in Time, solely?

He is GARUDA, the Sun Bird, the Phoenix, the Solar Lion - the flying
Swan, HAMSA, descended into Time and Manifestation.   He is a symbol
only, and an allegory.   He is mystically associated with the high-
soaring, sun-loving, strong-pinioned eagle.   He is linked to the Lord
of Manifestation, VISHNU the AVATÂRA, the Preserver, and he is with
all this still the Life, the Never-Dying and the Never-Resting. He
is the Bird of Far Flight, flying on powerful sure pinions.

-*- -*- -*- -*- -*- -*- -*- -*- -*- -*- -*- -*- -*- -*- -*- -*- -*- -*- -*- -

"Om, amitayat measure not with words
      Th' Immeasurable: nor sink the string of thought
Into the Fathomless.   Who asks doth err,
      Who answers, errs.   Say nought!

"The Books teach Darkness was, at first of all,
      And Brahm, sole meditating in that Night:
Look not for Brahm and the Beginning there!
      Nor him, nor any light

"Shall any gazer see with mortal eyes,
      Or any searcher know by mortal mind,
Veil after veil will lift - but there must be
      Veil upon veil behind."

                    THE LIGHT OF ASIA
                        by Sir Edwin Arnold

The world languished under the curse of hidden evil, crime unpunished, unchecked deception, and wrong concealed.   Men had not begun to form the laws of justice and to provide the means of self-government.   The murderer could walk abroad unharmed, the seducer escaped retribution.   Men were yet too primitive, Pandora's box of evil circumstances yet too recent for comfort. The gods were half regretful, and the Fire bestowed by Prometheus still burned unheeded in the human mind.

The council of High Heaven debated.   Should they destroy?   Should they have patience?   Should they alleviate, or spur, or soothe, or punish? Should they forget and laugh on in the festal mood, and dream in their own splendour?   Always they were haunted by Prometheus, who - suffering but not silent - reminded them that it was such a small piece of divine Fire, and could not be expected to create an instantaneous miracle; and they were never certain that they knew better than Prometheus.   For he could still see the humans, still watch the trend of being, and they were high - as high as Mount Olympus.

They decided to delay destruction, but to take action to protect the growing good in Man, to punish evil and to provide justice until Man could take this into his own hands and stand upon the side of Law and Order.

They called for volunteers to act as agents, and they found the three earth goddesses Alecto, Tisiphone and Megaera, ready and interested.   They became special guardians, to those upon Olympus, but the Greeks called them the Erinyes, the Avengers, the Gracious Goddesses.   Later still the Romans called them Furiae, the Furies.

They dealt out justice in the fashion of Olympus.   They fell upon the wrong-doer and drove him by stinging energy to death, distraction, confession, repentance or restitution.   They uncovered crime and exposed secret guilt. They roused the wronged to retribution.   They cast the thought of self-protection into the spark of Fire within the mind of Man.   They wrought the will of the high gods, but wrought it by the method Prometheus would have suggested.   They never rested, being true Immortals.   No hour of day or night might find them sleeping.   Day and night, the wrong-doer found the Avengers upon his foot-steps.

Men learned, in time, to choose the way of justice, and set up laws to govern the community.   Incited thereto by the goddesses, they devised punishments for wrong action.   The courts of justice became the representatives of the three Gracious Ones who - like governesses - had guided growing Man to part maturity of mind.

Prometheus watched this, half believing that the gods were now relenting, but Zeus undeceived him.   He said:

>"Old friend, we do not alter the decision.   We make the man-
>creature aware of what he does, so that he may be given fair and
>benevolent opportunity.   He still must choose.   He may be worth
>it - how do I know? - you stake so much - I can do nothing less
>than give you satisfaction.   For Man would sink into the purely

(continued on page #139)

CHAPTER EIGHTEEN

EMOTIONAL CONTROL

"Let the Heart seek always for the more perfect
Love and more perfect will be the comprehension."

Padma Hiranya Surangama.

When the student has adjusted the physical body to the new habits and has made the change permanent, he may consider the next step. He may take into account his environment and his Karmic responsibilities, then make up his mind where his best chance lies for the next attack.

What he may decide to do he must do in full responsibility and understanding. Only those who are not on The Way take steps of self-improvement blindly, from morality or environment or self-disgust or hope of heaven. The one who treads The Way knows why he does the things he chooses to do. This is one mark of the really earnest and - in a sense at least - initiated pupil. He always has a perfectly reasonable and thoroughly admirable explanation for what he does. There is no guesswork, no vague groping toward principles and ideals.

The student may make his next attack upon the emotions, if he has not started before this to apply the curb. If he has started, probably he can concentrate upon both emotions and mind, since the physical body is now in line with the Soul. For clarity, however, as we did with the body, let us deal with the emotions and mind one at a time.

Of necessity, the student must analyze himself. Pitilessly, without attempting to evade, he must expose the faults he finds to this analysis. Very little can be done to change a fault unless it is clearly understood. Where he finds imperfection he must build perfection. Where he finds weakness he must develop strength. Where he perceives weeds he must uproot, and he must be untiring in his efforts.

No one who approaches The Way does so totally unprepared. Some of the work, always, has been begun in previous lives. Often a pupil will have to his credit a great deal more than he realizes. He may have wrestled long with an overwhelming pride or egotism, for example, or a love of possessions. He may have done much to curb these undesirables, yet not completed the task.

When such a pupil comes to The Way in a succeeding incarnation he is always helped by Those who guard The Way, and though he may not be conscious of it, much is done to help him. He is surrounded with circumstances which actually bring out the worst tendencies, the faults and vices he is striving to uproot. He is, then, cast into the very hardest part of the struggle, for his own good, because if he does not resume the struggle in each life the weeds may grow quietly and become a greater problem later.

He, realizing the difficulties he is facing and his own weakness, may have a very much distorted idea of his own status. He may not think he is

a seasoned veteran of The Way, but consider himself only a beginner.   He may
not realize he is nearly victor, and may imagine he is beginning the struggle
with a particular fault.   But what he thinks of himself or his ability or
his status is of no importance, if only he resumes the struggle and prevents
delay.   In time he will reach a point where he does understand the importance
of the work he has been doing, and likewise the value of the help given him
along The Way, and he will marvel at his own attainments.

Therefore, let no one despair who begins a struggle with the really
hard-to-eliminate emotional habits, for he may be nearly at the end of the
struggle instead of at the beginning, and he may have lives of splendid per-
severance and attainment behind him.

Many have thought that to be "impersonal" is the great goal of this part
of the battle, but it is not desirable to eradicate emotion.   Such a being
is devoid of heart or feeling and can be only on the left-hand path.   What
is desirable is that the emotions are under complete control and cannot escape
the leash.   What is absolutely imperative is that the good emotions are
retained and the undesirable, selfish ones banished.

How is this to be accomplished?   As ever, by forsaking the lower and
turning to the higher.   By foregoing the selfish and choosing the unselfish
course.   By emphasizing the spiritual guidance of the body and the emotions,
and by minimizing the animalistic or instinctive tendencies.   By acting
more like a divine being, and less like an impulsive, passional and irresponsible being.   Such is the path toward emotional control.

-*- -*- -*- -*- -*- -*- -*- -*- -*- -*- -*- -*- -*- -*- -*- -*- -*- -*- -*-

♫ OLIDAY

Beside the River laughing dryads dance
And close upon their footsteps satyrs prance.
The swift-hoofed fauns are frolicsome in play;
The gnomes and elves have clambered into day.
Along the water all the birds sing sweet;
The balmy zephyrs race on cloudlets fleet;
The grasses quiver where the earth-folk mass;
The flowers bend where'er the air-folk pass.
Within the shallows water-beings crowd
Intent though frolicsome, their bearing proud.
The lords of rivulets stand at their posts
Behind them, close-ranked, all the small stream's hosts.
The region lords swoop in their power where
The deeper water makes a center pathway there,
But each leaf shimmers, every stone has sheen -
The rain lords' dew has washed the Valley clean.

Along the River highway the Water Lords approach
So on that royal pathway no lesser folk encroach.
The river-folk of Water, in happy mood and gay
Give welcome to the Triton who comes to holiday.

-*- -*- -*- -*-

Part II - The Dharma or Doctrine

132. Q. But some people imagine that Nirvâna is some sort of heavenly place,
a Paradise. Does Buddhism teach that?
A. No. When Kûtadanta asked the Buddha "Where is Nirvâna," he replied
that it was "Wherever the precepts are obeyed."

133. Q. What causes us to be reborn?
A. The unsatisfied selfish desire (Sk., TRISHNA; Pali, TANHA) for
things that belong to the state of personal existence in the
material world. This unquenched thirst for physical existence
(BHAVA) is a force, and has a creative power in itself so strong
that it draws the being back into mundane life.

134. Q. Are our re-births in any way affected by the nature of our unsatisfied desires?
A. Yes: and by our individual merits or demerits.

135. Q. Does our merit or demerit control the state, condition or form in
which we shall be re-born?
A. It does. The broad rule is that if we have an excess of merit, we
shall be well and happily born the next time; if an excess of demerit, our next birth will be wretched and full of suffering.

136. Q. One chief pillar of Buddhistic doctrine is, then, the idea that every
effect is the result of an actual cause, is it not?
A. It is: of a cause either immediate or remote.

137. Q. What do we call this causation?
A. Applied to individuals, it is Karma, that is, action. It means that
our own actions, or deeds bring upon us whatever of joy or misery
we experience.

138. Q. Can a bad man escape from the out-workings of his Karma?
A. The "Dhammapada" says: There exists no spot on the earth, or in the
sky, or in the sea, neither is there any in the mountain-clefts,
where an (evil) deed does not bring trouble (to the doer).

139. Q. Can a good man escape?
A. As the result of deeds of peculiar merit, a man may attain certain
advantages of place, body, environment and teaching in his next
stage of progress, which ward off the effects of bad Karma and
help his higher evolution.

140. Q. What are they called?
A. GATI SAMPATTI, UPADHI SAMPATTI, KALA SAMPATTI and PAYÔGA SAMPATTI.

141. Q. Is that consistent or inconsistent with common sense and the
teachings of modern science?
A. Perfectly consistent: there can be no doubt of it.

142. Q. May all men become Buddhas?
     A. It is not in the nature of every man to so become in one Kalpa, or
        world-period; a Buddha is developed, under Nature's general ad-
        justment of demand to supply, only at long intervals of time, when
        the state of humanity absolutely requires such a teacher to show
        it the forgotten Path to Nirvâna.

143. Q. Does Buddhism teach that man is re-born only upon our earth?
     A. As a general rule that would be the case, until he had evolved beyond
        its level; but the inhabited worlds are numberless.   The world
        upon which a person is to have his next birth, as well as the
        nature of the re-birth itself, is decided by the preponderance of
        the individual's merit or demerit.   In other words, it will be
        controlled by his attractions, as science would describe it; or
        by his Karma, as we, Buddhists, would say.

144. Q. Are there worlds more perfect and developed, and others less so,
        than our Earth?
     A. Buddhism teaches that there are whole Sakwalas, or systems of worlds,
        of various kinds, higher and lower, and also that the inhabitants
        of each world correspond in development with itself.

145. Q. Has not the Buddha summed up his whole doctrine in one gâthâ, or
        verse?
     A. Yes.

146. Q. Repeat it?
     A.   Sabba pâpassa akaranam
                            Kusalassa upasampadâ
                            Sachitta pariyo dapanam-
                            Etam Buddhânusâsanam.

                        "To cease from all evil actions,
                         To generate all that is good,
                         To cleanse one's mind:
                         This is the constant advice of the Buddhas."

147. Q. Have the first three of these lines any very striking characteristics?
     A. Yes: the first line embodies the whole spirit of the VINAYA PITAKA,
        the second that of the SUTTA, the third that of the ABHIDHAMMA.
        They comprise only eight Pali words, yet, as the dewdrop reflects
        the stars, they sparkle with the spirit of all the Buddha Dharma.

148. Q. Do these precepts show that Buddhism is an active or a passive
        religion?
     A. To "cease from sin", may be called passive, but to "get virtue",
        and "to cleanse one's own heart", or mind, are altogether active
        qualities.   Buddha taught that we should not merely not be evil,
        but that we should be positively good.

149. Q. Who or what are the "Three Guides" * that a Buddhist is supposed
        to follow?

149. A. They are disclosed in the formula called the TISARANA: "I follow
Buddha as my Guide: I follow the Law as my Guide: I follow the
Order as my Guide."   These three are, in fact, the Buddha
Dharma.

    * SARANAM.   Wijesinha Mudaliyar writes me:- "This word has been
hitherto very inappropriately and erroneously rendered Refuge, by
European Pali scholars, and thoughtlessly so accepted by native Pali
scholars.   Neither Pali etymology nor Buddhistic philosophy justi-
fies the translation.   Refuge, in the sense of a fleeing back or a
place of shelter, is quite foreign to true Buddhism which insists on
every man working out his own emancipation.   The root Srî in
Sanskrit (sara in Pali) means to move, to go; so that Saranam would
denote a moving, or he or that which goes before or with another -
a Guide or Helper.   I construe the passage thus: Gacchâmi, I go,
Buddham, to Buddha, Saranam, as my Guide.   The translation of the
Tisarana as the "Three Réfuges" has given rise to much misapprehen-
sion, and has been made by anti-Buddhists a fertile pretext for
taunting Buddhists with the absurdity of taking refuge in non-entities
and believing in unrealities.   The term Refuge is more applicable
to Nirvâna, of which Saranam is a synonym.   The High Priest Sumangala
also calls my attention to the fact that the Pali root Sara has the
secondary meaning of killing, or that which destroys.   Buddham
saranam gacchâmi might thus be rendered "I go to Buddha, the Law,
and the Order, as the destroyers of my fears - the first by his
preaching, the second by its axiomatic truth, the third by their
various examples and precepts."

150. Q. What does he mean when repeating this formula?
     A. He means that he regards the Buddha as his all-wise Teacher, Friend
and Exemplar; the Law or Doctrine, as containing the essential
and immutable principles of Justice and Truth and the path that
leads to the realization of perfect peace of mind on earth;
and the Order as the teachers and exemplars of that excellent
Law taught by Buddha.

151. Q. But are not some of the members of this "Order" men intellectually
and morally inferior?
     A. Yes; but we are taught by Buddha that only those who diligently at-
tend to the Precepts, discipline their minds, and strive to
attain or have attained one of the eight stages of holiness and
perfection, constitute his "Order".   It is expressly stated
that the Order referred to in the "Tisarana" refers to the
"Attha Ariya Puggala" - the Noble Ones who have attained one of
the eight stages of perfection.   The mere wearing of yellow
robes, or even ordination, does not of itself make a man pure,
wise or entitled to reverence.

152. Q. Then it is not such unworthy bhikshus as they, whom the true
Buddhist would take as his guides?
     A. Certainly not.

(to be continued)

"Man is not animal in origin?"

This, and related questions, are impossible to prove by scientific data. Theories are advanced and accepted by the scientific world but they meet an impassable wall of mystery at the very essential point of supporting evidence or surviving fossils.   It is very evident that the animal kingdom has a close resemblance to the human kingdom in body structure, and it is not surprising that Man should think himself to be a superior branch of the tree of life, and class himself as a primate of the higher order.

Yet there is no evidence to support the theory that Man grew from a lower animal level.   The evidence tends to point to the unending improvement of species, or else extinction.   It does not show anywhere that a large ape became a man, not in our historical times at least.   Many such proofs would be near us today if this process were in progress, therefore we can only conclude that if it happened at all it was in the very remote past, how remote we cannot even estimate.

Nature moves in one direction, upward and onward, refining and perfecting.   She does so slowly.   No species leaps from half intelligence to full intelligence suddenly.   Where, then, was bridged the chasm of mind existing between the human and the animal kingdoms?   Self-Consciousness is a quality of mind, and this is possessed by Man only.   Where did he find this quality?   In any animal species, now in existence, or extinct?   Or must we look for it at higher levels than we recognize as Man's?

Man is a complex being, a combination evolution.   He has the divine latent, the half-divine evident, and the animal submerged.   He balances upon three levels, and extends his being into the higher and more subtle worlds above him?   Rather, let us note, the divine reaches down from the subtle planes to grasp and ensoul an instinctive form or vehicle.   There lies the explanation.   The animal-like body is appropriated, or built, and directed by a Self-Consciousness.

The combination is like rider and horse, one and yet two.   Evolving as a unit the two progress more rapidly, each supplementing the other.   The form is quickened and enlightened, and the Self-Consciousness enriched by the duality.

Situated as it is in a complex world evolved by the Self-Consciousness acting upon the environment, the body and animal soul is not aware of the duality, does not understand the partnership.   It calls itself "I", but does not recognize the divine materializing through it.   It calls its baser instincts "I", and calls its noblest aspirations "I", and is not very far wrong in so doing, for it is a duality.

Over it, and guarding it, the Self knows it is not the lower being, and that it comes to share this dual evolution as a quick and necessary step in Time.   It may be that the Self sheds this wisdom on the lower being, but it does not penetrate the lower mind.   Therefore Man thinks he is a body and a body merely, linking himself to the ephemeral utilitarian vehicle, when all the splendid flaming Glory of the Sun-Spark shines above him, irradiating him, drawing him toward it, into the Sun of Being, and the Source of Life beyond.

THE THEORY OF MANU - The Manus:

1st PLANETARY DAY

Sandhya		) 1st Dawn or	1,728,000	
1st Manvantara	SWAYAMBHÛVA	) Root Manu	306,720,000	
Sandhya		(1st Twilight	1,728,000	
2nd Manvantara	SWAROCHI	(or Seed Manu	306,720,000	616,896,000

2nd PLANETARY DAY

Sandhya		) 2nd Dawn or	1,728,000	
3rd Manvantara	UTTAMA	) Root Manu	306,720,000	
Sandhya		(2nd Twilight	1,728,000	
4th Manvantara	THAMASA	(or Seed Manu	306,720,000	616,896,000

3rd PLANETARY DAY

Sandhya		) 3rd Dawn or	1,728,000	
5th Manvantara	RAIVATA	) Root Manu	306,720,000	
Sandhya		(3rd Twilight	1,728,000	
6th Manvantara	CHACKCHUSKA	(or Seed Manu	306,720,000	616,896,000

4th PLANETARY DAY

Sandhya		) 4th Dawn or	1,728,000	
7th Manvantara	VAIVASVATA	) Root Manu	306,720,000	
Sandhya		(4th Twilight	1,728,000	
8th Manvantara	SAVARNA	(or Seed Manu	306,720,000	616,896,000

5th PLANETARY DAY

Sandhya		) 5th Dawn or	1,728,000	
9th Manvantara	DAKSHA SAVARNA	) Root Manu	306,720,000	
Sandhya		(5th Twilight	1,728,000	
10th Manvantara	BRAHMÂ SAVARNA	(or Seed Manu	306,720,000	616,896,000

6th PLANETARY DAY

Sandhya		) 6th Dawn or	1,728,000	
11th Manvantara	DHARMA SAVARNA	) Root Manu	306,720,000	
Sandhya		(6th Twilight	1,728,000	
12th Manvantara	RUDRA SAVARNA	(or Seed Manu	306,720,000	616,896,000

7th PLANETARY DAY

Sandhya		) 7th Dawn or	1,728,000	
13th Manvantara	ROUCHYA	) Root Manu	306,720,000	
Sandhya		(7th Twilight	1,728,000	
14th Manvantara	BHOUTYA	(or Seed Manu	306,720,000	
Sandhya			1,728,000	618,624,000

	4,320,000,000

This is the end of the KALPA, or Day of BRAHMÂ,
followed by the PRALAYA, or Night of BRAHMÂ,
also lasting 4,320,000,000 years.

Compiled from H. P. Blavatsky's
list of The Manus, page #309, Volume 2, Original Edition,
THE SECRET DOCTRINE

From Rangoon, Burma, a noted scientist, philosopher, missionary and lecturer sends a contribution to THE GOLDEN LOTUS, very interesting to the scientific mind.   It is too long for our pages, unfortunately, but the author has given permission to quote extracts.   The Venerable Thero would be glad to hear from correspondents who are interested in the scientific approach to truth, and we will accept names of readers to forward to him.

The treatise is called "THE GREATEST PROBLEM OF THE UNIVERSE".   After discussing and defining the six theories of consciousness adopted by philosophy and modern science - (1) the anthropistic; (2) the neurological; (3) the animal; (4) the biological; (5) the cellular; (6) the atomistic - the Thero comments:

"However divergent are these six different theories as to the nature and origin of consciousness, they, nevertheless, on a clear and definite examination of the mental science, may be reduced to nothing."

He then proceeds with the main theme -
"Solution of the Mystery of Consciousness"

"The problem of consciousness is far beyond the reach of the human mind; being abstract, conceptual, profound, intrinsic, and subtle phenomena of the mind.   It is a field of the Enlightened One, the Buddha, who alone is capable of solving the impregnable mystery of consciousness having thoroughly penetrated into the material and mental phenomena, through His Supreme Enlightenment.   It is impossible to be acquired by thinking or meditating, nor could it be obtained by experiments on the material objects, either hard or smooth, neurolotic or microscopic, cellular or atomic ......

"Just as the curry which is made of many ingredients, even so, a consciousness is never a single factor, but it is a combination of essentials, mental-factors, objects, awareness, duality, understanding and passing-away.   And just as one finds it quite impossible to pick out the taste of different ingredients from a curry, even so, it is quite beyond the capacity of the human mind to pick out the different qualities of essentials, mental factors and concomitants from a single combination of consciousness, which is not visible even to the sight of the best microscope ......

"In fact there is no consciousness of any kind whatsoever within the entire frame of the body, nor does it arise from within, but from without, by the simultaneous supply of the respective essentials in each consciousness of the eye, ear, nose, tongue, body and mind ......

"Life, especially the life we term conscious existence, is indeed like the current of a river, which still maintains one constant form, one seeming identity, though not a single drop remains today of all the volume that composed that river yesterday.   A person standing on the bank of such a river would, of course, think that the river is the same, though not a particle of water which he sees at any point remains where

"it was a moment ago; and as the beginning and the end of a river receive the special name of 'source' and 'mouth', though they are still
composed of the same materials of the body of the river itself ......
even so the source and the mouth of the 'River of Life' are respectively
termed 'birth' and 'death' ......"

After discussing the "Eye-Consciousness" at length, the Thero includes a chart
on "The combination of the consciousnesses of ear, nose, tongue, body and mind".

"In conclusion I should like to draw the attention of my kind readers to
the fact that Buddhism is not a religion but Science:- Science of the
Universe and beyond Universe - so it stands as the most predominent and
irrevocable authority of the material, physical and mental Science of
the Universe, and that of Perfect Deliverance and Permanent Bliss
beyond the Universe, called N I B B A N A.

"N I B B A N A itself is the greatest of all the problems, which is not
even known and properly understood by the majority of the Buddhists; but,
it could be understood easily by intellectual minds, provided the lecturer
is able to explain it scientifically.   In my sincere opinion those who
want to know about the true and real aspects of Nibbana ought to be properly acquainted with the eight real qualities of the entire Universe;
and when the said eight real qualities are turned topsy-turvy, Nibbana
is found.

"The eight principal qualities of the entire Universe are: Birth, Decay,
Disease, Death, Pain, Impurity, Impermanence, and Formation ......
Now therefore, on turning over the aforesaid eight real qualities of the
Universe we find N I B B A N A; hence, in the ULTIMATE-TRUTH Nibbana
means the Perfect Eight Qualities of: Non-Birth, Non-Decay, Non-Disease,
Non-Death, Perfect and Feelingless Bliss, Perfectly-Pure (being free
from impurities of matter and mind) ...... Absolutely-Permanent (being
totally free from Feeling, Perception and Formation) ...... and
Non-Formation ......

"May all my kind readers soon acquire the true and perfect knowledge of
Mental Science; may the entire World be pervaded with the Light of Truth,
the Perfect Knowledge hailed, Ignorance dispelled; may the entire world
be totally released from the pangs of war, famine and pestilence; and
instead, let the entire world be restored with permanent peace, happiness, harmony and prosperity; and let all mankind unite in a Great-
Family of One-Fold.

"With Universal-Loving-Kindness.
        In the Fraternity of The Brotherhood of the Holy Sangha,
                Ariyo Dhamma Thero, B.A., H.B.S."

-*- -*- -*- -*- -*- -*- -*- -*- -*- -*- -*- -*- -*- -*- -*- -*- -*- -*- -*-

        "It is not more surprising to be born twice than once;
        everything in Nature is resurrection."
                                        Voltaire

SUN GODS: (August, 1947, p. #126)

   All of them, in the Egyptian mythology, are connected with the Hawk, tho
only at times is a Sun God shown with a hawk's head, most frequently in the
early days.   The Bird is often symbolized by the hawk wings outspread.   The
goddess Mut, wife of Amen-Ra, King of the Gods, was symbolized by the Vulture,
but the Sun Hawk was reserved for the potent Sun Gods of the Cosmic Mysteries.
This association has long puzzled the modern world, but the beautiful allegory
of the Bird and its strong-pinioned flight through the Uncreated to the
Created, and again returning, should be admired.   Many such allegories of
beauty are to be found in the ancient symbols.   Associated with the Sun Gods
the Bird represents Immortality, marks the god as Cosmic or Aeonic, existing
from "Eternity to Eternity", i.e., from MAHÂ KALPA to MAHÂ KALPA.

MILKY OCEAN: (August, 1947, p. #126)

   "Milky" is commonly applied to the Milky Way, consisting of countless
stars, because of its appearance of white light in the sky.   Occultism, however, takes another meaning in its use of "milky".   The composition of curds
is the simile, referring to the condition of the Cosmos during PRALAYA.   The
pre-manvantaric churning into a partially solidified but still liquid poten-
tiality produces the star-stuff, the Cosmic Matter, as yet undistinguished
and unappropriated to any particular form.   This is the Milky Ocean of the
Cosmic Night, and of the early Manvantaric Dawn.

PHOENIX: (August, 1947, p. #126)

   A mythical bird, returning at the end of a cycle to its nest, where it
destroys itself by fire, only to spring again from the ashes.   Various
periods of time are given as the cycle (500, 600, 1,200 years, etc.) evidently
representing lesser cycles, or representing the full cycle of the MAHÂ KALPA.
Without going further, one must observe the obvious connection with a cycle
of time, with periodical renewing of life in a new form, and a periodic return
to the nest.   The connection with GARUDA is not difficult to trace.

SOLAR LION: (August, 1947, p. #127)

   SIMHA (Sanskrit), Lion.   The astrological assignment of the lion symbol
to the constellation of Leo is not clear in connection with GARUDA, at first
glance.   It is, however, a derivation of the ancient myth or glyph of
GARUDA.   Many abstractions of the astrological system are descended from
ancient Mystery teachings, or were originally pure teachings of the Mystery
schools.   Symbols such as Leo have been called fanciful, but the meaning is
only half-revealed.   The signs of the Zodiac are - again - the story of the
Cosmos, hidden under glyph and symbol.   Leo is the "Fiery Lion", the Life,
and the symbol of the Solar Cycle, as GARUDA is the symbol of the MAHÂ KALPA.
The Bird may not be clear, as Leo or SIMHA, but nevertheless, this Sun
symbol refers back to GARUDA and the HAMSA.

-*- -*- -*- -*- -*- -*- -*- -*- -*- -*- -*- -*- -*- -*- -*- -*- -*- -*- -*-

            "To live to benefit mankind is the first step."

                        THE VOICE OF THE SILENCE,
                             by H. P. Blavatsky

spiritual world.   He cherishes the half-gods as the accustomed companions of
his day, and he relies upon them for the daily protection, but they fall away
and leave him helpless in the night of his despair, for then he gropes and
stumbles towards the great gods - half understood and loved, half feared - and
calls on them for aid.

        Yet, he never learns the truth thereby - that both the gods and the half-
gods are Man, the worshipper himself expressed at different levels of his
being, and that he calls upon himself to save himself -for all of these creations are created by Man's mind.

-*- -*- -*- -*- -*- -*- -*- -*- -*- -*- -*- -*- -*- -*- -*- -*- -*- -*- -*- -*-

MYTHOLOGY - continued from page #128

        "animal, but that we rouse the Fire, and fan it into Flame again
        ..... How say you, friend?   Do you still think the creature
        worth the pain and waiting?"

        Prometheus looked long at the mighty Zeus, smiling, re-estimating him.
He was worth following, thought Prometheus; he would do well to have his counsel in the future.   The two parted, with affection deep between them.

        Meantime the three implacable ones pursued the secret malefactors, and the
tribunals of Man arraigned the known or detected offenders.   To this day
the stinging rebuke of the Fire-Spark, wakened and made aware by the goddesses,
cries out against the wrong.   Men call it Conscience, and only the gods,
Prometheus, and the Avengers know that flaming arrows of the goddesses have
taken Man unaware, and set on fire that small spark of the Mind-Flame, so
that it wars upon injustice, cruelty and blood-guilt.

        The goddesses still exact penalties for crimes against the innocent, and
Prometheus makes no protest against the long delay.   He knows he now has
allies, and that the justice of the mighty Zeus is enlisted in the battle.

-*- -*- -*- -*- -*- -*- -*- -*- -*- -*- -*- -*y -*- -*- -*- -*- -*- -*- -*- -*-

        "The mysteries never were, never can be, put within the reach
        of the general public, not, at least, until that longed for
        day when our religious philosophy becomes universal.   At no
        time have more than a scarcely appreciable minority of men
        possessed nature's secret, though multitudes have witnessed
        the practical evidences of the possibility of their possession.

        "The adept is the rare efflorescence of a generation of en-
        quirers; and to become one, he must obey the inward impulse
        of his soul irrespective of the prudential considerations of
        worldly science or sagacity."

                                        THE MAHATMA LETTERS TO A.P.SINNETT
                                                page #6

BUDDHISM IN TRANSLATIONS, by H. C. Warren

Since 1896, when it was first published, this has been one of the leading, if not the leading book dealing with the life of Gautama Buddha, the Dharma or teaching, and the Sangha or Buddhist Brotherhood. The eighth edition has been out of print for some time, and the ninth edition printed in 1947 will be welcomed by students the world over.

While there are thousands of books and articles on Buddhism, the majority of them give the author's opinions of various aspects of the Teaching.   The author-compiler of BUDDHISM IN TRANSLATIONS presents the Buddhist scriptures themselves for the reader to study and without doubt it is for this reason - because the author refers the reader directly to the sources - that the book has held its place so long.   It is endowed with an enduring value.

There are only five chapters, but they cover five hundred pages.   Chapter One gives the "Life of the Buddha".   This Chapter was published separately for distribution in the Orient, and was reviewed in The Bookshelf for April, 1947.

Chapter 2	"Sentient Existence"	pages	111-202
3	"Karma and Rebirth"	"	209-274
4	"Meditation and Nirvâna"	"	280-389
5	"The Order"	"	392-481
Appendix	"The Five Groups"	"	487-497

The Chapters are divided into sections which contain translations of extracts from the Pali writings.   For example, Chapter Four on "Meditation and Nirvana" opens with a five-page "Introductory Discourse" by Professor Warren and is followed by lengthy extracts from Buddhaghosa's famous Commentary - The Way of Purity (Visuddhi-Magga) on Concentration, The Forty Subjects of Meditation, The Earth-Kasina, The Impurities, Reflection on the Buddha, World Cycles, Wisdom, The Attainment of the Paths, Nirvâna to be attained at Death, and The Attainment of Nirvanâ.   This Chapter also contains translations from -

ABHIDHAMMATTHA-SANGAHA	on The Thirty-One Grades of Being,
CULLA-VAGGA	on the Sublime State of Friendliness,
ÂKANKHEYYA-SUTTA	on The Six High Powers,
MILINDAPANHA	on Spiritual Law in the Natural World,
KEVADDHA-SUTTA	on The First High Power,
UDÂNA	on "Sariputta and the Two Demons,"
ANGUTTARA-NIKÂYA	on Wisdom,
MAJJHIMA-NIKÂYA	on "The Summum Bonum",
SAMYUTTA-NIKÂYA	on "Mara as Plowman" and "The Trance of Cessation"
MAHÂ-VAGGA	on "The Fire-Sermon"
DÎGHA-NIKÂYA	on "The Four Intent Contemplations".

From this description of the contents of Chapter Four one may judge the other Chapters.   Assuredly BUDDHISM IN TRANSLATIONS is worthy to hold its place for many more years to come, as the most convenient book for study, reference, and quotation by teachers and students of the Dharma.

Available from The Golden Lotus Press, price $3.00, including postage.

WORLD POLITICS

World-wide confusion has been created by the ever-contending national interests, never more active and intense than in an after-war period.
Consistent with the national characteristics, the representatives or
political leaders have followed the age-old pattern of bargain, exchange,
defraud and misrepresent, accuse and counter-accuse, seize and retain,
or conceding under compulsion.

Economic barriers remain unlevelled and rigid. · Economic relationships
remain unstabilized and uncertain.   Communications are not normal.   Very
much the same conditions exist now as when the war ended, and the immediate
recovery of some of the exhausted combatants would appear to be doubtful.

Considerable uneasiness is evident among the world's peoples, strong and
deep enough to influence the actions of statesmen and leaders.   Very
little dependence is placed upon the ability of the United Nations Organization to maintain peace, and latterly no attempt is being made to dis-
guise the resulting disillusionment.   Out of this uneasiness there is
coming a return to alliances for defence and mutual advantage, thus con-
tributing to a weakening of the only form of world government available
at present.

Opposing forces clash and antagonistic ideologies create impasse, yet
over there is the strong desire for world harmony deep-rooted in many
lands.   Though the world's peoples view the future with misgivings,
coalitions of peace-lovers are to be found in many places.

Coming into vogue may be noted a return to national isolationism, to
political divisions by group alliances, to frigid self-dependence and
rigid self-government.   Clusters of satellite subjugated nations replace
the once-free peoples, and the old dream of world empire emerges once
again in the new guise of Communism.

Struggling with the aftermaths of war - destruction, destitution, disease
and disillusionment - the nations meet the new political debacle with
heavy hearts, yet with deep underlying courage and resolution.

The burdens of political leaders are almost unendurably heavy, for the
issues they encounter are complicated and fraught with destiny.   The
future is in the making, but the decisions must be made by men of merely
fallible human minds, to whom the Wisdom of the Infallible is denied.
The world must therefore accept failure, injustice, mistakes and prejudiced decisions, as well as noble-hearted patriotism and altruistic
world service, for all of these may be expected from political leaders
in the present political mêlée.

We must not be unthinkingly optimistic.   We must not expect Utopia
tomorrow.

SAMYAG-DRSTI - Right View

Some translators have called this Direction the most important, therefore the first, arguing that a mental comprehension of MÂRGAH - The Way - is
the first step.   There have been many translations of the term, such as
Right Understanding, Right Belief, Right Faith, Right Outlook, Right Comprehension, Right Opinion, and so on.   All of them are near to the meaning,
but, as is often the case in translation, many terms are used instead of
one, thus indicating an absence of the exact equivalent.

DRSTI is from the verb DRIS - To View.   It might be used to mean Clear
Vision, the comprehension that comes from Right View.   It might be called
Right Skepticism or Right Unbelief in superstition and dogma and creeds.
It might be said to mean Right Thought, as some say it does, but thought
does not cover the entire subject, as more than thought is included.   It
might mean Right Comprehension, if it were not that the essential quality
of seeing clearly what is Wrong and what is Right is indicated by the use
of the verb-root DRIS.

Being first, this Direction must be given careful study, as it is usual
to place the first essential first.   A reason for the tabulation of Eight
Directions in order must be accepted, and that reason must be studied in
conjunction with each Direction.

Hundreds of writers have written commentaries upon these Eight Directions.   Scarcely a student, in the West, but has at some time or another
found them and pondered, has been moved to write about them.   Not very
many of them have undertaken to analyze the reason for the tabulation,
seeming content to assume the order was compiled by chance, that it has no
significance other than the words, or that the significance needs no comment.

Right Skepticism or Unbelief is an absolutely necessary first requirement.   Were it not for this coldly unemotional analysis and evaluation,
upon which understanding may be based, it would be impossible to proceed
very far without mistakes.   The usual tendency to build dogma, creed, traditions and blind belief is difficult at all times to eradicate, yet it is
by the resolute destruction of these extraneous props that the Right View
appears.   Undue skepticism and unbelief is not intended, as the word
Right is always present as a counter-balance and prevents a swing to the
extreme of destructive and unbalanced rejection.

Right Understanding is not acquired by one strenuous effort to achieve
the finally perfect attitude of mind.   It is achieved by slow, laborious
degrees, searching and weighing, proving and disproving, groping toward the
sure foundation of Truth by steps of cautious feet.   No haste is expected.
Many people believe that Right Understanding may be acquired by one supreme
attainment, but it is to be noted that life-long effort is never absent in
such a case.   The Understanding may seem to come suddenly, but in reality
it has been building for many long and patiently active years.

Other definitions are extensions or synonyms of the meaning expressed
in Sanskrit by DRSTI.

The guarding power of Right View, including within it the discriminative
and constructive use of Skepticism and Unbelief, is an excellent weapon with
which to encounter the monsters of Custom, Religious Fanaticism, and Falla-
cious Thought.   Indeed, one cannot conceive a first step upon The Way
without the necessary ability to put aside, to disbelieve, to view clearly
and to discriminate with exactness.   How else could anyone proceed upon
The Way?

Clear Vision, then, and Right Belief, are the most needed qualities,
and the attainment of these is therefore urged upon the follower of Gautama
Buddha in this, the first of the Directions that he gave for travel upon the
Path which leads toward NIRVÂNA.

(to be continued)

-*- -*- -*- -*- -*- -*- -*- -*- -*- -*- -*- -*- -*- -*- -*- -*- -*- -*- -*- -

From "TRANSACTIONS OF THE BLAVATSKY LODGE"

"Q.   Is it possible to say that MANU is an individuality?

"A.   In the abstract sense certainly not, but it is possible to
apply an analogy.   MANU is the synthesis perhaps of the
MANASA, and he is a single consciousness in the same sense that
while all the different cells of which the human body is composed are different and varying consciousnesses there is still
a unit of consciousness which is the man.   But this unit, so
to say, is not a single consciousness: it is a reflection of
thousands and millions of consciousnesses which a man has
absorbed.

"But MANU is not really an individuality, it is the whole of
mankind.   You may say that MANU is a generic name for the
PITRIS, the progenitors of mankind.   They come, as I have
shown, from the Lunar Chain.   They give birth to humanity,
for, having become the first men, they give birth to others
by evolving their shadows, their astral selves.   They not only
give birth to humanity, but to animals and all other creatures.
In this sense it is said in the PURANAS of the great Yogis
that they gave birth, one to all the serpents, another to all
the birds, etc.   But, as the moon receives its light from
the Sun, so the descendants of the Lunar PITRIS receive their
higher mental light from the Sun or the "Son of the Sun".
For all you know VAIVASVATA MANU may be an AVATAR or a personification of MAHAT, commissioned by the Universal Mind to
lead and guide thinking Humanity onwards."

by H. P. Blavatsky   (p. #100)

-*- -*- -*- -*- -*- -*- -*- -*- -*- -*- -*- -*- -*- -*- -*- -*- -*- -*-

"Let your heart be impartial and wide of range."

THE TRACT OF THE QUIET WAY
Yin Chih Wen

JATÂYU

What is JATÂYU?

Exoterically called the "King of the Vultures".   In the RÂMÂYANA he is
called "King of the Feathered Tribe".   He is symbolized as a vulture.
His connection with HAMSA is obvious.

What is he, esoterically?

He is the symbol of the Cycle of 60,000 years, the "son" of GARUDA
the man-bird symbolizing the Grand Cycle of the MAHÂ KALPA lasting
311,040,000,000,000 years.

Is this an allegory?

Yes.   The relationship of the lesser cycle to the Grand Cycle is expressed by the sonship, and is allegory purely.   It is obvious that
all the lesser cycles are "sons" of the Grand Cycle, being contained
within it.   It is also obvious that this particular cycle of 60,000
years has especial significance, since it is symbolized, named, and
used in epics such as the RÂMÂYANA, and in exoteric writings.

What is the especial significance?

Not given in exoteric writings, beyond the facts stated above.   The
period is related to the race cycles, and geographical changes, and
those are not made available to the public.

Why is JATÂYU a vulture?

The relationship to the sacred sun-bird, the hawk, is thereby shown.
He is "King of the Feathered Tribe", i.e., the Hawk in the particular
cycle of 60,000 years.   This is a further "descent" of the HAMSA,
in the sense that only the small cycle of time is represented.
Indeed, in the RÂMÂYANA, he is said to "turn his back to the sun"
and die, when he is slain by RÂVANA.   The cycle of time passes.

Why do the Eastern Philosophies speak of man-birds and these bird-forms?

All the allegories of the ancient schools of Wisdom were alike.   They
may have added characteristic racial differences in form, in story,
in name, and illustrative artistry.   The underlying principle is
ever the same.   Allowing for these racial changes, the allegory may
be traced through many ancient nations.   The Bird is still
symbolized today, and is in modern form accepted.   Underneath the
modern veneer, there is the HAMSA still.   Underneath the Vulture, in
Indian and in Egyptian art, there is the mythical JATÂYU.   The allegory borrows merely from the world of form.

Why does JATÂYU die?

In contrast to GARUDA, the man-bird, or hawk?   The obvious assumption

is that a cycle of 60,000 years must end, and a new cycle must begin.
Therefore JATÂYU must die at the end of his cycle.   But a new cycle
begins.   There is, therefore, always JATÂYU - 72,000 of him in one
KALPA, or Day of BRAHMÂ, lasting for 4,320,000,000 years.

Are other cycles symbolized?

Not in Bird form. They are, of course, important, but the series of
the Bird allegories ends with JATÂYU.

Could the allegory be extended further into other cycles?

Doubtless.   What need?   A hint is enough for the alert student.   In
all lands the Mystery Schools furnished these hints.   Remember the
occult maxim, "As above, so below".

Has this occult teaching meaning for today?

JATÂYU means little to a race immersed in the immediate present, deaf,
blind and mute concerning other periods of time, not interested beyond
its own small cycle.   Its indifference to the occult traditions has
closed the vista of the Cosmos.   But JATÂYU wings on, also indifferent,
relentlessly pursuing his own flight into the future.

And does he symbolize our race?

Somewhat - to those who cannot visualize the cosmic sweep of Time, who
must particularize, who cannot comprehend the impersonal symbolism of
the allegorical representations, who do not know the race is deathless.   Like JATÂYU, it is different or evolving from cycle to cycle.
It is co-existent with JATÂYU - the cycle of the moment, or the Age.

Has "King of the Feathered Tribe" significance?

Of course.   Such titles always have a profound meaning.   This one
means the race or geological cycle, which includes all lesser cycles
within it - thus, "King".

Do the bird forms mean more than Illustration?

No.   They serve only as nucleus for thought, or as an apt symbol in
carvings, paintings, poems or writings.

Can Man learn Cosmology without the symbolism?

He can, but the long series of ciphers dull all but the mathematical
minds.   The symbols are useful, as well as beautiful, and rich in
poetic colourings.

JATÂYU, then, is Time?

No.   A Cycle of the World Period or KALPA, a length of time, a definite measure of the emerging World Pattern, a specific step in the
continuous evolutionary procedure, and a certain status of the races
of mankind - that is JATÂYU.

None but the most high Gods could have summoned the three Goddesses into the High Council. No one but the mighty Zeus could have demanded their attendance. Therefore, when the three sisters drew near to Mount Olympus astute divinities and men deemed it a matter of importance.

The Moirai were beings of importance. Not exactly high, they were not low in the divine scale of being. Related to the completely baffled elemental gods and to the equally curious ranks of High Heaven, the three were yet unique and hard to duplicate, each being in a measure on the fringe of the circle of the Inner Heaven.

Whatever the council of the gods discussed ever remained a mystery, except perhaps the last decision. So it was that from the audience came forth three specially commissioned agents of the gods, who took into their capable hands the fate of all that lives. Later the Greeks called them Klothes, the spinners, as well as Moirai, "a share". The Romans adopted the latter name, in their language Parcae, but also called them Fata, the Fates, so it is they are best known as The Fates. In Teutonic mythology they are called the three sister goddesses, Past, Present and Future - the Norns.

The Fates were needed, for the box Pandora had opened had contained the problem of death, and it had become time in the evolutionary cycle for the race to meet this new condition. The Goddesses arranged their duties to their liking.

The oldest one, Atropos, assumed the most imperative task first, that of ushering beings into the passive, temporary sleep and rest called death. She slowly drew the shears of Fate across the thread of life and ended with exactitude the life-span of every mortal. For this, some people call her a great blessing, but others dread to meet her face to face. Her name means "Inflexible", as her decrees are irrevocable.

The second goddess, Lachesis, measured the shining thread of life, determined its true length, its end and its beginning, its straightness or its knots, its strength or weakness, and its justice to the being's merit, then laid the measured threads within the grasp of the stern older sister who wielded the shears with surgical exactitude. Therefore her name means "Lot".

The youngest sister, Klotho, pitiful and tender-hearted, could not assume the task of the two high-hearted and impersonal executors of justice, and she turned sorrowfully from the task. She stopped to touch the threads of shining light Lachesis handled, and then, seeing with divine sight the tangled skein of threads - the lives of beings - she bent attention on the web of life. From this she passed to helping Lachesis, and became the one who drew the shining threads apart and wove them into some cohesion. She then gave them to her sisters in some order and less confusion. Therefore the ancient peoples said she "spun" the threads, but that is allegory, for no one can spin a thread of life, not even a great goddess, not even Zeus in High Heaven. But still, her name is "Spinner", because she spins the fate.

The threads are lives - that is, the life in body. The body falls from the thread when it is cut apart, and that is what the goddesses were asked to do. They came to supervise and oversee the passing into body,

(continued on page #157)

CHAPTER NINETEEN

COMPASSION

"Let the Heart hear the plea of the unfortunate."

Padma Hiranya Surangama.

Undue emphasis has been laid upon many instructions and precepts to the exclusion of others, but the ones enjoining Compassion are most emphasized. In connection with Emotional Control, attention is called to the necessity for discriminative judgment in dealing with the ideal of Compassion.

"Compassion", in many cases, is too often sensuous and emotional expression of superiority, and as such it should be eradicated. It is well to avoid the extreme sentimentality and gushy wordiness displayed by many pupils who stop there - with the emotional satisfaction of telling others to be "compassionate". The true Compassion is not that.

To the Western mind the word compassion carries the meaning of superior knowledge, kindness or mercy. In the term itself there is no equality whatever. No one can express compassion, by any stretch of the imagination, toward a superior being, or an equal, or someone absolutely unknown. In the student, compassion may be expressed to unfortunate and needy people - but in the BODHISATTVA the true Compassion is expressed to all beings.

In order to begin to acquire the true Compassion (KARUNÂ) of the BODHI-SATTVA, extended to all beings, one may strive to practise MAITRÎ (Sanskrit) but in the Pali METTA. The generally accepted English equivalent for MAITRÎ is Loving-Kindness, and this is or should be well within the reach of all students.

The word MAITRÎ, as used in Buddhist terminology, has nothing whatever to do with the Western conception of compassion. MAITRÎ is different.

It is the name of an all-embracing attitude of mind evidencing itself as Loving-Kindness towards all beings, and implies unvarying conduct and action to match it. It does not qualify itself, or limit itself, or restrict itself to the unfortunate. It radiates in all directions, like the sun's rays, embracing all creation. It misses no one. It joyously swoops up to envelop the Most High, and it swoops downward to embrace the Most Low. It has no superiors and it has no inferiors. It knows no necessity for differentiation. It exists, seated in the mind, unchanging, not surging out in waves, as the emotional impulse to be compassionate does when it arises from time to time.

MAITRÎ comes into being when the emotions are under control. The emotional approach to it is doomed to failure. An emotional enjoyment of mingled superiority and generosity is never to be found in the true quality of MAITRÎ.

Seated in the mind, MAITRÎ is beyond the need for speech, and is best

expressed in living, in thought, and in action.   It cannot be secured except by comprehension, therefore it does not express itself through emotion.
Thrusting down into the daily life as a strong and undeniable force, it
evidences itself in many ways, momentarily depriving the emotions and the
physical body of the ability to act contrariwise when it exerts its control.

        Loving-Kindness does not mean a passive, negative and optomistic day-
dream, or speculative building of word-forms, or highly altruistic sermons
without experience or real achievement behind them.   These may be for the
student who has not progressed very far, but they are not for the aspiring
student who begins to seek for true values, and in so doing sets aside the
popular misconceptions to be met at every turn of the Path.

        Complete and perfect the quality of MAITRÎ must be in the Adept.   He
must be able to call all that lives into the circle of unfailing Loving-
Kindness.   It is not easy, and in a very much diversified World-Scheme such
as ours it requires some practice before it is accomplished to any degree
of usefulness.   It is not usually exhibited as a faculty or mastery of self
beyond the ranks of ARHAT, but many people possess it in some degree, and
many aspiring students have begun to reach toward it.   Such small innate
degrees of it as may be found in unawakened people indicate the progress of
humanity toward a higher spirituality.   The conscientious server of
humanity, however, must possess it, and must understand the necessity for
its coming into flower slowly.

        Many lives may be lived before MAITRÎ is fully acquired.   It is well to
begin at once to acquire it, practising it at every breath, and by extending
it toward all beings near so learn that in the lives to come the impersonal
KARUNÂ, the Compassion of the BODHISATTVA, may be extended toward and include all beings.   At this stage of the Path, however, the student must
become cognizant of MAITRÎ.

-*- -*- -*- -*- -*- -*- -*- -*- -*- -*- -*- -*- -*- -*- -*- -*- -*- -*-

OUR WORLD

What though to you this World is but a toy
For fate to play with and after play destroy,
Or though to you this world is but a grave
Wherein the base are buried with the brave,
Where though the noble with ignoble sinks to nothingness
You weep no tear nor sing one song the less -

To me this World is that majestic steep
Whereon Heaven's glories well may meet
With Love's triumphal music and make one,
And where, when Time is set and Years are done,
O glorious World, your perfect work shall light
The wonder of the Thronéd Infinite!

                            from "The Immortal Dweller"
                            by Ernest Fewster

Once, in the untold story of mankind's coming into body, there were no gods at all. Men were yet nebulous, not confined to a dense physical vehicle - that is, the planet and all life within it was in a very early stage of development. The core of earth was not yet hard. The luminous human units were not able to conceive the idea of a hidden heaven, because no concealed corner and no prisoning horizon prevented them from seeing all they willed to see. They were unable to invent a hell because the earth itself, such of it as was hard enough to cohere, was open to their gaze. The concentrated physical eyesight was not developed, but they could and did behold through other organs, whatever there might be in vision. They found the planet one of intense interest, but they did not erect images of themselves, called gods, for these creations were many ages into the future.

Men - we may call them men for want of a more satisfactory name - were shadowy and formless, like the planetary substance. The vegetable kingdom nourished them by way of moving fronds, and living tissues were not absorbed by them. Curious and unfamiliar were their shapes, a kind of loosely knit and tenuously molded sphere, not always in that form. Sometimes the circular nucleus extended itself flat-wise, elongated itself upward, compressed itself or expanded itself, to suit its environment or the emergency of the moment.

Naturally, social life was very elementary, for these beings built no houses and required no covering, depending on the elemental environment for all their needs. Their mentality was excellent, not dull nor witless. They were the sparks of the Undying Flame, descended into the World-Scheme called BHUMI, but they were for all that inexperienced as dwellers in their particular environment, and they were therefore very much disgruntled with the shapeless, shadowy forms. The spheres were so hard to manage, and so very inept at all the magnificent maneuvers the man-creatures had in mind.

They had come so recently, within the early Manvantaric Morning, into the World-Scheme, and settled on the planet just beginning to emerge from the slow sleep state of the last PRALAYA. They could remember, dimly, what they had been in the last bright Day of the last MANVANTARA. Their impulse, wakened, was to make the planet like the last one, somehow. They were not yet at home, they had not yet caught the tempo, they had not comprehended their own destiny, they did not realize their altered position in the evolutionary ladder. They were, then, infants, and the young world around them, new and humming with the new note of the Manvantaric Lords, was tuned to their capacity for action.

They were not animal in body. Some people question that, and wonder why the two kingdoms have resemblance. The shadow-men were men in essence. They built, however, in the succeeding Ages, bodies denser, and the animal evolution built bodies likewise, moving upward in the scale, of the special composite for building furnished by the Planetary Lords who supervised and helped the builders. Therefore, the close resemblance in the substance of the bodies.

These beings lived in constant wakefulness. There was no sleeping. The day passed and the night passed, but they required no rest - the shadow body was untiring. Death did not know them, and the long centuries

(continued on page #157)

Part II - The Dharma or Doctrine

153. Q. What are the five observances, or universal precepts, called the Pancha Sila, which are imposed on the laity in general?
A. They are included in the following formula, which Buddhists repeat publicly at the vihâras (temples):-

I observe the precept to refrain from destroying the life of beings.
I observe the precept to refrain from stealing.
I observe the precept to abstain from unlawful sexual intercourse. *
I observe the precept to refrain from falsehood.
I observe the precept to abstain from using intoxicants.

* This qualified form refers, of course, to laymen who only profess to keep five Precepts: a Bhikshu must observe strict celibacy. So, also, must the laic who binds himself to observe eight of the whole ten Precepts for specified periods; during these periods he must be celibate. The five Precepts were laid down by Buddha for all people. Though one may not be a Buddhist, yet the five and eight Precepts may profitably be observed by all. It is the taking of the "Three Refuges" that constitutes one a Buddhist.

154. Q. What strikes the intelligent person on reading these Silas?
A. That one who observes them strictly must escape from every cause productive of human misery. If we study history we shall find that it has all sprung from one or another of these causes.

155. Q. In which Silas is the far-seeing wisdom of the Buddha most plainly shown?
A. In the first, third and fifth: for the taking of life, sensuality, and the use of intoxicants, cause at least ninety-five per cent. of the sufferings among men.

156. Q. What benefits does a man derive from the observance of these Precepts?
A. He is said to acquire more or less merit according to the manner and time of observing the precepts, and the number observed. That is, if he observes only one precept, violating the other four, he acquires the merit of the observance of that precept only: and the longer he keeps that precept the greater will be the merit. He who keeps all the precepts inviolate will cause himself to have a higher and happier existence hereafter.

157. Q. What are the other observances which it is considered meritorious for the laity as such to undertake voluntarily to keep?
A. The ATTHANGA SILA, or the Eight-fold Precept, which embraces the five above enumerated (omitting the word "unlawful" in the third), with three additional; viz.:-

I observe the precept to abstain from eating at an unseasonable time.
I observe the precept to abstain from dancing, singing, music

and unbecoming shows, and from the use of garlands, scents,
perfumes, cosmetics, ointments, and ornaments.
I observe the precept to abstain from using high and broad
beds.

The seats and couches here referred to are those used by the
worldly-minded for the sake of pleasure and sensual enjoyment. The celibate should avoid these.

158. Q. How would a Buddhist describe true merit?
      A. There is no great merit in any merely outward act; all depends
         upon the inward motive that provokes the deed.

159. Q. Give an example?
      A. A rich man may expend lakhs of rupees in building dâgobas or
         vihâras, in erecting statues of Buddha, in festivals and pro-
         cessions, in feeding priests, in giving alms to the poor, or in
         planting trees, digging tanks, or constructing rest-houses by
         the roadside for travellers, and yet have comparatively little
         merit if it be done for display and to make himself praised by
         men, or for any other selfish motives. But he who does the
         least of these things with a kind motive, as from love for his
         fellow-men, gains great merit. A good deed done with a bad
         motive benefits others, but not the doer. One who approves of
         a good deed when done by another shares in the merit, if his
         sympathy is real, not pretended. The same rule as to evil
         deeds.

160. Q. But which is said to be the greatest of all meritorious actions?
      A. The "Dhammapada" declares that the merit of disseminating the
         Dharma, the Law of Righteousness, is greater than that of any
         other good work.

161. Q. What books contain all the most excellent wisdom of Buddha's
         teachings?
      A. The three collections of books called TRIPITAKAS or "Three Baskets".

162. Q. What are the names of the three Pitakas or groups of books?
      A. The VINÂYA PITAKA, the SUTTA PITAKA and the ABHIDHAMMA PITAKA.

163. Q. What do they respectively contain?
      A. The first contains all that pertains to morality and rules of dis-
         cipline for the government of the Sangha, or Order; the second
         contains instructive discourses on ethics applicable to all; the
         third explains the psychological teachings of the Buddha, in-
         cluding the twenty-four transcendental laws explanatory of the
         workings of Nature.

164. Q. Do Buddhists believe those books to be inspired, or revealed by a
         Divine Being?
      A. No: but they revere them as containing all the parts of that Most
         Excellent Law, by the knowing of which man may break through
         the trammels of SAMSARA.

165. Q. In the whole text of the three PITAKAS how many words are there?
      A. Dr. Rhys-Davids estimates them at 1,752,800.

166. Q. When were the PITAKAS first reduced to writing?
      A. In 88-76 B.C., under the Sinhalese King, Wattagamini; or 330
          years after the Parinirvana of Buddha.

167. Q. Have we reason to believe that all the discourses of the Buddha
          are known to us?
      A. Probably not, and it would be strange if they were. Within the
          forty-five years of his public life he must have preached many
          hundreds of discourses. Of these, in times of war and perse-
          cution, many must have been lost, many scattered to distant
          countries, and many mutilated. History says that enemies of
          the Buddha Dharma burnt piles of our books as high as a coco-
          nut tree.

168. Q. Do Buddhists consider the Buddha as one who by his own virtue can
          save us from the consequences of our individual sins?
      A. Not at all. Man must emancipate himself. Until he does that he
          will continue being born over and over, and over again - the
          victim of ignorance, the slave of unquenched passions.

169. Q. What, then, was the Buddha to us and all other beings?
      A. An all-seeing, all-wise Counsellor; one who discovered the safe
      p   path and pointed it out; one who showed the cause of, and the
          only cure for, human suffering. In pointing to the road, in
          showing us how to escape dangers, he became our Guide. He is
          to us like one leading a blind man across a narrow bridge over
          a swift and deep stream and so saving his life.

170. Q. If we were to try to represent the whole spirit of the Buddha's
          doctrine by one word, which word should we choose?
      A. Justice.

171. Q. Why?
      A. Because it teaches that every man gets, under the operations of
          unerring KARMA, exactly that reward or punishment which he has
          deserved, no more and no less. No good deed or bad deed,
          however trifling, and however secretly committed, escapes the
          evenly-balanced scales of KARMA.

172. Q. What is KARMA? *
      A. A causation operating on the moral, as well as on the physical and
          other planes. Buddhists say there is no miracle in human
          affairs: what a man sows that must and will he reap.

      * Karma is defined as the sum total of a man's actions. The law of
      Cause and Effect is called the PATICCA SAMUPPADA DHAMMA. In the
      ANGUTTARA NIKAYA the Buddha teaches that "my action is my possession,
      my action is my inheritance, my action is the womb which bears me,
      my action is my relative, my action is my refuge."

173. Q. What other good words have been used to express the essence of
          Buddhism?
      A. Self-culture and universal love.

(to be continued)

THE THEORY OF MANU:-

Each new Day of the planet begins like every other Planetary Day, with dawning, when the root life awakens to the new period of activity. At dusk the seed life is ready and is falling into rest, to await its period of activity in the new Manvantaric morning, but the old root form which produced the seed will die.

The poetic fancy of the Hindu thought pictures the MANU as a husbandman who sows the seed, rooting it, and tending it through the long Day, garnering the seed at twilight and putting it carefully away for the next Day. That the Root and Seed mentioned are Lives (the garnered Experience and Growth of all the Evolutionary Wave inhabiting the planet) is of course understood, but the beautiful simile of grain is used for illustration.

The List of MANUS (August, 1947, The Golden Lotus) gives the names of the Seed and Root MANUS of the seven Planetary Days. Each period represents a certain cyclic swing - one toward construction and perfection, and one toward the maintenance of perfection long enough to permit the new seed of higher life to develop. The Root MANU and the Seed MANU are co-partners, part of the Planetary Day. They are not individuals, but specific periods of time.

The work of each period is different, and therefore it is helpful to think of a MANVANTARA (and also a Planetary Day and a KALPA) as composed of JYOTSNÂ - Dawn, AHAN - Day, SANDHYÂ - Twilight, and RÂTRI - Dusk or Night.

The MANUS merge into each other without perceptible difference, even as dawn fades slowly into early morning, for example. The change in the planet or the race also comes slowly. During the lifetime of a man the change is imperceptible to him, even at the most critical point. A larger stretch of time is required to observe the difference. Even the physical characteristics of the planet do not vary much in one hundred years, whereas in the known geological period of thousands of years it is perceptible.

No conclusions, then, should be drawn about the life of Man or the evolution of Man through the Seven Days by the observation of one lifetime, because to do so is impossible, and the attempt has resulted in some very sad delusions. It should be remembered that the Seven Days are different, and there are wide differences in the stages of the evolutionary journey.

Man, as he is seen at this moment, in the midst of the Fourth Day, is not quite like this in each MANVANTARA. Though there is a pattern and a similarity of experience, there is nowhere duplication. A rough idea may be gathered from the experience of a child in school, passing through different classes in the graded work, meeting new problems every day, even within the year's grade or class. Yet, each course or grade is constructed like the others, perhaps is situated in the same building or space.

So moves the evolutionary Life Wave upon the evolutionary pathway through the MANVANTARA, guided by the MANU - that is, the monitor of experience designed to meet the need at that particular period, designed by the evolutionary path of great intricacy and detail. For, this is "MANU".

UPASAKA Walter Persian, President of the Buddhistische Gemeinde Deutschlands, writing from Germany, speaking of the work of the German Buddhists, says:

"The German Buddhist Society, with permission from the military authorities on religious affairs, is endeavoring to spread the Buddhist Philosophy and way of life, and also Buddhist texts and translations. After the years of restrictions, we are engaged in a religious and cultural revival in Europe. We have to start from the beginning again. Any literature will have to be newly printed, as the old literature was either destroyed by the invaders or confiscated by the Gestapo. ... Please do not forget that all Buddhist publications, written in German, Pali or English, have been destroyed by the Nazi Government, as well as those of the Christian, Jewish and Mohammedan societies. Therefore it is necessary to begin anew, and for this reason the assistance of Buddhist friends in the United States will be greatly appreciated. Please help us. Books can be sent, food can be sent, clothes can be sent. Ronald Fussel has written in the 'MIDDLE WAY': 'above all, write those few lines of brotherliness that our common humanity demands, let alone our common aspiration. Less than this would be inaction in a deed of mercy. But if you can, send books or food or clothing as well. A very thin trickle of help of this kind is going over to them now ...' "

We print this for the information of readers. The address is 22A Dusseldorf, Brunnenstrass 56, British Zone, Germany.

-*- -*- -*- -*- -*- -*- -*- -*- -*- -*- -*- -*- -*- -*- -*- -*- -*- -*- -*-

The BHIKKHU ANURUDDHA, writing from Ceylon, announces a change of name for the organization of which he is the Honourable General Secretary. The new name is INTERNATIONAL BUDDHIST STUDY CIRCLE. He is, also, Editor of its publication - "The Buddhist Herald". We hope to review this publication, when the first copy reaches us.

-*- -*- -*- -*- -*- -*- -*- -*- -*- -*- -*- -*- -*- -*- -*- -*- -*- -*- -*-

Before her departure for India, Dr. Judith Tyberg, M.A., author of "Sanskrit Keys to the Wisdom Religion", announced the founding of PORT ORIENT BOOK COMPANY, in San Diego, Calif. This Company is publishing and selling Correspondence Courses in Sanskrit, and a Course in Egyptology. Books on the Eastern Philosophies are available from this Company.

-*- -*- -*- -*- -*- -*- -*- -*- -*- -*- -*- -*- -*- -*- -*- -*- -*- -*- -*-

THE BUDDHIST VISION

Upon the summit of the mount He viewed,
With vision bright, a pure, celestial world,
The flag of Truth was to the breeze unfurled,
Far in the realm of Mind's infinitude.
Matter was but a mist ... a dream soon spent ...
Which disappeared when Love's eternal rays,
Revealed the dawn of bright, Nirvanic days,
And Truth alone remains omnipotent.

Edmund K. Goldsborough

"Can a man of average understanding become a pupil of the Adepts?"

So much on this subject of chelaship has been written for Western consumption, and so often is it misleading in its implications, that it is almost useless to speak briefly, considering the many versions extant and the very many different opinions held by occult students. A common understanding of the conditions of chelaship is not to be found.

"Average understanding" we take to mean the man or woman, mature, well balanced, not illusioned, who is in command of self, without pledges to any human being of equal stature, who is in earnest, aspiring to the Path in his or her own mind, already endeavoring to live the requirements in so far as they have been realized. In this case, yes; these are the preliminary requirements for aspirants. The "average citizen" would be unsuitable for this step, obviously, simply from lack of mental comprehension. He is not entirely qualified.

Why is he disqualified? Because his interests are not such as would warrant his acceptance.

Supreme Wisdom must be earned. No one is likely to tell a child in the first grade what the mathematical laws are, for he must first learn arithmetic. To tell him more than the rudiments would be a waste of time, and the effort would meet a blank incomprehension.

At each point of the evolutionary journey every being is immersed in or concentrated upon a phase of existence or a period of experience, like a step in graded instruction. To take his concentration from a particular lesson ere it is learned means to deprive the individual of a link in education. To force a higher step upon him ahead of his capacity is cruel, useless and actually dangerous to many.   Consequently, the effort is demanded of the individual only at his time, not at the Adept-Teacher's time, and each individual must bring himself into the preliminary condition before he is said to reach his time.

Once understanding that there is no mass production in the department of occult endeavor, and that it is an individual effort, a lonely and sometimes persecuted pathway, the inquirer will comprehend why the "average" is not good enough for pupilage.

The "unusual" should be the measure. However usual the circumstances, the appearance, the background, and the perceptible brain quality, there is always a very unusual quality in any pupil, whether it may be recognized by others or not recognized.   It should be recognized.   It is this quality of unusual adaptability and potential perception that is the final factor in acceptance.

Of course this question is forever unanswerable in the impersonal general application, since it is a personal individual equation that cannot be expressed in words nor defined by "not this", "not that", that wins or loses for the aspirant the coveted and much-desired post of pupil.

MAHAT: (Sanskrit)   (September, 1947, p. #143)

The literal meaning is "the Great".   Unthinking people prefer to call the Mind matter, or physical reaction, or a part of the body.   The Eastern Philosophy defines Mind as Divine, states it originates in the Divine, and is part of the Divine Mind and Consciousness.   MAHAT is that Divine Mind from which comes MANAS, the thinking principle in Man.

MANU: (Sanskrit)   (September, 1947, p. #143)

All legends personalize in time.   This one of the DHYÂNI CHOHAN hosts, the condemned to live in body by Karmic necessity, has been converted into a very interesting superhuman being or beings.   Named for easy reference, these periods of time spent by the DHYÂNI CHOHAN hosts in evolutionary stages have emerged as Divine Guardians or Rishis.   The legend is much cherished in India, where the MANU is credited with a long set of Rules called MÂNAVI DHARMA SÂSTRA.   The truth is often unattractive in its simple beauty.   It is adorned with tinsel often.

PURÂNAS: (Sanskrit)   (September, 1947, p. #143)

The very ancient manuscripts collected under this title of "Ancient" are exactly that, so old their authorship is uncertain.   They are not, thus collected, to be taken as the work of one pen, or as a related series, but as a collection of very old teachings they are valuable.   They contain old thought, expressed symbolically or allegorically.   Many valuable records are to be found in these manuscripts, though disguised and sometimes obscure in language to modern minds.

RÂMÂYANA: (Sanskrit)   (September, 1947, p. #144)

This epic poem of old ÂRYÂVARTA, much treasured because of its great age, is a companion to the MAHÂBHÂRATA, another epic.   The RÂMÂYANA is a tale of Indian heroes and their adventures.   RÂMA, the hero, is still a model to the Hindus today, and the events of his adventures are more widely known than current world events.   Although it is much exaggerated as a teaching medium, it has poetic merit, and is one of the world's artistic treasures.

MIND: (April, 1946, p. #51)

Used as an English word familiar in its implications, it is really a substitute for the Sanskrit MANAS - that is, the thinking principle or mental faculty.   However, esoterically MANAS is said to be triple, and at its highest in Man almost Divine, whereas in its lowest aspect it has been rendered almost animal.   Distinction should be made between the triple aspects of the Mind, linking the Spirit with the Body.   The mental faculties use the physical brain as center and tool for many ages, and it is only at the end of the long evolutionary journey that the brain is transcended and the Mind uses its higher vehicle.   At that point, the Mind becomes responsive to the higher principles and the Man transfers the center of his being to the Mind.   He is not yet centered in the Soul, the Causal Principle, and it is this which is the work of those who take THE WAY.

the life span, and the passing from the body, determining the fate of every mortal, and dispensing justice for the mighty Zeus.

Klotho presides at births.   She holds the shining cord and watches all is well - or else as well as may be.   Lachesis watches life, and how the life is marked depends on the imponderables presided over by the Goddesses.   The oldest and most wise, Atropos, holds the shears, and wields them when the life span ends.

Prometheus, observing this, as he observes all beings from his high post on Mount Caucasus, concluded that the gods had once more held it fitting to be helpful to his proteges, the human creatures.   He grew a little thoughtful, and wondered if his friend Zeus would not reverse himself ere long, if this continued.   He settled back against his prison crag and looked to see if, maybe, Zeus might be near him.   But this time only silence and the empty space before his summit was the answer.

The mortals grew accustomed to death, parting, and the new disasters. The Goddesses grew busy, and the web of life hummed with activity.   Still, the mortals had not stormed Olympus, yet the giant Titan hoped, for after all the gods had not forgotten and they were just.   They fanned the flame by much adversity.   Prometheus was happy, as the supreme Zeus in his usual inscrutable fashion had duly noted.

-*- -*- -*- -*- -*- -*- -*- -*- -*- -*- -*- -*- -*- -*- -*- -*- -*- -*- -*- -*-

THE HISTORY OF GODHOOD - continued from page #149

passed without much perceptible difference.   The shadow-bodies grew a little denser, that is all that happened, and the shadow-men grew a little wiser as they learned to know the planet.

They had no need for gods, because the Gods were present.   The Progenitors, the Teachers, and the Lords moved always in plain view among the Shadows, the Seed-Men of the First Day of the Planet.   No one of them could have imagined gods, for Gods there were among them, who taught them wisdom, who brought them slowly to the point of utmost growth and stature possible for that Day, who helped them when the Day ended, who watched them as the SANDHYA swept them into sleep.   By that time the planet and all life within it required a sleep and a forgetting, and a new Day dawning.

-*- -*- -*- -*- -*- -*- -*- -*- -*- -*- -*- -*- -*- -*- -*- -*- -*- -*- -*- -*-

"Avoiding all extremes, Buddha Dhamma represents the Middle Way of
sanity and self-mastery.   It demands nothing in the way of
conduct that is contrary to good sense or detrimental to physical
and mental health.   The body is important in that it is the
vehicle of the mind, and the mind is the instrument of liberation.
The mind alone defiles or purifies itself, and it must function
healthily as the first essential to progress."

from "Buddhism as World-Religion"
by Francis Story

THE THEOSOPHICAL GLOSSARY, by Helena P. Blavatsky

The word "Theosophical" in the title is held to mean the Wisdom of the Ages taught in the ancient Mystery Schools, but as these Schools have disappeared from the Western world students are compelled to seek the inner teachings in the Eastern writings, where they have survived for many, many centuries.

During the past century scientists and scholars discovered the spiritual wealth of the Eastern writings, and the Western civilizations became acquainted with them in the form of translations and commentaries. Some Christian missionaries in Burma, Ceylon and China were impressed with the wisdom and nobility of the Buddha's Dharma and won adherents to the Dharma by their very fine writings. Diplomats and army officers added their quotas of writings and translations from India, Tibet and Nepal.

Madame Helena P. Blavatsky was a Buddhist who visited Ceylon and Tibet and lived in India for several years. She had a number of learned associates and was on friendly terms with leading authorities on the Eastern Philosophies. One of her associates, Colonel H. S. Olcott, wrote "The Buddhist Catechism", which has been in demand for sixty years. Madame Blavatsky took up the task of explaining the Eastern Philosophies to the West, and wrote a few very important books, the last of which was "The Theosophical Glossary".

It can safely be said it is the only book of its kind, and so has stood alone since its publication in January, 1892. Its purpose is to explain the terms used in present-day occult literature, as well as those used in the ancient teachings. Thus, a number of terms are in Latin, Greek, Pâli, Tibetan, Hebrew, etc., but most of the terms are Sanskrit for obvious reasons.

The Buddhist literature has been translated from Pâli, Sanskrit, Tibetan and Chinese into Japanese and modern European languages. But Pâli is very similar to Sanskrit, and Sûtras have been restored into the Sanskrit from the Chinese and Tibetan. Therefore students must turn to the Sanskrit for proper understanding of the Buddha's Dharma. Also, it should be remembered that the principal literature of India - the VEDAS and PURÂNAS, SÛTRAS and SÂSTRAS, the epics and philosophical systems - are in Sanskrit. Truly Sanskrit is a key to the Wisdom. Sanskrit deals with subject-matters for which there are no exact English equivalents, so that long explanations are necessary.

As Madame Blavatsky was a Buddhist, the "Glossary" abounds with Buddhist terms. It is a mine of information for the Buddhist student, but it is also invaluable to every student of the occult - to quote:

"Occultist: One who studies the various branches of occult science. The term is used by the French Kabbalists (See Eliphas Lévi's works). Occultism embraces the whole range of psychological, physiological, cosmical, physical, and spiritual phenomena. From the word 'occultus', hidden or secret. It therefore applies to the study of the Kabbalah, astrology, alchemy, and all arcane sciences." (page #238)

We recommend the photographic reproduction of the Original Edition, as first issued at London, England, in 1892, containing 389 pages. Obtainable from The Golden Lotus Press, price $3.00.

ANACHRONISMS

Politically the future is uncertain and economically the present
is unstable.   Beyond that no one will venture to predict or to
foresee the outcome, so complicated is the world problem.

Statesmen mutter darkly about the use of force and their opponents
glower over threats of non-cooperation.   Nations strain the
frayed edges of diplomatic language to the breaking point, and
polite consideration is a custom long abandoned by the impatiently
frustrated congress of the delegates.   Diplomacy and peaceful
discussion have failed to settle the questions of the after-war
years, and in some cases the application of force has failed
to solve the difficulties.

Too much attention has been given to the appearance of amity.
Only now the unexpressed unrest, aggression, oppression and ar-
rogant invasion have found themselves exposed and openly opposed.
Too many polite speeches at variance with the conduct of national affairs have been accepted as genuine and valid.   Too
many times the weaker nations have been sacrificed to the chimera
of united action, and as might have been expected the smaller
nations are uniting for self-preservation.

Long separated by distance, customs, language, economic indepen-
dence and difficult travel, the nations for the first time meet
in a world united by the speed of communication and the toppling
barriers of race, creed and custom.   They meet but to measure
swords again, in most cases continuing the border disputes or the
age-old persecutions.

Under the pressure caused by the disappearance of that seclusion
afforded by isolation, some nations attempt to pursue the methods
of the centuries of separation, and still depend upon these
anachronisms - archaic, injurious and altogether barbarous in these
more modern times.

But, will they be convinced of that in time?   Will they combine
in time?   Will they adopt more civilized methods?   Or, must we
resort again to a world melée, to a world holocaust, and an un-
precedented world horror?

SAMYAG-DRSTI - Right View

Motive has been ever the underlying cause for action, or for absence of action.   Stressing the necessity for Right Action, the Buddha nevertheless considered the motive for Right Action of supreme importance, the subtle differences in the various motives behind action being pointed out by him in many Sûtras.   Realizing that behind the motive there is comprehension, and behind that comprehension an all-embracing view of life and living, the Buddha placed Right View first of all the Eight Directions.

No one, he said, should attempt to proceed further without Right View, and no one should expect to obtain the desired results until after he acquires Right View.   Indeed, upon this one uncompromising condition is dependent every other condition, for hardly can one be expected to act rightly if the View - understanding, judgment, motive - is unable to visualize and direct Action.

Comprehension is an actual necessity.   Due to the multitude of dogmas, speculations, superstitions, half-beliefs and half-truths, comprising the religious teachings of the times, very many people have erroneous ideas of the cause of life, the cause of death, and the futility of depending upon an outside source for salvation has not become apparent to many adult intelligences.   Under the resulting misunderstanding, such people are acting in a manner not in accordance with Right Action.   They do so, however, because they do not possess Right Knowledge and they do not have Right Understanding of conduct and its results.   Because they do not possess Right View they are unable to achieve Right Action.

Due to the erroneous teachings of a perpetual hereafter, people discard the personal effort to achieve Perfection.   They assume their perfection will arrive automatically and effortlessly in the hereafter, so that they may safely disregard the proper rules of living in the present.   Or, being ignorant and untaught, they do not understand the proper rules of living, and thereby follow the whims of their selfish wills or their own emotional, sensual natures.

Such fallacies must be discarded.   The proper understanding of the recurring cycle of being, the perpetual action of Karma, the ever-present necessity for haste and attention to the steps of the evolutionary pathway, and the inevitable consequences of selfishness, must be acquired.   Hundreds of people today would be horrified at their own actions if they could be convinced of the consequences these actions would produce in the next rebirth, but the delusion of non-returning blinds them, and they pursue their disastrous dallying, feeling secure in the delusive safety of an unfailing, magic system of salvation.

No compromise, the Buddha said, with self-deception.   No reliance upon another, no ritual, no dogma, no sacrifices, and no self-indulgence.   No turning to the right, no turning to the left, no dalliance, no leisure - and no haste.   How wise the words he spoke, beyond the gates of what men call NIRVÂNA, lingering a moment at the end to say to those still dear to him - "Work out your own salvation with diligence."

Right View is like that - without compromise.   It does not have attraction for the self-indulgent.

KÂLA

What does this mean?

It is the Sanskrit word equivalent to Time, but expressing much more.
It would be best to explain KÂLA by two English words - by Duration,
and by Time.   The first is Infinite, Eternal and Universal Time, the
second is finite and conditioned.   The Sanskrit word for conditioned
time is KHANDAKÂLA.

Is KÂLA endless?

In the sense that there is forever change and that nothing endures
unchanged, no.   In the sense that there is forever Duration, the
Boundless, Unlimited and Infinite aspect of Time, it is endless.

Is KHANDAKÂLA endless?

No, never.   It is bounded, definite, finite, limited by Manvantaric
duration.   It may seem to be endless to our perception, but it is
only a period, a cycle.   It endures through a temporary manifestation of the material universe.

What time is meant by KÂLA?

All Time.   The Finite is contained within the Infinite, the Limited
within the Limitless.

What time is meant by KHANDAKÂLA?

All Time, finite and cyclic, in the sense that however long it may be
it must end.   It applies to every lesser cycle, for even the smallest
division known to Man - the second - is still Time.

Is KÂLA personified?

In the East, not by any special form.   Necessarily, it is closely
associated with BRAHMÂ and the Age of BRAHMÂ.   KÂLAHAMSA is a title
of GARUDA - "the Swan in Time".   KÂLA is also a title given to YAMA,
who presides over the Element of Earth and judges the dead.

Why does it become associated with YAMA?

BRAHMÂ is the manifested Universe, the outward-turned aspect of the
neuter BRAHMA, the Source of Being.   BRAHMÂ, as such, properly has
KÂLA as an aspect.   Exoterically however the popular fancy attaches
attributes, and YAMA, as King of the Underworld is a much lower God
than the great BRAHMÂ, so that during the centuries he could com-
fortably assume various attributes such as this one.   BRAHMÂ being
a temporary expression of BRAHMA, existing for only a period of the
Infinite Duration, is both Time the Infinite and Time the Finite.

(to be continued)

The Second Morning of the World-Scheme, the Second Dawning, found the planetary body much advanced along the spiral.   Changes could be noted in the density, and changes in the composition or balance of distribution of the elements comprising the field of force.   Contraction had eliminated the unimpeded passage of some bodies.   Gases had risen to the outer envelope, and within this the more solid atomic structure was cohering.   Into the fluidity of the centrifugal vortex appeared a waxing and waning tide which produced the orbit of the mass of the vast nebula.   Over the whole there hovered the Builders, the Sons of Manvantaric Morning, fiery and splendid and powerful, as they wrought still the changes and the motion.

Life flowed again into the cooling mass, and found itself plunged into airy substance, no longer fiery.   The World-Scheme had descended yet another note within the scale of seven.   The Life within it followed pattern.

The lower kingdoms wakened, drew the robe of body close about them, and made progress.   The Day grew into Brightness, and then at their own time the higher kingdoms wakened.   They came into a newly furbished world, a new and different condition.   They were still aerially formed, although more dense than the fine, luminous sheaths of the preceding aeons.

They grew accustomed to the denser world, and found themselves again the lords of all the planet.   They were instructed slowly by the Builders. They required nothing, for they were attuned to what they found around them. They gathered fiery energy direct from the still throbbing fiery centers. They drew in air and watery vapour from the atmosphere.   They rested never, for there was nothing really solid.   They were still spheroid, although a little more substantial, not able to float lightly, not able to dart quickly, yet not immobilized.   They were much slower, more specialized, more material, though that is not applicable for there was yet no matter solid.

They still possessed immortality.   They did not die, though sometimes they developed sleepy stages, and somnolent, they were quiescent.   They were more nearly shadows than they had been, but not as yet opaque.   Their bodies were translucent still, and luminous, and highly sensitive, the keen-ness of their subtle knowing not blunted or refracted.

Space was their home, the special space provided by the Builders. Moving through the mass, the Builders brought it toward the goal of density. They were like Gods, and they were Gods in actuality, much older, much wiser, much nearer to the mighty Cosmic Powers.

The Life within the nebula was happy.   They were not lonely, not lost, not separated, and quite satisfied to be where they could learn and bring themselves a little nearer to Perfection.   They were not satisfied with the still clumsy shadowy body, but they made progress.   In their own fashion they spoke sometimes, one to another, of their future.   And they were, to the end of Day, still clear about that future.   They passed into the sleep between the Days with certainty about that Future, and passing left that place of growing denser in the form.

They knew no gods, for Gods in subtle form were always with them.

by Rev. Gyomay M. Kuboso
(Reprinted from "NIRVANA", May, 1947)

The future of Buddhism here in America is of great concern to all Buddhists.
It is urgent, now, for us to think, formulate, and spread the teachings, so
that our religion will integrate into the culture of America.   If Buddhism is
to flourish in America, it must grow from the soil of America and it must be
one with the American culture.   Since Buddhism was brought from Japan, it has
been like a plant being transplanted; its roots are not firmly set to grow.
In this message, I would like to suggest a few points which I hope may help
towards our effort in the establishment of American Buddhism.

Until the present day, most of the young Buddhists were brought up as nominal
Buddhists not receiving much of the fundamental teachings and philosophy of
Buddhism.   Because of this fact, many of the Buddhists, who were scattered
throughout the country during and after the last World War, were afraid and
even hesitated to say freely and proudly, "I am a Buddhist."   They did not
know Buddhism, and, furthermore, they thought of it as a religion only
among Japanese.

Buddhism prospered in centralized Japanese communities; it was progressing
among the Japanese people.   Surely, there are Buddhist Caucasians here in
America, but they became Buddhists by reading books and studying Buddhism.
We, Buddhists, didn't spread the teachings to them.   Some have, perhaps; but
I speak of the majority of the Buddhists.

Buddhism is an universal religion.   We must not cling to the old Japanese
form of presentation as it came from Japan and confine it among the Japanese
people.   We must make Buddhism part of the American culture by changing its
interpretations and presentations and making it more adaptable to the American
way of life, spreading it among all people.   Now, more than ever, we,
Buddhists, must learn, understand and practice Buddhism.   We have the responsibility of carrying on Buddhism; we are the true representatives of
Buddhism in the current of American culture.

When we view the history of Buddhism, we clearly see how Buddhism became
Chinese Buddhism when it migrated there from India and how it benefited and
was appreciated by the Chinese people as part of their lives.   Later, when
it spread into Japan it became part of Japanese culture and enriched the
lives of the Japanese people.   Now, we should readily see why Buddhism must
grow as American Buddhism if we wish to make it progress as part of the
American way of life.   We cannot conform too strictly to Japanese traditional presentation.   It must be changed!

I would like to suggest the following ten point program for the establishment
of American Buddhism:

1. Intellectual rather than emotional.
2. Philosophical rather than mere faith.
3. Non-sectarian rather than sectarian.
4. Understanding and practice rather than formalism.
5. Stress on lay leaders.

(continued on page #164)

      6.   Use of simple, direct and understandable language.
      7.   Uniform teachings of fundamental Buddhism.
      8.   Unification of organizations under one Buddhism.
      9.   Establishment of unified independent Y. B. A.
    10.   Establishment of Buddhist Colleges in America.

American Buddhism should start from Gautama Buddha rather than from the
branched out sectarian teachings.   The sectarians must go beyond the founders
of sects and its teachings and go directly to Gautama Buddha.   The spirit of
this movement is not new -- it is a rediscovery of fundamental Buddhism.

-*- -*- -*- -*- -*- -*- -*- -*- -*- -*- -*- -*- -*- -*- -*- -*- -*- -*- -*- -*-

LITTLE ELVES

The little Elves are friendly folk
    In woodlands, glens and dells.
They know the caverns of the gnomes
    And where the satyr dwells.

The little Elves are very old
    But yet so quaint and wee
They hardly reach above the shoe
    And never to the knee.

The little Elves have tendencies
    As human beings do.
They have a liking for the strange
    And also for the new.

The little Elves are curious
    About their human friends.
They like to be included, so
    They weep when friendship ends.

The little Elves - of many kinds -
    Are fond of someone gay
Who likes to saunter through their haunts
    And often stops to play.

Their little faces shine with joy
    And out they march in glee,
When they can find a human friend
    Who likes their company.

So very happy are they then
    It is a sight to see!

-*- -*- -*- -*-

CHAPTER TWENTY

MENTAL CONTROL

"Let the Mind serve as the mirror of the Soul, and so
reflect the Spirit."

Padma Hiranya Surangama.

The Mind is called in some books the "Slayer of the Real", and many are
those who quote this, entirely misunderstanding it, thinking if they "slay
the slayer" they will attain Illumination.

Those who read the books of Eastern origin should remember the East
speaks in a different language. They should read the beautiful, elaborately imaginative symbolism of the words with intent to perceive the meaning
behind the sentences and phrases. For those who read Eastern thought in
terms of the literal-minded Western languages, who take the Eastern words as
meaning what they say exactly, who take the shadow for the substance, are
often very much misled, and they may never begin THE WAY because of their misunderstanding.

In some cases Western students come to think the words "slay the slayer"
mean to obliterate or suspend thought. They think by some magical procedure, or mantram, or breathing, or what not, to displace intelligence, and
to find NIRVANA. Now, a true understanding of the place of Mind in the complex being would prevent such misunderstanding.

Truly, no pupil approaches THE WAY without a developed intelligence and
a thoughtful, discriminating Mind. He is equipped with the preliminary
requisite of an efficient brain controlled by a Mind capable of concentration
upon a goal or idea, used to assimilate new information, or serve as a store-
house for experience. He has the advantage of many lives of development
behind him, gained in the competitive physical world, in which the necessity
for survival has forced him to evolve this tool.

In some books this controlling mental apparatus has been called the
SARIRA - the sheath - and in others MANAS, the Mind. It is impossible to
speak of the "mental body", but it is necessary to adopt some designation for
the subtle link, distinguished as higher than, different from, and in control of the physical brain.

It is now the task of the pupil to bridge the gap between the Mind and
the Soul and Spirit. The Soul always has had moments when it was able to
send its inspiration through the Mind to the physical brain, and thus for
the moment at least combat the reactions, impulses and emotions aroused by
contact with the physical world, but, not always was the gate open to inspiration from above. Urgent and imperative fear, hunger, thirst, weariness, sex and the emotions, the crowding attractions and interests of the
every-day life - any one or all of these - may have clouded the lower being,
leaving no opportunity for the finer vibrations to register. The Mind,
imprisoned in Matter, dealt most of all with Matter, and because of this

it has been described as the "Slayer of the Real", because the Soul impulses
and commands were "slain" as they entered the sheath of MANAS.

All that comes through to the physical being from Soul and Spirit must
come through the MANAS, which is the gate, the bridge, the link. It must be
trained, therefore, to refrain from "slaying the real", and to permit the
passage of the spiritual vibrations. It must become a vehicle, it must be
conquered, held at command, and in this sense only the "slayer" must be
"slain".   Nevertheless it is to be used, not eliminated. It is to be a
servant, not banished. It is to be useful and to assist, not to be broken
and destroyed.

No one attains NIRVÂNA - nor even the first step of THE WAY - without
the aid of intelligence and without a keenly developed discrimination, and
for this MANAS is required to control the physical brain, its instrument.
Therefore the pupil should begin his mental habit forming early on THE WAY,
and to understand wherefore and why he makes certain habits. He requires
the full cooperation of the Mind, and this he can acquire, though slowly.

This is a difficult task.   It never has been easy.

Subtle and volatile, mercurial and fiery, scintillating with brilliance,
that which is called a "sheath" is the cloud-form of the MÂNASA, enveloping
and inspiring the grosser, heavier atomic structures of the being. Restless
and powerful, ever active, the volatility of Mind enwraps the focal center
and reacts upon it, surging like a wave-tossed powerful ocean. Mind has
its tides and rhythms, but it is powerful and never leashed by any save the
Adept. It surges unchecked in the undeveloped being.

This uncontrolled and almost irresistible untamed ocean must yet be conquered. It is the task of tasks, and it must not be underestimated. Sweep
through the denser being as it will, it must be met and limits set; it must
be understood; it must be yoked to serve the Will; it must be called into
alignment.

Many people have begun this task unknowing. Many students have begun
to understand the nature of MÂNASA. Many, therefore, attempt to bring the
Mind into control, and in so doing take the first step toward Self-Mastery,
for he who rules MÂNASA is beyond the need of Precepts.

-*- -*- -*- -*- -*- -*- -*- -*- -*- -*- -*- -*- -*- -*- -*- -*- -*- -*- -

THOUGHTS OF THE OVERSHADOWER

I know, O Elder Brother, I have gone the way
That all poor flesh goes; and have earned all dire
And fretful things -- until the One Far Day
Brings end to Maya and the grasping mire;
But, now that I have rounded past the Lower Turn
And know where lies my home - though harrowing the climb -
O Warrior, be Thou present while I really learn
What I, now, know -- that Your great Way is mine.

                                        John Lamarr

Part II - The Dharma or Doctrine

174. Q. What doctrine ennobles Buddhism, and gives it its exalted place among
        the world's religions?
     A. That of MITTA or MAITREYA - compassionate kindness. The importance
        of this doctrine is more-over emphasised in the giving of the
        name "MAITRI" (the Compassionate One), to the coming Buddha.

175. Q. Were all these points of Doctrine that you have explained meditated
        upon by the Buddha near the Bo-tree?
     A. Yes, these and many more that may be read in the Buddhist Scrip-
        tures. The entire system of Buddhism came to his mind during
        the Great Enlightenment.

176. Q. How long did the Buddha remain near the Bo-tree?
     A. Forty-nine days.

177. Q. What do we call the first discourse preached by the Buddha - that
        which he addressed to his five former companions?
     A. The DHAMMACAKKA-PPAVATTANA SUTTA, - The Sutra of the Definition of
        the Rule of Doctrine. *

   * After the appearance of the first edition, I received from one of the
     ablest PALI scholars of Ceylon, the late L. Corneille Wijesinha, Esq.,
     Mudaliar of Matale, what seems a better rendering of DHAMMACAKKA-
     PPAVATTANA than the one previously given; he makes it "The Establish-
     ment of the Reign of Law". Professor Rhys-Davids prefers, "The
     Foundation of the Kingdom of Righteousness". Mr. Wijesinha writes
     me: "You may use 'Kingdom of Righteousness,' too, but it savours more
     of dogmatic theology than of philosophic ethics. DHAMMACAKKA-
     PPAVATTANA SUTTAM is "the discourse entitled 'The Establishment of
     the Reign of Law'." Having shown this to the High Priest, I am happy
     to be able to say that he assents to Mr. Wijesinha's rendering.

178. Q. What subjects were treated by him in this discourse?
     A. The "Four Noble Truths," and the "Noble Eight-fold Path". He con-
        demned the extreme physical mortification of the ascetics, on
        the one hand, and the enjoyment of sensual pleasures on the other;
        pointing out and recommending the Noble Eight-fold Path as the
        Middle Path.

179. Q. Did the Buddha hold to idol-worship?
     A. He did not; he opposed it. The worship of gods, demons, trees,
        etc., was condemned by the Buddha. External worship is a fetter
        that one has to break if he is to advance higher.

180. Q. But do not Buddhists make reverence before the statue of the Buddha,
        his relics, and the monuments enshrining them?
     A. Yes, but not with the sentiment of the idolator.

181. Q. What is the difference?
     A. Our Pagan brother not only takes his images as visible representa-
        tions of his unseen God or gods, but the refined idolater, in
        worshipping, considers that the idol contains in its substance a
        portion of the all-pervading divinity.

182. Q. What does the Buddhist think?
      A. The Buddhist reverences the Buddha's statue and the other things you
          have mentioned, only as mementoes of the greatest, wisest, most
          benevolent and compassionate man in this world-period (Kalpa).
          All races and peoples preserve, treasure up, and value the relics
          and mementoes of men and women who have been considered in any
          way great.   The Buddha, to us, seems more to be revered and be-
          loved than any one else, by every human being who knows sorrow.

183. Q. Has the Buddha himself given us something definite upon this subject?
      A. Certainly.   In the MAHA PARI NIRVANA SUTTA he says that emancipa-
          tion is attainable only by leading the Holy life, according to the
          Noble Eight-fold Path, not by external worship (amisa puja), nor
          by adoration of himself, or of another, or of any image.

184. Q. What was the Buddha's estimate of ceremonialism?
      A. From the beginning, he condemned the observance of ceremonies and
          other external practices, which only tend to increase our
          spiritual blindness and our clinging to mere lifeless forms.

185. Q. What as to controversies?
      A. In numerous discourses he denounced this habit as most pernicious.
          He prescribed penances for Bhikkhus who waste time and weaken
          their higher intuitions in wrangling over theories and meta-
          physical subtleties.

186. Q. Are charms, incantations, the observance of lucky hours and devil-
          dancing a part of Buddhism?
      A. They are positively repugnant to its fundamental principles.   They
          are the surviving relics of fetishism and pantheistic and other
          foreign religions.   In the BRAHMAJALA SUTTA the Buddha has
          categorically described these and other superstitions as pagan,
          mean and spurious. *

      * The mixing of these arts and practices with Buddhism is a sign of
      deterioration.   Their facts and phenomena are real and capable of
      scientific explanation.   They are embraced in the term "magic,"
      but when resorted to, for selfish purposes, attract bad influences
      about one, and impede spiritual advancement.   When employed for
      harmless and beneficent purposes, such as healing the sick, saving
      life, etc., the Buddha permitted their use.

187. Q. What striking contrasts are there between Buddhism and what may be
          properly called "religions"?
      A. Among others, these: It teaches the highest goodness without a
          creating God; a continuity of life without adhering to the super-
          stitious and selfish doctrine of an eternal, metaphysical soul-
          substance that goes out of the body; a happiness without an
          objective heaven; a method of salvation without a vicarious
          Saviour; redemption by oneself as the Redeemer, and without
          rites, prayers, penances, priests or intercessory saints; and
          a summum bonum, i.e., Nirvana, attainable in this life and in
          this world by leading a pure, unselfish life of wisdom and
          compassion to all beings.

188. Q. Specify the two main divisions of "meditation," i.e., of the process
          by which one extinguishes passion and attains knowledge?
      A. SAMATHA, and VIDARSANA:
             (1)   the attenuation of passion by leading the holy life and
                     by continued effort to subdue the senses;
             (2)   the attainment of supernormal wisdom by reflection:
             each of which embraces twenty aspects, but I need not here
             specify them.

189. Q. What are the four paths or stages of advancement that one may at-
          tain to?
      A. (1)   SOTÂPATTI - the beginning or entering into which follows
                 after one's clear perception of the 'Four Noble Truths';

         (2)   SAKARDÂGÂMI - the path of one who has so subjugated lust,
                 hatred and delusion that he need only return once to this world;

         (3)   ANÂGAMI - the path of those who have so far conquered self
                 that they need not return to this world;

         (4)   ARHAT - the path of the holy and worthy Arhat, who is not only
                 free from the necessity of re-incarnation, but has capacitated
                 himself to enjoy perfect wisdom, boundless pity for the ig-
                 norant and suffering, and measureless love for all beings.

190. Q. Does popular Buddhism contain nothing but what is true, and in ac-
          cord with science?
      A. Like every other religion that has existed many centuries, it cer-
          tainly now contains untruth mingled with truth; even gold is
          found mixed with dross.   The poetical imagination, the zeal,
          or the lingering superstitions of Buddhist devotees have, in
          various ages, caused the noble principles of the Buddha's moral
          doctrines to be coupled more or less with what might be removed
          to advantage.

191. Q. When such perversions are discovered what should be the true
          Buddhist's earnest desire?
      A. The true Buddhist should be ever ready and anxious to see the false
          purged away from the true, and to assist, if he can.   Three
          great Councils of the Sangha were held for the express purpose of
          purging the body of Teachings from all corrupt interpolations.

192. Q. When?
      A. The first, at Sattapanni cave, just after the death of the Buddha;
          the second at Valukarama, in Vaisali; the third at Asokarama
          Vihara, at Pataliputra, 235 years after Buddha's decease.

193. Q. In what discourse does the Buddha himself warn us to expect this
          perversion of the true Doctrine?
      A. In the Sanyutta Nikaya.

194. Q. Are there any dogmas in Buddhism which we are required to accept
          on faith?
      A. No: we are earnestly enjoined to accept nothing whatever on faith;
          whether it be written in books, handed down from our ancestors,
          or taught by the sages.
                                      (to be continued)

THE THEORY OF MANU - ROOT MANUS:

  One must not strain the simile of the husbandman too far. If one uses
a poetic illustration, it is not necessary to conclude the illustration has
actuality. For this reason, it might be well to caution the student not to
use the titles of the fourteen MANUS except as names for that particular
period or MANVANTARA with which they are associated, distinguished from every
other MANVANTARA.

  Similarly, if one must have a simile to indicate the difference in the
pairs of MANVANTARAS - Root and Seed - each pair comprising one Planetary Day,
it is not necessary to imagine an individuality or personality in charge of
the periods in question. To do so is to return to anthropomorphism and the
worship of superhuman beings.

  The student should hold always in his mind the impersonality of the Cosmic Scheme, as visualized and realized by that indomitable body of Seers and
Adepts who have, through the ages, revealed the Cosmos to the initiates of
the race. This impersonality has been turned, so often, into a personality
that it has become a habit of the non-thinking. Whatever it may be to
initiates, the MANU is exoterically a cycle and an evolutionary rhythm.

  In the beginning of a KALPA - it is immaterial what the mind may be able
to accept as the condition at that time - there is always a preliminary period
between PRALAYA and the KALPA. This period passes slowly. The work of
the Planetary Builders in the Morning of the First Day is to cohere, to com-
press, to assemble, and to root the Life coming from the preceding worlds,
gathered into the planetary field of force from surrounding space in the vortex of world formation. Much of the sphere is fiery, gaseous, tenuous and
ethereal. The awakening life is subtle-formed, or embryonic, latent and
unconscious. The kingdoms of life lower in the scale awaken first, and
find conditions to their liking first.

  That which is called Root MANU consists of this work of beginning, developing and fostering, perfecting, as far as may be the Life of the entire
planetary chain of seven worlds, and of each planetary body's seven spheres.
This is explained in detail in "The Secret Doctrine".

  The Day begins, the MANU roots the Life. Each Day thereafter has a new
beginning, and each Root MANU begins a higher spiral of the round of planets,
and the time of growing. Each Root MANU, in turn, alters the surface of
the planet, or the composition of the elements, so that each Day has an entirely new and different condition. Each Round or Day, the planetary body
thickens, settles, densifies. Life within it follows pattern, until the
balance turns, and once again the planetary body passes from density with
equal slowness.

  Each Root MANU, then, fosters, even as it destroys the work of previous
MANUS. Each Root MANU builds ever more refined and complicated forms, and
consciousnesses suited to them. Each Root MANU hands over into the SANDHYÂ
of cataclysm, destruction, change and deathless sleeping, its charges of

(continued on page #173)

Deep within the heart of a heavily wooded land of hills and valleys,
beautiful and undisturbed by mortals, dwelt a Princess of the Water Kingdom,
in a waterfall of unusual loveliness.   She had come upon it quite by accident, for, like many Water beings, she often wandered by way of stream and
river.   The deep ocean was her home, and she was kin to many royal lines
of Water Rulers, but in the long lifetime of such an Immortal there is desire
for change and for seclusion, and sometimes even an Immortal may have a
curiosity.

This daughter of a prince of the Atlantic Ocean, being weary, sought
solace in a journey, and purely by chance she visited a mighty river flowing
into the ocean.   She spent a long time in its deep waters, but sometimes followed tributary rivers, and so one day she entered the delightful little
rushing stream called "Crystal Water".   She found its course in the deep
woods among the hills entrancing, and by and by she came to love the waterfall, and made its sparkling cascade her home and center.

The waterfall was triple.   It tumbled from the heights into a deep,
wide pool, as still as the long cataract itself was turbulent.   The water
fell again, with thunder, into another pool, and then again it fell toward
the lower valley.   Here was the throbbing power center of the stream, and
here the Water Princess loved to be.

The beings of the valley - the birds and animals, the races of immortals-
found her wise and tender.   They told her tales of land, and she was never
tired of hearing.   The creatures came to drink of the clear water, and she
would call them closer and the long tales would begin.   They asked her sometimes of the depths of ocean, but she said it was not very pretty, not like
the valley.

Sometimes she slept - as the Immortals do - in winter.   The pool was
frozen and the water chilly - not that that mattered to her, but the woodland
creatures suffered - and she made a place beneath the fall where depth would
be a refuge, there spending the cold winter.

The Princess missed her kinsfolk, but she had for court the little water
undines, and the teeming life of the valley.   There were no older, no important Water beings nearer than the depths of the great River.   They knew
she sought seclusion and they left her, being tactful, used to moods like
hers in the high ranks of the Immortals.

 The long years passed and then the red race of men grew slowly in the
region.   They found the lovely waterfall and called it Moon-bright, or
Cloud-mist.   They liked to spend time near it, sensing the deep peace of its
power and the special benediction of the Princess flowing out like balm upon
all in the country near her.   They called it Place of Being Peaceful, but
more often, Pool of Deep Reflection.

So time passed and the Princess learned of mortals, even as she had
learned of land and water animals and birds and the valley's other evolutions.

At last war came to the Princess.   The red invaders came down from the

(continued on page #173)

"What is the nature of Compassion?"

Is it pity? If so, it should be called pity. Is it mercy? If so, it should be called mercy. If it is not mercy, pity, and other common definitions of the term, then what is it?

Compassion is obviously one of the hard to define complex words, not easily replaced by any other word. It is also a word used in various moods or shadings, and it is the variety of its meanings that prevents it from being limited to any one of the synonyms or allied words connected with it. Nevertheless, it is commonly understood to mean pity for those afflicted, distressed, or in trouble.

The meaning "to suffer with" or "to sorrow for" another is a little higher, but even here a difference in status is implied, no equality of state being necessary. Indeed an inequality of state is necessary to call it forth.

MAHÂ KARUNÂ, the true Compassion, is not this. It has no need for cause; it pours forth upon the world regardless of the individual need. It does not contemplate another's misery, in order to rush to be helpful and sympathetic. It does not alter its own joyousness to call another miserable or less happy, but retains its state of balance and of poise and joy. It does not "sorrow with", being above the emotion of sorrow. It is not contemplative and unemotional mental waves, and it is not emotionally stirred heart waves. It is from the high realm of the perfected being that the true Compassion comes, and it is not the ordinary compassion in any sense of the word.

What is MAHÂ KARUNÂ? The Buddhas of Compassion, turning toward the world of action, ray forth the Truth in Their Compassion for all beings. They seek to point The Way. They seek to call men Home. They strive to spread Enlightenment. They act, with all Their mighty strength, to strike at cause, but not at the effects. They do not waste time upon pity, regret, sorrow or commiseration. Seeing the underlying causes of the world's suffering, They seek to relieve the suffering by removing the Cause of Suffering. They are not anxious to make men well, happy, rich, amused, and satisfied. They take the ills of life as natural reactions from evident causes, and they judge rightly that the true Compassion seeks to break the chains fettering the being to the cause of his particular - and yet general - misery.

Perhaps this is the true distinction between the ordinary human compassion and the divinely practical Compassion of the Bodhisattvas and the Buddhas. One, seeing the effect, sorrows and seeks to alleviate it. One, seeing the cause, seeks to eradicate that cause forever.

One, being human, is sporadic, excited by another's misfortune, nonexistent in the absence of suffering, limited and visionless and emotionally based. One, being divinely based, is all-seeing, all-wise, all-embracing, never-ceasing, never-wavering, never withheld, never non-existent.

The true Compassion comprehends the Cause of Suffering and brings its strength to bear against it.

the races and all Life within the planet.   The charges pass into a new condition, with their experience and knowledge, taking with them all the gains
and losses, all the rich heritage of ages.

    The Root MANU is BRAHMĀ in his aspect of the Creator, and his other as-
pect of VISHNU, the Preserver, let us say.   But what is BRAHMA?   And what
is MANU?   They are the impersonal and incorporeal Forces of the Universe,
suspected by the uninitiated of possessing body.

-*- -*- -*- -*- -*- -*- -*- -*- -*- -*- -*- -*- -*- -*- -*- -*- -*- -*- -*-

THE PRINCESS - continued from page #171

north and there was slaughter in her valley.   She wept and wrung her hands,
impotent.

    Last came the Sachem, surviving all his people, retreating, resisting
capture, spent and sore wounded, wearily following the trail to the upper
pool secluded.   Laying his beloved weapons down, he flung one arm to the sky
in salutation to Manito, and with a last thought of peace and liberty, of
taking refuge with "the spirit of the water", plunged into the pool and there
departed body.

    The quiet pool held him until the red invaders followed, and would have
drawn the body forth for mutilation.   But the Princess, horror-stricken,
drew it gently down by a strong current - for the Water has strange powers.

    The conquerors would have persisted, seeking trophies, but that the
Princess, rising unseen, invisible and terrible in her wrath and Water Power,
at long last the mighty one of ocean, hurled the invincible and impregnable
shield of Water between them, driving terror into their hearts.   Crying
"the place is spirit-haunted", they fled to safety beyond the pressing shield
of Water, spreading over the triple fall and claiming territory in the land
and air adjacent.

    The Princess laid the Sachem's body on a pebbly shelf, within the depths,
and there it rested, in deep sanctuary, behind the shield of Water.   And
through the stained and murder-haunted valley the stream flowed red, but
yet as calmly as before.

                                                (to be continued)

-*- -*- -*- -*- -*- -*- -*- -*- -*- -*- -*- -*- -*- -*- -*- -*- -*- -*- -*-

        "The angels keep their ancient places;-
         Turn but a stone, and start a wing!
         'Tis ye, 'tis your estrangèd faces,
         That miss the many-splendoured thing."   . . . . .

                            "Not where the wheeling systems darken
                             And our benumbed conceiving soars! -
                             The drift of pinions, would we hearken,
                             Beats at our own clay-shuttered doors."

                                            Francis Thompson

SLAYER OF THE REAL: (October, 1947, p. #165)

A symbolic and poetic expression, often construed literally. The Mind
is not the slayer. It is Ignorance - of spiritual values, of spiritual laws,
of spiritual reality - that slays the Real. For Ignorance of spiritual
values drives the Mind to rely upon the Unreal world of manifestation, thus
shutting out the guidance of the Spirit.

SPIRIT: (October, 1947, p. #166)

This is a word used in the West to mean, among other meanings, "The immortal part of man". Therefore, Spirit is an English word used for convenience, instead of the Sanskrit word ÂTMA which it replaces. The word ÂTMA
is used to indicate the highest principles in Man - ÂTMA manifesting through
BUDDHI and MANAS, forming what is known as the Reincarnating Principle, or the
Permanent Sheath, or the Wayfarer through the MANVANTARA. These, from time
immemorial, have been understood by all the Initiated to be beyond any contact
with Matter.

CONSCIOUSNESS: (October, 1947, p. #170)

This is a term which may be said to cover all Life, for all Life is conscious on its own plane, in its own place, according to its capacity. It is
used to name the imperishable directing Life that inhabits bodies, and through
them contacts and experiences the manifested Universe. The Consciousness is
the energy, the force, the responsible agent, directing the form. It is the
Consciousness that evolves and carries with it, onward and upward, the garnered experiences of the many incarnations of its journey. It is not to be
thought of as intelligence or knowledge, for those are tools of the Consciousness. It is, rather, the intangible and eternally manifesting evidence of
what the West calls "Spirit", the East "ÂTMA", and it is common to all Life,
for it is Life itself.

Below Man's feet, upon the Ladder of Being, climbing toward the portal
of self-consciousness, climbs the One Life in many forms, from the mineral to
the animal. From Man's place upon the Ladder springs the liberated Consciousness to freedom in still finer, nobler, more ethereal realms, until the
Ladder vanishes beyond his sight into the Cosmos. On each round of the
Ladder Consciousness and Life find means to garner the experiences in order
at that level. The evolution of the form is interesting and a study in itself, but it is the evolution of the Consciousness that is important, which
should be the most important study made by Man.

TANHÂ: (Pâli)   (August, 1947, p. #131)

TANHÂ is Desire - the Thirst for experience, for sensation, for satisfaction, for life and being in the form. "It is clinging to life on the earth,
the direct cause of rebirth or reincarnation," says H. P. Blavatsky in "The
Theosophical Glossary". It forms the fourth NIDANA, or Fetter, being called
TRISHNA in the Sanskrit. Each one of the twelve Fetters stands alone, is
spoken of separately by Buddhist commentators, as well as enumerated in the
list of the Chain of Twelve Fetters. Hence, the use of the one Fetter in
"The Buddhist Catechism", and the use of the PÂLI term.

"NIRVANA" - published by The Eastern Young Buddhist League

Nirvâna signifies a culmination in human progress.   "NIRVANA" as the title of
an American Buddhist magazine signifies a culmination in the progress of the
Dharma of the Buddha.

Gautama Buddha had many titles, one being the "Great Plowman", for he sowed
the Dharma in North India twenty-five hundred years ago.   From India the seeds
were carried to take root in many lands.   Moving eastward the Dharma reached
Burma, Siam and China, where the Sûtras were held safe, awaiting translation,
whereas the literature in India was destroyed.   The Dharma then reached Japan
and finally was brought to America by Japanese Buddhists.   Moving westward
from India the Dharma travelled rapidly in the past hundred years, for with the
coming of a knowledge of Buddhism into Europe a number of Buddhist organizations
were formed, and from there the Dharma reached America.   It may be said that
two streams of Buddhism - that of the European and American scholars (principally from the Pâli or Hinayâna) and that of the Japanese Buddhists (principally from the Chinese or Mahâyâna) - have remained apart.   "NIRVANA"
heralds the meeting of the two streams in the New World, and symbolizes the
encircling of the world by the Buddhadharma.   May it have a bright future.

"NIRVANA" is a publication issued quarterly by the Eastern Young Buddhist League
of The Buddhist Churches of America, with headquarters in New York.   The
number here reviewed is Volume III, Number One, published under the auspices
of the Eastern Young Buddhist League by the Publications Committee of the
Chicago Buddhist Church.   This is the Spring Quarter Issue.

"NIRVANA" is modern in tone and typically American.   The outstanding articles
are the Editorial by K. Arthur Hayashi, the "Foreword", "A Message to American
Buddhists" by Rev. Gyomay M. Kubose, and "The Census of American Buddhism",
because they deal with the aspirations and hence the future of Buddhists in
America.   The authors remind readers that the teachings must "integrate into
the culture of America", that there is need to study the "fundamentals of the
Dharma", that "American Buddhism should start from Gautama Buddha rather than
from the branched out sectarian teachings", and should be a "rediscovery of
fundamental Buddhism".

The contents include:
    "The Buddhist Movement in America", by Rev. Julius A. Goldwater;
    "The Responsibility of Buddhists", by Rev. Sunya N. Pratt;
    "Christianity and Buddhism", by Philipp K. Eidmann;
    "The Divinity of Life", by Marie M. Biehl;
    "Six Buddhist Thoughts in Japan", by Rev. Nyogen Senzaki;
    "The Dharma and the World Today", by Stephen Bela Renovich;
    "The ABC of Buddhism", by Gyosei Wm. Flygare.

Though the Editors state it is by no means complete, a "Directory of Buddhist
Organizations in America" is included.   A complete Directory would be valuable
in unifying American Buddhists.   A list of "Buddhist Publications" is also
given, and it is gratifying to note there are at least seventeen of those
published in the United States at present.

Copies of this particular number, dated May, 1947, may be obtained at the
price of twenty-five cents per copy, by writing to the Editor, Mr. K. Arthur
Hayashi, 5487 South Dorchester Avenue, Chicago, 15, Ill.

Sentinel's Signals

RE-ARMAMENT

The last resort of nationalism is again to be invoked.

Freed from the threat of World Imperialism and World
Conquest, emerging victorious and dominant, the World
Democracies have waited in the interval for some co-
operative uplift to remove the threat of war and its
attendant horrors.   Arbitration, discussion, diplomatic procedure, exchange and barter - all these are
under way, for they may be considered policies per-
manently adopted by the great Democracies as means to
effect peaceful settlements.   Still the unduly pro-
longed exchange of world amenities produces for the
nations only stalemate and dissatisfaction, and by it
no question of the slightest importance to the present
day or to the future has been answered.

Under the circumstances, one may say fairly that the
nations arm to meet the threat of an immovable objec-
tion to the peaceful settlement of any world problem.
The will of the preponderance of the assemblage of
nations is set aside and held at bay and flouted
openly by a small group of erstwhile allies.

This is no time to think of parliamentary procedure
and diplomats' agreements.   This is a time to strive
to hold the unprotected smaller nations safe from
more aggression and interference, from compulsion
towards an undemocratic mode of living.

The cause is clear - to be or not to be - to live or
not to live - for many smaller nations.   Therefore
the world re-arms itself, in measured movements,
with firm intent to hold the frontiers of Democracy,
if need should be and there is no alternative.

-*- -*- -*- -*-

SAMYAG-DRSTI - Right View

Complete understanding of the Way to travel - that is SAMYAG-DRSTI.

It is a state of mind to be reached by the slow process of discarding wrong views - MITHYĀ-DRSTI - or swiftly by one supreme and instantaneous assimilation of the Dharma. No other methods are possible, though often an individual progresses slowly, gathering wisdom through a lifetime, only to leap forward into realization and the full state of SAMYAG-DRSTI when he first hears or reads the Dharma.

The perfect state of SAMYAG-DRSTI is remarkable in its serenity and calm acceptance of the blows of fortune, as well as in its most intent dedication to a purpose. It holds one true to self and true to others, and true to the great Way. It demands all and accepts all as due, content with nothing less than utmost effort.

The self-indulgent dreamers never have acquired it, nor have they known the diamond-clear and brilliant realization of the mind it brings to its possessor. The lazy poseurs and mind-grasping intellectuals never have the outward signs, because they have not realized the culminating inner stage upon which the outer signs depend. The talkers do not know; the state of inner understanding transcends the need to garble words and meanings. The complete silence of the inner knowing is broken only to express the Dharma, or to communicate with others on the mundane, every-day affair of living.

The possession of this understanding wisdom, although it is based upon Mind aligned with and in some cases supra-mind, does not complete the libera-tion of the being. Its task is to guide, direct, sustain and undertake the sometimes miserable task of liberation from the toils of MĀRA. It is en-during, never departing, being a growth of inner faculties, therefore a per-manent possession, not subject to the whim or fancy of the lower, more material Mind-essence. No one who once possesses SAMYAG-DRSTI is capable of retraction or conversion from or desertion of the Way toward the Heights.

It has a firm grasp upon the lower being always. Not in connection with it are found the lower vices, the baser passions, the meaner habits. It will not brook their presence - even if the stained, polluted lower being would permit the upward aspiration necessary to acquire the understanding. The two extremes are never to be found within one being.

The lure of wordly gain and wordly fame is worthless to the Understan-der. He does not stoop to practise selfishness or self-aggrandizement. He sinks into the background, well content to take himself in hand and to work out his Karma. He is benignly selfless, but his selflessness is of such a nature it passes often for indifference to others, simply because he holds himself aloof from time-wasting and unnecessary occupations.

SAMYAG-DRSTI works a complete revolution in the life and habits. It is a quiet revolution, but comprehensive. No drifter, dreamer, speculator, incoherent mystic, idler, or dabbler in the occult arts may be associated with it, even by those who do not know its nature. The SAMYAG-DRSTIN and SAMYAG-DRSTI are the exact and eternal opposite of these - being respec-tively Right Viewer and Right View, the Understander and the Understanding.

KÂLA (continued)

Does KÂLA have an esoteric meaning?

Very many words, if traced to the source, have esoteric meaning. Is the
outer world ever separated from the subtle realms, and is there anything
unrelated to the cosmos, or outside of cosmos? Whatever the relationship of words may be to the actuality, the esoteric teachings are confined to certain basic thoughts generally inclusive in their application. Starting at the level of Cosmos, they include all microscopic
portions of the Cosmos. One such esoteric teaching is this one of Time.

Can we realize KÂLA - Duration?

The only time apparent to our minds is the man-made scale we call the
calendar. Any other race of evolutionary beings would perceive a different scale of time, according to their particular perceptions. An
indication of this is given in the ancient system, in the scales or
computations called Divine Time and Cosmic Time. The same scales of
time were used by various ancient nations, each calling them by different names, but the modern world has eliminated this recognition of
the existence of other consciousnesses within the Universe.

Is the scale called Cosmic Time important?

The little that we can know or can realize through the measure called
"Brahmâ's Age" and "Years of Brahmâ" is an indication of the Duration
beyond - the realm of the Infinite, the Beginningless and Endless
BRAHMA. That which is called Cosmic Time is BRAHMA'S Time, the time
of the creative period when BRAHMA wakes or "breathes outward". These
interludes of cosmic activity are important - our short lives occur
within them.

Our time scale is an artificial, arbitrary one?

Yes, one suited to the human comprehension, but the time scale does not
recognize the ancient reckonings based upon the research of the ancient
seers. No human mind, of course, can encompass the Infinite, but
human minds absorb as much as they can encompass. The measure of the
student's understanding of the World-Scheme is his conception of Time -
either it is a liberating factor, or it binds the mind to the immediate present.

What is the thought behind the Sanskrit word?

It is not a title, label or name of a man-made period. KÂLA is from
the root word KALA - to urge forward, to impel, to accomplish, to complete. It is, fortunately, not confused by personification, and has
remained abstract, an idea undeified.

Time is the remorseless equalizer, the undeflectable summator of the moving pageant, the divisor and the moderator of the races, the inscrutable systematizer and implacable calculator.   As the great weigher, holding the destiny of all the worlds, KÂLA is Fate.

Time is.   During the MAHÂKALPA it is an aspect of BRAHMÂ.   Remaining when the manifested universe dissolves into the Milky Ocean and BRAHMA "sleeps" during the long PRALAYA, KÂLA endures through the long Night. Ever, through the ages and the eternities of the Cosmos, endures the mystery called KÂLA - Duration.

Not simple is this explanation, but not simple is this Cosmic Unalterable called KÂLA.

-*- -*- -*- -*- -*- -*- -*- -*- -*- -*- -*- -*- -*- -*- -*- -*- -*- -*- -*- -*-

Reprinted from "The Canadian Theosophist", October, 1947.

MIDNIGHT

There comes a night breath bringing
    The fragrance of the hay,
There comes a star-beam flinging
    A blessing for the day.

There comes a thought of dying
    To me who cannot die;
The whippoorwill is crying,
    A fire-fly flickers by.

What storm of Fate's provoking
    Sweeps from the depths remote,
In surging grief-tides choking
    All nightlong at my throat?

Is it the summer's glory
    That must be laid away,
Or dread of winter hoary
    Above the church-yard clay?

Or in the heart-deep stirring
    Some woe of other lives,
Whose harvest time recurring
    Out of the chaos strives?

In Memoriam   by A. E. S. Smythe
Died October 2, 1947

by The Ven. Palane Siri Vajiranana Maha Nayaka Thera
(Reprinted from "The Maha Bodhi", May-June, 1946)

Who does things carefully, he, alone, is capable of thoroughness of action.
To do a thing thoroughly there must be preparation and devotion. Preparation makes for dexterity, and devotion brings steadiness. Preparation
saves energy. It is the foundation of all true economy. Devotion produces singlemindedness, the great antidote to loose behaviour.

The whole purpose of culture is to make us thorough in the use of our bodily
and mental limbs. To the extent a man is master of his inner and outer
faculties of control he is a man thorough in his doings.

If one has no mindfulness one will not develop thoroughness of action. And
he who is not capable of doing things thoroughly will be lopsided of character, will not achieve much, and will not make a success of this human
existence.

Thoroughness should characterize not merely a few of our actions but our
whole behaviour. Thoroughness of behaviour really means profundity of conduct. Thoroughness is the great enemy of superficiality. That is because
to be thorough in anything one must be mindful and act scrupulously and
circumspectly, without skipping any essential details which constitute
completeness.

In order to achieve anything of value one must be thorough. Especially is
this true in the sphere of religion.

If a Buddhist wants to know his religion well so that he may be able to
apply it effectively to life and realize the highest possible happiness, he
must first of all read the Buddha-word with complete awareness, and well-
established mindfulness; he should not read without proper attention or
half-heartedly. He must bring to bear on the Pavacana the whole body of
his inner faculties with concentrated attention. Who reads thus does a
good deal towards retaining what he reads and becoming a receptacle of
knowledge (suta dhara). For such a person the Truth does not go in at
one ear and out at the next. His mind is not like a leaky pot or a sieve.
What is taken into his mind stands there long though unrehearsed.

In this way through attentive reading one stores the Buddha-word in one's
mind, inscribes it indelibly in the tablets of one's heart, and places the
lion fat of the Truth in the golden vase of one's spirit, and becomes a
living hoard of knowledge (suta sannicaya).

The Buddha-word is verily "the life-blood of a master-spirit," and must not
be lightly read over but learned by heart in the sense of letting it sink
deep into one's consciousness so that it may become something like the very
flux of the essential factors of embodiment in the course of becoming
(bhavanga sota sadisa) and be capable of being called up to memory at will
without any hesitation or reference to that or this book or teacher. One
who has come to such proficiency of recollection is called truly a bearer
(dhata) of the Aryan Norm.

CHAPTER TWENTY-ONE

MENTAL DISCIPLINE

"The Mind reflects the entire being; the two worlds meet
therein. The Body meets the Spirit through MÂNASA."

Padma Hiranya Surangama.

The Mind is a delicate and easily moved apparatus. It is more easily
controlled by gentle persuasion than by the iron hand of Will. Control
does not mean rigidity, nor a perpetual critical self-analysis. Less pressure should be used and less intensity of effort than is generally supposed.

The wise student begins his discipline at the underlying mental impulse
motivating all his actions, and from there regulates his actions. He does
this because thereby he maintains the control. Once acquired, he maintains
it thenceforward automatically.

How is this control to be acquired, and how maintained?

The student must raise his thought during waking hours and thus set the
rhythm and the pattern for his hours of work in sleep. In his Mind he can
be constantly revolving knowledge acquired, until it is part of his consciousness. This sets the Mind to work in those idle moments when the work
or interests of the everyday world release the brain and Mind, and it
prevents waste of time in uncontrolled, idle thinking.

He must keep his aspiration fixed on some great Being, or on some aspiration of his own, or some ideal of service, and this dedication will
prevent his thought from dropping to the level of the surrounding indifferent
humanity, and thus being pulled back toward lower levels of thought.

He must bring the Mind to cleaner, higher levels, and keep its normal
there, thus clearing from the gate or bridge the clouds of heavy, coarse
vibrations, without beauty, which "slay" the finer vibrations. No one, not
even the most humble beginner, can fail to prove this is true if he but
makes the effort and observes results.

The student who does this can be sure of help from unexpected sources.
He will be aided though he may not realize exactly how. He will make
friends who vibrate to the new wave-length of his mentality. He will find
mental stimulants, he will find new interests, he will find friends to help
him. He will come gradually into the clearer realms of the Soul, and
through the Soul he will find contacts who will help him to sustain the
effort.

Those who are ready for The Way cannot fail to understand the foregoing procedure. They will understand the kind of work necessary - the
daily, persevering, unfailing guard upon the information taken into the Mind
from the printed page, the constant refusal to read the many unnecessary
words conveying unclean, degrading, wrong thought. They will understand the
constant refusal to listen to others who speak words that degrade by un-
cleanness, by cruelty, by bigotry and fanaticism, by error and lack of
beauty of all kinds. They will avoid such people - who will find the higher
levels of thought in their own time.

They will avoid the terrible effects of the primitive in music, the harsh-
ness of undeveloped and uncultured voices, the shattering vibrations abounding
in civilization at present, for these hurt and shock the more sensitive and
refined mentality.   They will avoid, also, environments without beauty, dis-
cordant colors, and drabness, surrounding themselves with beauty and harmony.

They will guard their words and try to make the spoken thought correspond
with the higher vibrations they deliberately select, drawing them within from
the encircling environment.   Here - in this choice of the higher and finer
in all things, in rejection of the lower and coarser - is the real meaning of
the proverb "As a man thinketh, so he is."

The pupil who guards his Mind as a jewel, refusing to allow it to be
sullied, merits much.   He has begun to control the bridge, to clear the
gate, and to call down the Soul to habitation there.   He has made it possible,
in time, to contact the mighty Spirit.

This is the first true step of progress.   It means that eventually the
pupil, in consciousness, because of this alignment, will be instructed by the
Elders who have so longed to help him for so many years.   He can now be
contacted through one or more of the methods the average man calls occult,
mysterious, magical, mystical, phenomenal, and many other names, but which
they are not.   The methods used are simply and naturally a consequence of
the pupil's own development, and he, himself, recognizes them as right and
natural, though perhaps he is not able to understand the method available for
use in his own case.

-*- -*- -*- -*- -*- -*- -*- -*- -*- -*- -*- -*- -*- -*- -*- -*- -*- -*- -*-

From "TRANSACTIONS OF THE BLAVATSKY LODGE" (page #99)

"Q.   Is MANU a unity also of human consciousness personified, or is it the
      individualization of the Thought Divine for manvantaric purposes?

"A.   Of both, since 'human consciousness' is but a Ray of the Divine. Our
      MANAS, or Ego, proceeds from, and is the Son (figuratively) of MAHAT.
      VAIVASVATA MANU (the MANU of our own fifth race and Humanity in
      general) is the chief personified representative of the thinking
      Humanity of the fifth Root-race; and therefore he is represented as
      the eldest Son of the Sun and an AGNISHWATTA Ancestor. As 'MANU' is
      derived from Man, to think, the idea is clear. Thought in its
      action on human brains is endless. Thus MANU is, and contains the
      potentiality of all the thinking forms which will be developed on
      earth from this particular source. In the exoteric teaching he is
      the beginning of this earth, and from him and his daughter ILA
      humanity is born; he is a unity which contains all the pluralities
      and their modifications. Every MANVANTARA has thus its own MANU
      and from this MANU the various MANUS or rather all the MANASA of
      the KALPAS will proceed. As an analogy he may be compared to the
      white light which contains all the other rays, giving birth to them
      by passing through the prism of differentiation and evolution.
      But this pertains to the esoteric and metaphysical teachings."

                                        by H. P. Blavatsky

Although it was unlike the Days preceding it, the Third Day of the World-Scheme brought the Life within it to another stage of evolution. The intervening time of cataclysm and regeneration had wrought important changes. The surface had cooled and hardened enough to form a skin of matter, and the core, still molten, built an atmosphere of hot and humid heavy water-air. The planet had descended yet another note in the scale of density; another element had come into the composition of the solidifying mass.

Water now dominated the entire field of force, from outer tenuous water-suffused air to inner, water-saturated core. The fiery core resisted the invasion, so that the contracting, cooling globe was thrown into convulsions and eruptions often, caused by the inner pressure on the cooling skin. The water accumulated on the crust and its great weight and cooling screen effected a still deeper hardening of the surface shell. The struggle of the elemental forces was titanic. Amid the tumult and upheaval Life wakened to a Day of rapidly changing atomic structure.

Man, when he awoke, was plunged into the Watery element, from which he drew his first, half-material, true body, though of it there were many stages. By slow development it took a shape more like the human in appearance, but it was not more than a mold or blueprint, rudimentary, not very beautiful. It was a hint of what might be. The spheroid shapes of other Days had vanished; the swiftness, brightness and luminosity had gone forever. The Third Day shapes were sylphid, and were suited to the Water element, their home - though how that might be is deep buried in the mysteries connected with the elements.

The sylphid shapes were men. That is, the Life progressed in that Day through a form or shape adapted to the circumstances. Not otherwise could Life have survived for a moment. In fact the growing Life had no discomfort and very little regret, for it had lost the memory of what had been in other Days, as density closed round it, causing it to forget the splendid meteor shapes and swiftly moving spheroids, the light and luminous vestures. The race remembered, nevertheless, affinity with Fire, and affinity with Air, and now responded to the stimulus of Water with an equal readiness and an equal ardor, filled with the zest of living and the spirit of adventure. Indeed, this particular race of beings has been always glad to meet the unexpected, curious and inquiring, mentally restless, alert, and quivering with the Will-driven desire to know, so that it cannot rest long in a static mood or concrete pattern.

They did not settle upon earth, for there was never solid land, the cooling crust beneath the sea becoming only ocean bottom. They dwelt in Water, as they had dwelt in Fire and in Air, and Water mothered them. There was never, in that Day, a place to build a temple, or to erect a statue, or to call upon a Deity, for there were no dry spaces, and the shallows were not liked by these intensely specialized, water-loving beings.

All Life was marine in that Day. The animal and vegetable kingdoms flowed with the tide or anchored in the muddy shallows. At the end of the Day, the drying crust rolled back the Water, by imperceptible stages, and

(continued on page #192)

THE THEORY OF MANU - SEED MANUS:

    The Seed MANU succeeds the Root MANU, after the SANDHYÂ of cataclysm,
change, rest and regeneration. The awakening Life is not different, nor in
some cases functionally altered, but the environment may be strange and
thereby compel an adjustment in the life habits.

    The Seed MANU brings the awakened Life by slow aeons of YUGAS to the
highest point of the perfection possible, and then begins the winnowing process of the seeded grain. The Life must take a higher step next time it
comes to meet the Day and Dawning. It must be fit to meet it. Somehow
the husbandman, the MANU, must set the crop in order, and put the sifted
graded seed away for the SANDHYÂ. Such operations are achieved by such long-
scale and wholesale methods that they were best described by allegory.

    The high peak of perfection comes, and with it passes all the finest,
best and highest of the races into the earned and well-deserved long sleep
between the Days. The civilizations fall by slow degrees, because the best
pass from them, and the less perfected are left to try to grow a little time
longer. They later pass onward, as they ripen, to the resting stage, as
the hour strikes for them. The civilizations fall still lower. The winnowing proceeds until at last, on the not yet deserted man-bearing planet,
the stock is very savage, very primitive, perhaps degenerated. These are
the laggards, given time to ripen as long as possible.

    The animal and vegetable kingdoms likewise change. They may be scanty
or stunted, not like the splendid springing glory of the early Morning. They
too are winnowed, fitted into a class or grade, and made ready for re-
rooting.

    The planet bears its last unripened crop of seed Life in the falling
Dusk. From the cataclysms of the SANDHYÂ only a very small percentage of
these scattered remnants of the races may survive to become misfits in odd
corners in the next Day's dawning, yet not dying until the Life proceeds into the higher forms available and ready, from the re-seeding of the Lives
in the next bright early Morning. Some linger long into the Day, however,
time being needed.

    No MANU is like another, as has been said, but the work is similar in
each MANVANTARA. The results never vary, the pattern never changes, the
system never alters, as evolution proceeds upon its inexorable cycle.
Only, as the Life is quite unpredictable and the individual units are unique,
each MANVANTARA produces multitudinous and endless variations of the
fluidic World Scheme.

    No superimposing Will of any Being is permitted to deprive the Life of
its inherent right to grow, to learn, to build, to mature, and to evolve
into the full and perfected liberated being.

    Under the guise of Seed MANU the VISHNU aspect of the mighty BRAHMÂ
matures and ripens and brings Life to the full perfection of the Day.
Under the SIVA aspect the mighty BRAHMÂ winnows and destroys, making all new
again when the seed Life is safe and warm within the enfolding, compassing
over-brooding carefulness of the Enduring BRAHMÂ.

Part II - The Dharma or Doctrine

195. Q. Did he himself really teach that noble rule?
     A. Yes.   The Buddha has said that we must not believe in a thing said
        merely because it is said; nor in traditions because they have
        been handed down from antiquity; nor rumours, as such; nor
        writings by sages, merely because sages wrote them; nor fancies
        that we may suspect to have been inspired in us by a Deva (that
        is, in presumed spiritual inspiration); nor from inferences
        drawn from some haphazard assumption we may have made; nor be-
        cause of what seems an analogical necessity; nor on the mere
        authority of our own teachers or masters.

196. Q. When, then, must we believe?
     A. We are to believe when the writing, doctrine, or saying is corrobo-
        rated by our own reason and consciousness.   "For this," says
        he in concluding, "I taught you not to believe merely because
        you have heard, but when you believed of your own consciousness,
        then to act accordingly and abundantly."   (See the Kâlâma
        Sutta of the Anguttara Nikâya, and the Mahâ Pari Nirvâna Sutta.)

197. Q. What does the Buddha call himself?
     A. He says that he and the other Buddhas are only "preachers" of truth
        who point out the way: we ourselves must make the effort.

198. Q. Where is this said?
     A. In Chapter XX of the Dhammapada.

199. Q. Does Buddhism countenance hypocrisy?
     A. The Dhammapada says: "Like a beautiful flower full of colour with-
        out scent, the fine words of him who does not act accordingly
        are fruitless."

200. Q. Does Buddhism teach us to return evil for evil?
     A. In the Dhammapada the Buddha said: "If a man foolishly does me
        wrong, I will return to him the protection of my ungrudging
        love; the more evil comes from him, the more good shall go from
        me."   This is the path followed by the Arhat.* To return
        evil for evil is positively forbidden in Buddhism.

     * A Buddhist ascetic who, by a prescribed course of practice has at-
     tained to a superior state of spiritual and intellectual development.
     Arhats may be divided into the two general groups of the
     Samathayânika and Sukka Vipassaka.   The former have destroyed their
     passions, and fully developed their intellectual capacity or mystical
     insight; the latter have equally conquered passion, but not acquired
     the superior mental powers.   The former can work phenomena, the
     latter cannot.   The Arhat of the former class, when fully developed,
     is no longer a prey to the delusions of the senses, nor the slave
     of passion or mortal frailty.   He penetrates to the root of what-
     soever subject his mind is applied to without following the slow
     processes of reasoning.   His self-conquest is complete; and in
     place of the emotion and desire which vex and enthral the ordinary
     man he is lifted up into a condition which is best expressed in the
     term "Nirvânic".   There is in Ceylon a popular misconception that

the attainment of Arhatship is now impossible; that the Buddha had
himself prophesied that the power would die out in one millennium
after his death.   This rumour - and the similar one that is everywhere heard in India, viz., that this being the dark cycle of the
Kali Yuga, the practice of Yôga Vidyâ, or sublime spiritual science,
is impossible - I ascribe to the ingenuity of those who should be
as pure and (to use a non-Buddhistic but very convenient term)
psychically wise as were their predecessors, but are not, and who
therefore seek an excuse!   The Buddha taught quite the contrary
idea.   In the Digha Nikâya he said: "Hear, Subbhadra!   The world
will never be without Arhats if the ascetics (Bhikkhus) in my congregations well and truly keep my precepts."   (Imeccha Subhadda-
bhikkhu samma vihareiyum asunno loko Arahantehiassa.)

201. Q. Does it encourage cruelty?
      A. No, indeed.   In the Five Precepts and in many of his discourses,
          the Buddha teaches us to be merciful to all beings, to try and
          make them happy, to love them all, to abstain from taking life,
          or consenting to it, or encouraging its being done.

202. Q. In which discourse is this stated?
      A. The Dhammika Sutta says: "Let him (the householder) not destroy,
          or cause to be destroyed, any life at all, or sanction the act
          of those who do so.   Let him refrain from even hurting any
          creature, * etc."

      * Kolb, in his "History of Culture," says: "It is Buddhism we have
      to thank for the sparing of prisoners of war, who heretofore had
      been slain; also for the discontinuance of the carrying away into
      captivity of the inhabitants of conquered lands."

203. Q. Does it approve of drunkenness?
      A. In his Dhammika Sutta we are warned against drinking liquors,
          causing others to drink, or sanctioning the acts of those who
          drink.*

      * The fifth Sila has reference to the mere taking of intoxicants and
      stupefying drugs which leads ultimately to drunkenness.

204. Q. To what are we told that drunkenness leads?
      A. To demerit, crime, insanity, and ignorance - which is the chief
          cause of re-birth.

205. Q. What does Buddhism teach about marriage?
      A. Absolute chastity being a condition of full spiritual development,
          is most highly commended; but a marriage to one wife and
          fidelity to her is recognised as a kind of chastity.   Polygamy
          was censured by the Buddha as involving ignorance and promoting
          lust.

206. Q. In what discourse?
      A. The Anguttara Nikâya, Chap. iv, 55.

207. Q. What does it teach as to the duty of parents to children?
      A. They should restrain them from vice; train them in virtue; have

them taught arts and sciences; provide them with suitable
wives and husbands, and give them their inheritance.

208. Q. What is the duty of children?
      A. To support their parents when old or needy; perform family duties
          incumbent on them; guard their property; make themselves worthy
          to be their heirs, and when they are gone, honour their memory.

209. Q. What of pupils to the teacher?
      A. To show him respect; minister to him; obey him; supply his wants;
          attend to his instruction.

210. Q. What of husband to wife?
      A. To cherish her; treat her with respect and kindness; be faithful to
          her; cause her to be honoured by others; provide her with
          suitable ornaments and clothes.

211. Q. What of the wife to her husband?
      A. To show affection to him; order her household aright; be hospitable
          to guests; be chaste; be thrifty; show skill and diligence in
          all things.

212. Q. Where are these precepts taught?
      A. In the Sigâlovâda Sutta.

213. Q. Do riches help a man to future happiness?
      A. The Dhammapada says: "One is the road that leads to wealth, another
          the road that leads to Nirvâna."

214. Q. Does that mean that no rich man can attain Nirvâna?
      A. That depends on which he loves most. If he uses his wealth for
          the benefit of mankind - for the suffering, the oppressed, the
          ignorant - then his wealth aids him to acquire merit.

215. Q. But if the contrary?
      A. But if he loves and greedily hoards money for the sake of its pos-
          session, then it weakens his moral sense, prompts him to crime,
          brings curses upon him in this life, and their effects are
          felt in the next birth.

216. Q. What says the Dhammapada about ignorance?
      A. That it is a taint worse than all taints that a man can put upon
          himself.

217. Q. What does it say about uncharitableness towards others?
      A. That the fault of others is easily perceived, but that of oneself
          difficult to perceive; a man winnows his neighbour's faults
          like chaff, but his own fault he hides, as a cheat hides the
          bad die from the gambler.

218. Q. What advice does the Buddha give us as to man's duty to the poor?
      A. He says that a man's net income should be divided into four parts,
          of which one should be devoted to philanthropic objects.

(to be continued)

Continued from October, 1947:

    The long years passed. The Sachem's spirit lingered. He made his
home beside the pool, and being spirit could converse with the much-interested
Princess. He had been lonely, many times, before he found himself able to
converse with her by slow degrees.

    The massacre had altered her a little. She wished to know the reason,
and why he of all his people still lingered near her. He did not know.
How could he understand the laws of being, though in retrospect he knew he
had been driven to an act of self-destruction?

    Still life was lovely to him, in the vale of Crystal Water. Why should
he hasten, look for other trails to follow, leave his land and all his heritage, and somehow seek his vanished people? What if the red invaders'
wigwams were established in the region? Would he stoop now to take the hand
of friendship? How could he sit beside the fire in council? He - might
be watching - sometimes - just for curiosity - but --- after all, this was
an alien people. And then, they did not see him, as he had very soon discovered. No, it was much better to be lonely in the valley, near the pool,
yet with the "spirit of the water" for companionship ---

    He was a stately Sachem. The years had given him nature wisdom, and
the responsibility of rulership had given him understanding, yet he loved
every aspect of the world around him, and he had simple-minded faith in what
he called "Manito", though what he meant by that the Princess could not
gather. They differed, do you see, in evolutionary backgrounds, and she
was really very much less versed in land and human ways than he was in the
nature ways, because his whole life had been spent so close to nature.
Yet, the under-water realm of ocean - he had never seen it - was not in his
understanding.

    The undines chided her, much discontented, wishful for their old-time
playmate, and pointed out the Sachem was no water being, and furthermore, a
mortal, one who continually required new bodies, for so the massacre had
taught them. They said:

    "But, there are River Lords. Why should you shield this mortal?"
Being true immortals, they possessed the eye of vision; they knew the Princess loved the Shadow-man, for so they called him. His name, however, had
been Flying Eagle, for so had his mother named him.

    She loved him, with the quiet brooding selfless tenderness that some-
times one of the race of DEVÂH gives to mortals. It is not yearning, and
it holds no hint of mortal passion. It brushed softly on the Sachem's
spirit-face as lightly as a passing butterfly on wing. It warmed him,
being lonely, and it made him happy, for he had been close to nature, loved
the serene "spirit of the water" unseen, in his lifetime. Also, the nature
of the bond created by his death, by accident and by force of circumstances,
had held him to the spot, and he was grateful for the sanctuary that he
sensed around him. But love - like humans - that had not been considered.
The Spirit-man was spirit, but though spirit unable yet to comprehend the
nature of the Princess. She held a veil between them.

The two were much together. She hovered sometimes, in the cataract, enjoying the wild water and the electric energy sweeping down in the watery air-cloud. She liked it best in heavy floods, and then was in a way a stranger to the Sachem. She was more like the Storm Kings of the Ocean, riding with the Tritons through a tempest. He could not join her, but he enjoyed the spectacle.

On sunny days, and summer dawns, and moonlight evenings, she took the mood of nature, less elemental, more childlike. She was inclined to make appearance like a lovely maiden, half hidden in fine mist water-draperies. Sometimes she looked as if she were a mermaid - part visible in air, part lost from vision in the water - leaning on a great rock near the Sachem's favorite corner, just at the edge of the quiet pool. They made attempt at converse, then, and so the two learned of the different levels of existence from each other.

The Sachem wore the spirit-body, exactly like his mortal body - and furthermore he clothed it in the appearance of his ceremonial robes of council. The Princess never had revealed her true appearance. She wove from fancy - all of them partly veiled and all of them partly true - more shapes than there were days, and he grew used to them, finding himself able to discern the one unwavering and subtle flame of being behind the veil of the appearance. She wove with protean power, and used the right of Water Royal to appear in many forms.

The shield stayed firm. Once placed, it held against all comers. The Princess held the conquering invaders at bay. They came to call it "deadman's pool" - though that was not exactly true, the Sachem lived - and dreaded it, as if their enemy could rise and strike them. Beneath it all was true dread of the ever-living Princess, the "spirit of the water", but that was not quite how their legends put it.

(to be continued)

-*- -*- -*- -*- -*- -*- -*- -*- -*- -*- -*- -*- -*- -*- -*- -*- -*- -*-

THE LAND OF THE SOUL
_____

There is a land my soul knows where -
    Where blue and white the Springtimes break,
Where man is more than self and clay
    And master of the thrust of fate.

There is a land my soul knows where -
    Where Summer is a world of gold
And Life is more than Time and Tide,
    The Past is not a tale that's told.

There is a land my soul knows where -
    Where life is in the very wind,
Where Ecstasy is day and night,
    And Love the substance of the mind.

In Memoriam   From "The Immortal Dweller"
Died October 18, 1947   by Ernest Fewster

_____

"Should many books be used in studying the Dharma?"

That is an individual decision. Many people are addicted to the research method, feeling that by reading and comparing everything obtainable
they are more secure in their opinions.   It would be impossible for such
minds to accept any one book as authority, and perhaps rightly so.

On the other hand, there is no guarantee an avalanche of tomes in agreement with each other contain the truth, or the whole truth, as they may be
subject to a delusion or delusions held in common by their authors.

A single authority may be considered sufficient by some students, yet
here the question is of quality, authenticity and insight, if not of actual
Illumination.   The single authority may be obscure and rare, only to be
discovered after research and exhaustive study.   Obversely, it may be in
plain sight, available in every book store, a well-known classic, overlooked
simply because of its familiarity.

Is there any rule possible for general application on this matter of
literature?   Evidently, no.   The student must follow his bent, must pursue
his own path, must achieve his own satisfaction.   The only counsel possible
is to use whatever books, study, research and inquiry into sources as may
be essential to the individual student's satisfaction.

Whatever is found unnecessary in the writings may be eliminated.   The
net result of much research should in the end be simple, reasonable, clear,
logical, and in line with the facts of existence, and with the visible world
around the student.   Mystical and incomprehensible jargon is of no practical use to anyone; and technical phrases copied from other languages are
like a smattering of learning, unless they are thoroughly comprehended.   The
scholar's speculations on the word-meanings are not absolutely final, and
the scholar's translations into English may not be logical and true to the
original in all cases.

The student should cultivate the insight into the worth of writings.
He may acquire it through continual reading, or he may possess it unsuspected.
If he can utilize it, he will find it more useful than an encyclopedia, as
it will enable him to classify and estimate by this method as well as by the
perusal of the written word.

No royal road is there to reach Illumination.   No one may reach it by
a formula, or by a lifetime devoted to much study.   Similarly, no one may
escape it, if it is his time, for then, whether he has read much or not, he
may be sure of reaching it.

Meantime, the student must be guided by his own decision, since he alone
possesses the right to make it.   He should accept, however, such assistance
as may come his way through recommendations, suggestions, and example.

-*- -*- -*- -*- -*- -*- -*- -*- -*- -*- -*- -*- -*- -*- -*- -*- -*- -*- -*- -*-

"Let me have sound knowledge and walk on the great way."

TAO TÊ CHING
Translated by Ch'u Ta-kao

Recently there appeared a new Buddhist periodical, founded and sponsored by the Alumni of the Mahadhatu Buddhist College of Siam in March 2490 Buddhist Era (1947), and we hasten to extend our best wishes to the newcomer - known as THE SÂSANA PADÎPA.

The Vasihakha number, Volume 1, Number 4, June 2490, is very artistically illustrated with the elaborately detailed small figures so carefully executed by Eastern artists, and has a lotus-decorated front cover in colors. All of its 35 pages are printed in the beautiful Siamese characters, except the Foreword by the Editor, which is in English. His sentiments might well be echoed by every Buddhist -

> "I myself believe that degradation can come equally to laymen or priests if we have no "Good Understanding" towards each other. Buddhism from the viewpoint of the new world could be proved by one thing, and that is to let everyone have "Good Understanding" towards each other ... Let the Blessing of the Holy Triple Gem protect our work as we remain, firmly, in this Dharma ... Let spiritual happiness be yours on this great day, full-moon day of Vaishakha."

To Sathira Bandharangshi, the Editor, to the Associate Editors, and to The Sâsana Padîpa Organization, greetings.

-*- -*- -*- -*- -*- -*- -*- -*- -*- -*- -*- -*- -*- -*- -*- -*- -*- -*- -*- -*-

From Hawaii comes a most interesting little publication called BODHI LEAF, published bi-monthly by the Junior Young Buddhist Associations, with Madge Honda as Editor. It contains news of local activities, clubs and Young Buddhist Associations, but also a merry little tale called "Gombei and the Scarecrow", and a noteworthy verse, as follows:

"Child's Morning Prayer
"I take my refuge in Lord Buddha and dedicate myself to His service.
May His Teaching guide me during the day, in my work and in my play."

-*- -*- -*- -*- -*- -*- -*- -*- -*- -*- -*- -*- -*- -*- -*- -*- -*- -*- -*- -*-

Bhikkhu M. Sangharatana, Secretary of the Maha Bodhi Society of India, writing from Sarnath, tells us that "the birthday anniversary of the late Venerable Dharmapala was held on the 17th of September, and the sixteenth anniversary of Mulagandha Kuti Vihara is to be held on November 27th. Her Excellency, Mrs. Sarojini Naidu, Governor of the United Provinces, will preside over the occasion. As you are aware, this is one of the most important festivals of the Buddhists in India. Thousands of Buddhist pilgrims from different parts of the world are expected to take part in the celebrations. The programme includes Holy Relics processions, exhibitions, meetings, lectures on Buddhist philosophy and culture, Buddha-pujas, illuminations, etc."

-*- -*- -*- -*- -*- -*- -*- -*- -*- -*- -*- -*- -*- -*- -*- -*- -*- -*- -*- -*-

THE LONE HEART

The lone heart wanders
In a new-found guise,
But the old soul wears
The same bright eyes.

V.I.S.

And when owing to such recollective power and such careful storing of the
Word, one is able to recite off-hand decads of discourses, decads of sections,
and decads of fifty-groups from the Scriptures, one is called a verbally
well-practised person (vacasa paricita) in the Buddha-word.

And the verbally well-practised man is bound to think of the Word and become
in time a scrutinizer in mind (manasanupekkhita) of the Doctrine. With that
scrutiny of the Word learned by heart every point connected with the Word,
every aspect of its meaning and every nuance of its significance must become
clear.   It is said that the knowledge of that man is like a direct vision
of objects before the eyes of a person holding high a great light.

When one has got to that clarity one steps out to master the very purpose and
heart of the Norm in its sense of realization and scientifically, by way of
cause and condition, becomes one who has well penetrated the Teaching through
right understanding and the wisdom of insight into actuality (ditthiya
suppatividdha).

Here has been given an example of what is meant by thoroughness, in the Dis-
pensation of the Buddha, and through this is given too an indication of
what thoroughness must be in the pursuit of other objects.

-*- -*- -*- -*- -*- -*- -*- -*- -*- -*- -*- -*- -*- -*- -*- -*- -*- -*- -*-

THE HISTORY OF GODHOOD - continued from page #183

left the Life to cling to Water, or to climb to Air, or to burrow into Earth,
so hastening the choices of the species.   For this is true, that lower
evolutionary waves must take long life cycles to progress.   Therefore they
begin the changes earlier at the end of each Day, and must be given preliminary growing time in each Day's Dawning.   The man-bearing planets do not
receive the Life called Man until the lower evolutions have prepared themselves and altered to the new note and the new conditions.   Man, everywhere
and in all time, where he develops, is a fluidity; he changes quickly, he is
adaptable, the added factor of the Fire of Mind alerting him and hastening
his progress.

The Builders grew the Water-skin of planet by condensation of the atoms,
as they had grown the airy envelope by similar procedure.   They swirled the
sediment of cohering matter into the center, and thus built the ball of
hardening atomic structure, with its inner fire and its outer crust.   They
were not visible except to Man, for Water covered all the core.   However,
Man was yet aware of them and of the elemental lives around him, busy with
the work of elements and forces.   Man was companionable, and could be found
in converse with these lives.   There was no separation and no blindness, for
Man had not lost his seeing eye nor dulled his fine-tuned hearing.   There
were no barriers to hold him prisoner.

He still has memory of these former playmates and comrades of the
elemental forces, and still remembers the sublimely stately Builders.   He
reminisces in his myths and legends, not knowing these were true tales in
another Day of the long lifetime of the planet.

-*- -*- -*- -*- -*- -*- -*- -*- -*- -*- -*- -*- -*- -*- -*- -*- -*- -*- -*-

"Long and weary is the way before thee, O Disciple."

"The Voice of the Silence"
by H. P. Blavatsky

CYCLES: (November, 1947, p. #184)

Used to mean a recurring period of time or round of years.   The life-span of Man is the basis for the computation of the human cycle - one hundred years.   The human mind accepts comparisons with what it knows.   Thus, a moth may have a life cycle of only a few hours of our time - but the planet's cycle is another story, and the time we call a life-time may be a second only in the larger cycles.   Cycles are innumerable, but for convenience some of the more important recurring cyclic periods have been given special names.

ILLUMINATION: (November, 1947, p. #190)

This is a term which becomes clear if it is translated "Spiritual Attain-ment."   It is correctly applied to the final initiation where Enlightenment is achieved.   There are, of course, partial preliminary illuminations.

MIRROR: (October, 1947, p. #165)

This is a metaphor.   It expresses the state of imperturbability of mind required before any true attainment is possible or even conceivable.   If the simile of a mirror reflecting the Spirit into the lower consciousness is clear, it is not clear how to hold the mental substance as a mirror,   In the long struggle to achieve the mastery lies the explanation of the many years of conflict.   It is best to resort to the directions of The Noble Eight-fold Path of Gautama Buddha.

ADEPT: (September, 1947, p. #155)

This title is a general one.   It may be used for anyone who has at-tained full Liberation, truly, but it should not be used for a lesser Initiate. It is not a title belonging to any one rank.   It is a general descriptive term, or title of respect where the exact status is unknown or unrevealed.

THE WAY: (September, 1947, p. #156)

The Buddhist and Taoist term for Evolution.   It has a special meaning to those who reach the higher ranks of Humanity, who seek to study the next step forward.   To the majority of human beings, it is best thought of as The Way, meaning the most practical and helpful Way to live upon the planet, and the ultimate achievement of Liberation.

FORBIDDEN FRUIT: (May, 1947, p. #76)

As each step of the Path has obligations and duties, as well as rewards and privileges, so has each one its "forbidden fruit" of actions, desires, thoughts which are beneath that level.   Each step requires acceptance of the conditions accompanying it.   Each step becomes harder, more steep, more dif-ficult to mount, and at each the candidate rejects forever the discarded pleasures, vices, practises he has outgrown.

A GIFT SUGGESTION

In Western lands a period of gift-giving comes at the end of every year, when a few days are devoted to remembrance, exchange of greetings, and wide-spread thought for others. It is, as it were, a time for observance of the DÂNA PÂRAMITÂ - selfless giving for the welfare of others - and the practise of DÂNAM is not unknown to any person at this one season of the year.

Thoughts of friends cross the mind at the approach of the annual festival, and people give consideration to the selection of gifts. Yet, what better gift is there, for one who is ready to welcome it, than an introduction to the Great Way which leads to Enlightenment?

However, the nature of the introduction is important. Many of the available books about the Dharma are not suitable for a new reader, or one critically versed in Western literature. The very exactness of some translations may be counted a disadvantage in the case of the casual reader, or the more dilettant acquaintances of students, so that care must be exercised in the selection of literature intended as gifts.

Because The Golden Lotus Bookshelf exists to guide readers to the best and most suitable literature, a suggestion is offered to students who may have such friends in mind. As an introduction, and as a guide and key to three important phases of the Eastern Philosophy, a set of small books is recommended. When regarded as related they explain much the student should understand, and they are invaluable in tracing the relationship between the seemingly irreconcilable - Hinduism, original Buddhism, and the later so-called MAHÂYÂNA Buddhism.

THE LIGHT OF ASIA, by Sir Edwin Arnold:
> This is a most useful book on the Buddha's Dharma, as it gives a poetic translation of the LALITA VISTARA (The Life and Teachings of the Buddha) with the true thought of the East in the West's own language. Sir Edwin Arnold's work should stand for all time, and this book should be of value to all students.

THE SONG CELESTIAL, by Sir Edwin Arnold:
> As it contains the earlier Indian thought, being a poetic translation of THE BHAGAVAD GITA, India's most famous scripture, and is illuminating in many ways, this book is also valuable. Though not Buddhist, it gives the earlier Aryan philosophy known to the Buddha's time, which formed the base of his own philosophical system.

These two books deserve study as a related pair.

THE VOICE OF THE SILENCE, by Helena P. Blavatsky:
> This is purely MAHÂYÂNA Buddhism. The author was a Buddhist who spent some time in Ceylon, India and Tibet. As the late Tashi Lama placed his approval upon this book no further recommendation is necessary.

These three books fit together, are uniform in size and binding, and are listed at seventy-five cents each, but readers who wish to acquire all three may have the set at the special price of $2.00, postage paid.

MODERN WARFARE

Only an unleashed imagination can conceive the horrors of
the consequences, if war is to be waged by the new weapons
of the Atomic Age.   Such devastations of the fertile sur-
faces and underwater structures as are contemplated in the
military circles are not limited to man's sphere of action,
and they cannot be excused by any necessity of human
beings.   These weapons would seem to be a deliberate and
intentional preparation to alter the world as it is now
constituted, for the atomic structure is the underlying,
at present static, condition upon which all Life depends.

Many unnoticed effects, as well as results directly traced
to the atomic bombs already used, are changing the world's
climate, and the imperceptible effects of these changes
will continue for many centuries.   Each atomic disturbance
must - by the law of being - bring such slow, long-
continued changes, for good or evil.   No one may predict
what these changes may be, how they will spread, how they
will affect Life, where they will end.

All Life is involved, for all Life is affected in a devas-
tated region.   No animal, insect, plant, tree or stone
but shares the damage, shock and dismemberment with the
human victims.   The birds of air and denizens of water
are sacrifices.   No one may say they have deserved it,
and we, who bring this terrible disaster upon the lower
lives of this our star - are the aggressors.

How can we do it?   How can we condemn one of ourselves,
our race called human, to this ordeal?   How can we visit
it upon one innocent and trusting lower life beneath us?
How can we blast one tree, one blade of grass, into a
cataclysm of disintegration?

How can we risk the undetected, slow and uninterrupted
chain effects, which may so alter all our world that it
will change the entire evolutionary process?

How can we inflict this upon our planet?

-*- -*- -*- -*-

SAMYAG-DRSTI - Right View

Invaluable as is the possession of Right View, that is, the complete Understanding of the Way comprising Right View, this possession is of itself unable to achieve the final victory.   Some students have achieved this Understanding easily - almost too easily - and valued it as not worth putting into practice.   Others have toyed with it mentally, tasting the flavor and finding it to their liking, yet not assimilating the essential essence. Others have found it useful as a soporific, and still others value it as a stimulant.

The imperfect application and use of the Understanding, or the failure to use the Understanding, prevent the student from achieving his Liberation, and he falls back again into the toils of MÂRA.

Though the Understanding illuminates the Path, the Wisdom dictates the direction, the Intelligence directs the movement, these being aspects of Right View, still the View of the Viewer must find fulfillment in action, or failing action must be frustrated.   The eight methods of the Noble Eightfold Path are interlocking and they support one another.   SAMYAG-DRSTI must call forth an ally to its aid before the Viewer may consider himself a traveller upon the Path through the three worlds of being.

The Viewer must continue to know what is the true Path to follow, and Understand the reasons why it must be followed, and express Wisdom in his manner of undertaking it, but these will be ineffective without CETANÂ, the Will to Action, and the second one of the eight methods, SAMYAK-SAMKALPA. It is sometimes called Right Motive, Right Undertaking, Right Resolution, Right Mindfulness and Right Aim - but is here interpreted as Right Intention.

The alliance and affinity between Right View and Right Intention is apparent to the casual glance.   SAMYAK-SAMKALPA is CETANÂ, the Will, in support of MANAS, the Mind, or the supreme ruler approving what is submitted by the Mind-Essence; and the decree of rulership is ever followed by some immediate action.

The Will engages in the enterprise because it has become allied to the intermediate Mind.   The two are understandably separable and yet understandably allied.   One may be present, active, and the other present though quiescent or entirely opposed.   One may be evident and the other non-evident, yet both be fully awake, aware and functioning.   One may be predominant and the other subordinate, yet, in all the stages of the Path, these two must act together, must be supporters of each other, must hold the wheel of action and steer to the wind of opportunity.   The Will and the Mind must be in agreement, otherwise there is a lack of energy, or a lack of balance, and both are absolutely essential to the treading of the Path.

"And the Exalted One said: 'Now what, brethren, is RIGHT VIEW?
The knowledge about Ill, the Arising of Ill, the Ceasing of Ill, and the Way leading to the Ceasing of Ill - that, brethren, is called RIGHT VIEW.'"

DÎGHA NÎKÂYA, II, p. 312.

MERU

Does this word mean mountain?

No. It is the name of the region known as the North Pole.

Does it refer to a mountain?

Popular and exoteric rumour speaks of it as the name of a mountain, alleged to contain the abodes of gods and devas. This tradition comes down from earliest Vedic times, and is probably the origin of the legend of Mount Olympus. Except that it is located geographically in the land of the Greeks, Olympus is similar.

Does MERU mean anything esoterically?

The exact meaning is that the first race, the first land or solid earth, was located at the Northern Pole, and there the Golden Age came into being, when gods mingled with men. The Sanskrit name of the "Land of Bliss" comes from that record of the esoteric schools. Nothing more than this is meant, except that geographically the region was and is a pole, one of the important focal points for the magnetic currents and the invisible forces that control the movement of the planet. Therefore the region is of importance always, whether it is inhabited or not inhabited by men.

Is there anywhere a region of gods and devas?

Yes: all beings, all life, have definite abodes. Gods and Devas likewise, though they do not crowd into one small region, and that one region is not connected with any particular mountain anywhere in the world. The LOKAS, or "worlds" of the Eastern Philosophy, are not small, some of these regions (within our sphere) being larger than the earth core itself. The name MERU, once historical and accurate, has descended into an absurdity, for what physical mountain might contain the "gods and devas", since it could not contain mankind?

Does the popular tradition name a geographical location for MERU?

Oh, many. Sometimes it is supposed to be an unknown or unidentified mountain in the Himalayan range. Sometimes it is an actual mountain in the center of the earth, and at other times in the region of SWARGA, the abode of the gods. Sometimes it is a mountain on the site of the North Pole. Sometimes it is simply referred to as an unidentified region, not physical, and carefully unlocated by those who have a little insight.

What use has this tradition?

None, except to the occult student. Then, he must come across it in his studies, and become aware of the significance. No others will be interested.

Will it help students?

All traditions based upon history, or records of the race, must be set into their proper place.   This one adds to the knowledge of the race, and is not without helpfulness.   However, the "gods" and "devas" mentioned in the tradition are not mysterious or fanciful.   Simply, the third eye of vision, still unclouded, beheld the denizens and dwellers of the subtle realms adjacent to our own.

Do we now?

Not ordinarily.   The student gradually recovers vision, in some cases quickly, in others slowly, in still others karmically unable to do so in the first lifetime of study.   However, the first glimpse, when it comes, dispels all doubts, and MERU as a tradition and a legend becomes most appallingly true and accurate, as do many other such traditions.

Is MERU the only name?

No.   "The Secret Doctrine" gives such names as HEMÂDRI, the golden mountain; RATNASÂNU, the jewel peak; KARNIKÁCHALA, the lotus mountain; AMARÂDRI, the eternal mountain; DEVAPARVATA, the mountain of the gods; KHARGAKKURRA, the world mountain; and SUMERU, Beauteous Light-giver. The East speaks in this poetry of simile.

Is there now an actual mountain?

If, for the moment of our time, there were no mountain, even no land to support it, at the exact geographical spot, if that were to be located, this would not prove there was no mountain and no land at the time mentioned in the occult tradition.   The time is the important factor, not the place, for time is here involved.   The mountain and the land existed in their time, but may not continue to occupy the place unchanged beyond their time.   Only when time and place coincide is there existence. Sometimes the occult tradition tells of time and place once coincident, but no longer coincident, therefore no longer existent.   Today, for instance, though there might be a mountain and a land upon that place, time being different, there would be no "Land of Bliss" existing.

Many such traditions are creating misunderstanding?

They need not, if the student is aware of the inevitable change that overtakes all phenomena of being in the manifested worlds.

-*- -*- -*- -*- -*- -*- -*- -*- -*- -*- -*- -*- -*- -*- -*- -*- -*- -*- -*-

"A wanderer is man from his birth.
He was born in a ship
On the breast of the River of Time."

from "The Future"
by Matthew Arnold.

We take pleasure in presenting in full, though serially,
the following article by the celebrated scholar and
author, Miss Isaline B. Horner, Hon. Secretary of The
Pali Text Society, London. Footnote references have
been omitted, for lack of space.

The Staff.

-*- -*- -*- -*- -*- -*- -*- -*- -*- -*- -*- -*- -*- -*- -*- -*- -*- -*- -*-

SOME ASPECTS OF MOVEMENT IN EARLY BUDDHISM

I. B. HORNER

One of the more striking features of Early or Pali Buddhism lies in the open
or implied stress it constantly lays on movement and motion. Although only
a few of the concepts which involve motion can be referred to here, they may
suffice to show, either by their direct statements or by the similes and
symbolism connected with them, that the Buddhist disciple, be he monk or layman, was thought of as moving from the low to the more excellent, or the reverse.

To arrive at the goal, for the sake of which it may be supposed that Gotama's
more ardent followers went forth from home and adopted the life of religion,
there was demanded an unceasing effort in a gradual going forward up to the
highest. Attainment of profound knowledge does not come straight-away, but
by a gradual training, a gradual doing, a gradual process, even as, in the
famous simile of the great ocean, the sea deepens, slopes and shelves
gradually, with no abruptness such as a precipice. Another simile of rivers
and the sea takes nirvana as the goal instead of profound knowledge: as the
great rivers tend, slide and gravitate to the East, to the sea (which happens
to be the case in India), so do monks tend, slide and gravitate toward
nirvana by means of cultivating the Way. This Way, the symbol of journeying
and moving, is for going and growth, not for standing still.

Again, as is the nature of even great rivers to lose their former names and
identities when they reach the sea, so do all former caste distinctions break
down when men and women go forth (another term of motion) into the teaching
and monastic discipline proclaimed and laid down by Gotama. Even if this
context were unsupported by others, it would be sufficient by itself to indicate Gotama's attitude to such caste distinctions as existed in his day in
North India. Former identities are lost or merged in the common determination to tread the Way, to cross the sea or the river, to go upstream to the
source or down to the sea.

Although it is stated in the VISUDDHIMAGGA, a work whose authorship is at-
tributed to Buddhaghosa, the celebrated commentator on the Pali canon, that
there is the Way but no one who goes on it, this is contradicted by a canoni-
cal passage which is almost certainly older. In this it is asked how is a
monk a "goer", or one who goes? And it is answered: "Inasmuch as he is
going quickly there where on this long road he has not yet been, is he a
goer". This is the context we must follow in talking about Early Buddhism;
for, preceding the other as it probably does by five centuries or more, it
regarded man as a reality and not squeezed out of existence by psychological
analysis into his component parts.

I shall assume then that there is a goer, a traveller, whose symbolic
journey leads him over land or over water.

(to be continued)

Continued from November, 1947:

    Such friendships as the one between the Water Princess and the Sachem
Flying Eagle are unusual.   The evolutions move upon their own distinctive
cycles.   Each is within hail of many other evolutionary life cycles, but
each is separated from the others.   Not until an untoward or accidental
dislocation of the cyclic progress is any evolutionary unit subject to delay,
to separation from his fellows, to temporary banishment in some secluded
corner.   These two were met in some such self-created exile and procrastina-
tion, in an arrested development of species.

    Such as the Sachem, who had created first the consequences of self-
destruction.   Outlived that may be.   It is not too long to cause an irreparable delay, unless as sometimes happens the human consciousness is frozen
into a place, a state, a similcrum of body, or makes itself a prison by the
shock effect of tragedy or sudden death or sheer frustration.

    Such as the Princess, long lost to her royal duty, stepping into the
lower stature of a cascade dweller, and enjoying freedom from such duties as
a Princess might have borne.   Not criminal or wrong - just weary - was the
Princess when she came for change and deep seclusion, and DEVÂH have long
cycles of full activity and of half seclusion for recuperation, but later
she was wrong in prolonging her seclusion, and in resisting the cyclic change
to full activity, for to change had been her duty.

    They drifted, half content, half restless, yet happy too, through cen-
turies.   The terrain did not change.   The great River did not alter course,
the red men seldom now intruded, but every now and then an adventurous Indian
lad or two would make the great adventure into the usually shunned valley,
and then the Sachem's heart would be stirred with old memories.   The Princess
watched him, and would call him musically and sweetly, but he would be at
such times walking with the lads, or nearby listening to their chatter, unseen
by them.   The "enemy" in this case were merely half-grown children - a
warrior such as Flying Eagle could be benevolent toward them.

    So time passed, until war came back to trouble the whole region.   A
strange race hunted in the River Valley.   The war canoes sped up and down
the River.   The leaders by the council fires were apprehensive, for weapons
powerful and swift to strike were used by these white strangers.   The River
region resounded with man-made thunder, and bright lightning flashes carried
swift death, riding on the air toward the victims.   The arrow and the toma-
hawk were good only in ambush, and even in hand-to-hand combat the thunder-
flash took lives.

    The race of red men slowly released its hold upon the region.   An era
ended.   The white men took possession, spreading outward.   A new era began,
and it brought so many changes to the region the Sachem often wondered if he
had been dreaming when his tribe's wigwams held his people, or if he dreamed
now a wild, senseless dream of a new world around the vale of Crystal Water.

    The Princess, only, was untroubled.   Men were another evolution, not
Water, and not kin to her, and they might come and go in certain limits,
secure from Water and its denizens.   Royal, she knew the Law of Water, and
the place it held in the great destiny of the sphere itself.   She made no

outward overture, no inward resistance.   She held the shield in place, as
heretofore.   Only, as time went and the red men passed she smiled more often
on the new race, who came infrequently to visit places of beauty such as the
Pool of Deep Reflection.   She sensed their admiration, peaceful mission -
and then, these strangers, tho guilty perhaps of warfare and massacre elsewhere, had not committed murder within her valley.   A difference, but to the
Water Princess a vast difference.

The shield stayed, nevertheless, a force to reckon with by all who entered the region of the waterfall.   Some of the visitors found that realm
of Ocean within the shield to be friendly, some fled in panic, some were un-
easy, some were quite happy.   People have close affinities to what are called
the elements.   Sometimes someone would enter who loved the Water, and that
individual would be happy, loath to leave the shelter of the shield.   Yet
even he would never understand that once within it he was no longer in his
native Air or Water-Air, the habitat of Man, but in the magic circle of an
artificial and unsuspected pocket of the Water Kingdom.

(to be continued)

-*- -*- -*- -*- -*- -*- -*- -*- -*- -*- -*- -*- -*- -*- -*- -*- -*- -*- -*- -*-

BONDAGE

How shall I walk your close and narrow streets
    Or wander down your narrow dusty roads -
I, whose glad heart the morning sunlight greets
    On glorious mountains and the storms' abodes?

How shall I sing your prisoning walls of brick
    Or chant the hours of earth's time-haunted homes -
I, who have watched the glittering stars shine thick
    About the vast where my winged spirit roams?

How shall I love the noisy halls of earth,
    The fretful cries that beat upon my ears -
I, who have dwelt where music hath its birth
    And heard the tonal vespers of the spheres?

I, who have known the everlasting skies,
    I, who have held the heritage of space,
Shall I, from hills where dawn forever lies,
    Accept the bondage of earth's time and place?

from "The Immortal Dweller"
by Ernest Fewster

CHAPTER TWENTY-TWO

DISILLUSIONMENT

"Let the Mind intercede for those who walk in darkness."

Padma Hiranya Surangama.

The student who is conscientious is apt to take himself to task for his failure to illuminate others near him, who are not interested in his studies. He thinks he should be able to approach all men with Truth and at once be given credence.   He often takes time from a busy life to bring the gift of knowledge to those whom he may consider to "walk in darkness".

Such is the heart of man, the gift may be rejected.   Consider, then, the disillusionment and ultimate withdrawal of the student, who tries to give his knowledge to his surrounding circle, or to point the way to better understanding of life's problems.   Influenced by this very common rejection by his immediate circle, he may abandon further efforts, thereby closing the door of opportunity to others in the future.

Is this avoidable?   It might be.   If the student were more versed in human nature, he would expect to speak to others as a duty when it seemed to be a duty, but to remain silent when it appeared to be unwise, or to be an intrusion to speak.   He would not expect to find all men ready to listen, and willing to approach The Way.   If he stopped to use analogy he would look for, in his circle, a cross section and fair representation of the world around him - that is, all grades of consciousness and preparation or lack of preparation for the Path.

This matter of the obligation to speak of The Way and to help others has been of such consequence, when withheld, that lives have been altered by the withholding.   In that case the Karma of the silence rests upon the cause of that silence.   If the one who remains silent does so in good faith, not maliciously, but discouraged and remembering rejection, suspicion, envy, betrayal and slander, the fault falls back again to some degree upon the ones who rejected him.

The Truth is like a jewel.   It shines clearly, and once offered cannot be mistaken.   The Karma of rejection must fall to the rejector's portion - even if through his good fortune it be only the Karma of his own delayed progress.

The long-lost cause of many students' isolation in the present is their participation in rejection in the past, or the infliction of hurt upon those who obey the law of helping.   By Karmic consequence those students are now unable to respond to light rays emitted from the helpers, having already struck at previous helpers through the healing beams that sought to enfold them.

No set and fast rule in this matter can be put before the student. Sometimes it is much better to leave a point a little hazy and to become a little indefinite.

The one point necessary to be distinct upon is that the Law of Service
calls for speaking at such times as true and sincere need is to be perceived,
and to continue speaking to the point of satiation.   The obvious conclusion
that there is no obligation to speak to every one, or to incur enmity by
speaking needlessly where minds are closed and prejudiced, or where personal
animosity is displayed, will be reached.   The wise student will guide himself accordingly, thus eliminating the discouragement and disillusion
created by rejection.

Indeed, the Path calls for a nice discrimination at all points, upon all
subjects and all actions, and it does not waver in its calm and inevitable
application of the consequences.   Those who travel on the Path are apt to
find that there are Rules, and that the consequence of discovering one is
the obligation to abide by it.   One of the Rules is: "Thou shalt not waste
the Truth upon unworthy".   The chela-student must observe it.

-*- -*- -*- -*- -*- -*- -*- -*- -*- -*- -*- -*- -*- -*- -*- -*- -*- -*- -*- -*-

GNOME-SPRITE

Green he was, and shiny -
    Very like a flame
Quivering and glowing,
    Never quite the same.

Quick he was, and merry -
    Very like a song
Musical and pretty,
    Lasting all day long.

Thin he was, and simple -
    Very like a child,
Curious and friendly,
    In the sylvan wild.

Queer he was, and lovely -
    Very like a tone
Blending shades of color,
    Bright against a stone.

Sweet he was, and wistful -
    Very like a pet
Missing someone often,
    With a deep regret.

Green he was, a beauty -
    Very like a flame;
Where he lives is secret,
    Gnome-Sprite is his name.

-*- -*- -*- -*-

The Fourth Day of the planet, breaking in iridescent dawns above a warm and gently surging sea, reflected all the glory of the first majestic Golden Age that comes with every advent of a sentient race upon a man-bearing sphere. The skies were fair, and the sunshine nourished the fertile tropic land near to the northern pole, which was the only land not under the wide-spreading ocean. A paradise was to be found there, where the waters lapped at the first continent, and all the rivers poured into the southern sea.

Into this paradise of beauty and profusion came the downward-darting Lives, prepared to take upon themselves shapes of whatever kind might be required - for new shapes are always built in the First Dawn, in every Morning of the planetary Days.   These Lives were the advancing ranks of the already self-conscious and self-dependent, who had made themselves ready to be present in the important working hours of this, the early Morning. The race then, in that time, was superior to its descendant races, for as the centuries rolled by the less evolved of mankind wakened to the Day. Each wave of Life brought with it an increasing deterioration and confusion into the ranks of the first dwellers in the Land of the Bright Morning.

Due to the necessity of helping even these superior and wisely-named Progenitors and Forefathers, the Builders and the DHYÂNI CHOHANS of the previous MANVANTARA were constrained to set the pattern of this, the new note of the planet. They were within the subtle realm, not corporeal, but still in form, and that form shone with all the brilliance of the unobstructed radiance of the light-body of these beings. Men called them, then, the Golden-faces, for there was radiance like bright sunlight aureoling their countenances, and so came into being the legend of the angelic halo. The halos were in truth no fancy, in that Age. Likewise the legends have come down to us of Edens, Paradises, Gardens, Celestial visitors, and of the keenly felt loss of this first Land of Beauty.

The planet had resolved itself once more, within its time for resting, and had come down a plane, a tone, a note, into the element of Earth, or solid matter. The core was round and firm and spheroid, and it was even then still hardening. The water had withdrawn, so far, as to uncover the first continent, but in the years to come it crept back farther. It leaves a certain quota of the surface to the evolving races of the Lives, for they require Earth and Air for sustenance, but though it changes space at times it does not change the quota. At all times Law is over all and Law says - so much space for Water.

These first seed-men were high in the more noble virtues. They quarreled not, and warred not, and they were not desirous of great riches. Therefore they were in all respects, save one, immune to gross temptations, but they had never conquered the perplexity of sex, and this proved their undoing.

Nevertheless, the centuries and centuries of this Land's existence was by far the brightest, brighter than those recorded in any later annals, therefore men call it the Golden Age, some of them remembering the golden aureoles of the faces of the mighty Builders, who dwelt near Man and taught him. They served as Kings, Leaders and Teachers of the still half-asleep but slowly awakening Humanity of this our present Planetary Day.

Part II - The Dharma or Doctrine

219. Q. What five occupations are said to be low and base?
     A. Selling liquor, selling animals for slaughter, selling poison,
        selling murderous weapons, and dealing in slaves.

220. Q. Who are said to be incapable of progress in spirituality?
     A. The killers of father, mother, and holy Arhats; bhikkhus who sow
        discord in the Sangha; those who attempt to injure the person of
        a Buddha; those who hold extremely nihilistic views as to the
        future existence; and those who are extremely sensual.

221. Q. Does Buddhism specify places or conditions of torment into which a
        bad man's Karma draws him on leaving this life?
     A. Yes.   They are: Sanjîva; Kâlasûtra; Sanghâta; Raurava; Mahâ-
        Raurava; Tâpa; Pratâpa; Avîchi.

222. Q. Is the torment eternal?
     A. Certainly not.   Its duration depends on a man's Karma.

223. Q. Does Buddhism declare that non-believers in Buddha will of necessity
        be damned for their unbelief?
     A. No: by good deeds they may enjoy a limited term of happiness before
        being drawn into re-birth by their unexhausted Tanhâ.   To escape
        re-birth, one must tread the Noble Eight-fold Path.

224. Q. What is the spiritual status of woman among Buddhists?
     A. According to our religion they are on a footing of perfect equality
        with men. "Woman," says the Buddha, in the CHULLAVEDALLA SUTTA,
        "may attain the highest path of Holiness" - Arhatship - that
        is open to man.

225. Q. What does a modern critic say about the effect of Buddhism on
        woman?
     A. That "it has done more for the happiness and enfranchisement of
        woman than any other creed" (Sir Lepel Griffin).

226. Q. What did the Buddha teach about caste?
     A. That one does not become of any caste, whether Pariah, the lowest,
        or Brâhman, the highest, by birth, but by his deeds. "By deeds,"
        said He, "One becomes an outcast, by deeds one becomes a Brâh-
        man" (See VASALA SUTTA).

227. Q. Tell me a story to illustrate this?
     A. Ananda, passing by a well, was thirsty and asked Prakriti, a girl
        of the Mâtanga, or Pariah caste, to give him water. She said
        she was of such low caste that he would become contaminated by
        taking water from her hand.   But Ananda replied: "I ask not
        for caste but for water;" and the Mâtanga girl's heart was glad
        and she gave him to drink.   The Buddha blessed her for it.

228. Q. What did the Buddha say in "VASALA-SUTTA" about a man of the Pariah
        Sopâka caste?
     A. That by his merits he reached the highest fame; that many Khattiyas
        (Kshattriyas) and Brâhmans went to serve him; and that after

death he was born in the Brahma world: while there are many
Brâhmanas who for their evil deeds are born in hell.

229. Q. Does Buddhism teach the immortality of the soul?
      A. It considers "soul" to be a word used by the ignorant to express a
          false idea. If everything is subject to change, then man is
          included, and every material part of him must change. That
          which is subject to change is not permanent, so there can be no
          immortal survival of a changeful thing. *

      * The "soul" here criticised is the equivalent of the Greek psyche.
        The word "material" covers other states of matter than that of the
        physical body.

230. Q. What is so objectionable in this word "soul"?
      A. The idea associated with it that man can be an entity separated from
          all other entities, and from the existence of the whole of the
          Universe. This idea of separateness is unreasonable, not
          provable by logic, nor supported by science.

231. Q. Then there is no separate "I", nor can we say "my" this or that?
      A. Exactly so. There is but one All, of which we and every being
          and thing are but parts.

232. Q. If the idea of a separate human "soul" is to be rejected, what is it
          in man which gives him the impression of having a permanent
          personality?
      A. Tanhâ, or the unsatisfied desire for existence. The being having
          done that for which he must be rewarded or punished in future, and
          having Tanhâ, will have a re-birth through the influence of Karma.

233. Q. What is it that is born?
      A. A new aggregation of Skandhas, or personality* caused by the last
          generative thought of the dying person.

      * Upon reflection, I have substituted "personality" for "individuality"
        as written in the first edition. The successive appearances upon
        one or many earths, or "descents into generation," of the tanhaically-
        coherent parts (Skandhas) of a certain being are a succession of per-
        sonalities. In each birth the personality differs from that of the
        previous, or next succeeding birth. Karma, the deus ex machina, masks
        (or shall we say reflects?) itself, now in the personality of a sage,
        again as an artisan, and so on through-out the string of births. But
        though personalities ever shift, the one line of life along which
        they are strung like beads, runs unbroken: it is ever that particular
        line, never any other. It is therefore individual - an individual
        vital undulation - which is careering through the objective side of
        Nature, under the impulse of Karma and the creative direction of Tanhâ
        and persists through many cyclic changes. Professor Rhys-Davids
        calls that which passes from personality to personality along the in-
        dividual chain, "character" or "doing". Since "character" is not a
        mere metaphysical abstraction, but the sum of one's mental qualities
        and moral propensities, would it not help to dispel what Professor
        Rhys-Davids calls "The desperate expedient of a mystery" (BUDDHISM,
        p. 101), if we regarded the life-undulation as individuality, and
        each of its series of natal manifestations as a separate personality?

We must have two words to distinguish between the concepts, and I find none so clear and expressive as the two I have chosen. The perfected individual, Buddhistically speaking, is a Buddha, I should say; for a Buddha is but the rare flower of humanity, without the least super- natural admixture. And, as countless generations - "four asankhoyyas and a hundred thousand cycles" (Fausboll and Rhys-David's BUDDHIST BIRTH STORIES, 13) - are required to develop a man into a Buddha, and the iron will to become one runs throughout all the successive births, what shall we call that which thus wills and perseveres? Character, or individuality? An individuality, but partly manifested in any one birth, but built up of fragments from all the births.

The denial of "Soul" by Buddha (see SAMYUTTA NIKÂYA, the SUTTA PITAKA) points to the prevalent delusive belief in an independent personality; an entity, which after one birth would go to a fixed place, or state where, as a perfect entity, it could eternally enjoy or suffer. And what he shows is that the "I am I" consciousness is, as regards per- manency, logically impossible, since its elementary constituents con- stantly change and the "I" of one birth differs from the "I" of every other birth. But every thing that I have found in Buddhism accords with the theory of a gradual evolution of the perfected man - viz., a Buddha - through numberless natal experiences. And in the con- sciousness of that individual who, at the end of a given chain of births attains Buddhahood, or who succeeds in attaining the fourth stage of Dhyâna, or mystic self-development, in any of his births anterior to the final one, the scenes of all these serial births are perceptible. In the JÂTAKATHAVANNANA - so well translated by Professor Rhys-Davids- an expression continually recurs which, I think, rather supports such an idea, viz: "Then the Blessed One made manifest an occurrence hidden by change of birth," or "that which had been hidden by," etc. Early Buddhism then clearly held to a permanency of records in the AKÂSA, and the potential capacity of man to read the same when he has evolved to the stage of true individual enlightenment. At death, and in convulsions and trance, the javana chitta is transferred to the object last created by the desires. The will to live brings all thoughts into objectivity.

234. Q. How many Skandhas are there?
      A. Five.

235. Q. Name the five Skandhas?
      A. Rûpa, Vêdanâ, Sannâ, Samkhârâ, and Vinnâna.

236. Q. Briefly explain what they are?
      A. Rûpa, material qualities; Vêdanâ, sensation; Sannâ, abstract ideas; Samkhârâ, tendencies of mind; Vinnâna, mental powers, or con- sciousness. Of those we are formed; by them we are conscious of existence; and through them communicate with the world about us.

237. Q. To what cause must we attribute the differences in the combination of the Five Skandhas which make every individual differ from every other individual?
      A. To the ripened Karma of the individual in his preceding births.

(to be continued)

THE THEORY OF MANU - VAIVASVATA MANU:

    Due attention should be given at all times to the remembrance that the words MANVANTARA, PRALAYA, KALPA, etc., etc., are used by the commentators of the Eastern Philosophy in a way that may create confusion to the Western reader. MANVANTARA - general - is used for various purposes in the technical esoteric meaning, and so are other general terms. It is sometimes impossible to perceive from the outside exactly what is intended, and therefore we find MANVANTARA - for instance - referring at times to the "reign of one MANU", at times to the KALPA, and sometimes to other obviously different periods of time. No hint whatsoever is furnished in the exoteric published works. The reader's own intuitive perception is his only guide.

    However, to avoid unnecessary confusion, the word MANVANTARA has been confined in The Book of Cosmos to the time "between MANUS", 308,448,000 years, its most obviously legitimate place. KALPA, or Day of BRAHMÂ, has been confined to its most obvious place, and PRALAYA to the Nights of BRAHMÂ, so that the reader's mind is not obliged to distinguish for himself between major and minor cycles. Students who refer to "The Secret Doctrine" and the Eastern Philosophy will kindly remember this statement.

    Another term used in a general sense exoterically, but in many other specific ways esoterically, is this one MANU. It is in the general and purely exoteric meaning that "The Theory of MANU" has been written, to fit the term into "The Book of Cosmos" as an integral part. Other meanings may be used by commentators, without, however, furnishing the key to the meaning, as the student may discover upon reference to the above-mentioned authorities.

    VAIVASVATA MANU, the MANU of our present MANVANTARA, is more frequently mentioned than the preceding MANUS. He - as he is spoken of in the personi- fied form - is subject to the various conflicting meanings and terms of time, therefore he may be an irritant to many who seek for themselves additional data to the outline given in these pages.

    If the student will remember that the enormous length of a MANVANTARA is involved, and that many legends arise within the shorter cycle of a sub- race, or under the influence of the vicissitudes of time, and that the eso- teric truths were never public property, he will be patient with the con- fusion resulting from the concealment of the keys to these general terms of inner esoteric knowledge.

    An effort to cast light upon the theory of MANU follows in succeeding numbers.

-*- -*- -*- -*- -*- -*- -*- -*- -*- -*- -*- -*- -*- -*- -*- -*- -*- -*- -*-

    "MANU: The great Indian legislator. The name comes from the
            Sanskrit root man 'to think' - mankind really, but stands
            for SWÂYAMBHUVA, the first of the MANUS, who started
            from SWAYAMBHU, 'the self-existent', hence the Logos,
            and the progenitor of mankind.

            MANU is the first Legislator, almost a Divine Being."

                        "The Theosophical Glossary", p. 206
                            by H. P. Blavatsky.

"Have the words of ancient sages meaning for today?"

Today Life is not different in essence. The modern problems are very
much like the ancient problems. The modern world still grapples with the
ancient enemies of greed, lust, envy, hatred, enmity, cruelty and ambition.
Neither the change in manners, customs and languages, nor the increase of
general knowledge has been able to remove any one of the basic obstacles and
imperfections. They have not lifted the clouds of Karmic penalties enfolding mankind.

This being so, there is one measure for the words of sages, whether they
are ancient or modern. The measure is their application to the daily problems of living. If this test were applied much of the nonsensical modern
cultism and senseless mysticism would be abandoned forthwith.

The words of ancient sages have survived through centuries simply because they meet this test, and it is likely they will continue to meet it in
the future. Conversely, it is likely that much of the modern writings will
vanish within one decade, unable to survive the test of application.

Some exceptions to the rule may be noted. That is, some ancient
writings were cast into a mold of thought appropriate to the age. They may
not be applicable to life in other centuries, because the need for that particular mold has passed, or because in breaking the mold to obtain the
thought the essence vanishes, understanding of the meaning having disappeared
in the intervening time. This is, perhaps, more true of writings in a
long-buried language such as the hieroglyphics, where the meaning is not
always clear, due to imperfect understanding of the original vowel system.

Success in translation, preserving the meaning and the essence, comes
generally in varying degree when writings of a still-living language are involved, such as the Hindu and Chinese manuscripts. Modern scholars of these
races have contact, through race sympathy, with the written words of their
venerated ancestors. They can interpret for us.

Always due appreciation should be given to merit, wherever it is found
to meet the test of application to life. It is axiomatic that the prophet
hath no honour in his own country - and time, more especially time. Nevertheless, there are in every generation such bearers of the Wisdom as are
Man's heritage, and it is the duty of the student to give credit to such
bearers when they appear.

It is not easy, in the welter of the flood of modern literature, to distinguish the modern seer or sage, when everywhere the spurious speak of their
importance and their ideas. The student must distinguish, and he generally
does so by the trial-and-error method. By the only practical and permanent
method, he learns to distinguish between the showy, frothy and temporary
nature of some types of "sages", and the sound, everlasting but unvaryingly
prosaic quality of the long-tested maxims of the Ancient Teachers. He
comes to the conclusion that the last are not likely to be misleading.

The wise ones use their own intelligence; they profit by the ancient
sages' writings and are not deceived by contradictory modern ideas.

Bhikkhu M. Sangharatana, Secretary of MAHA BODHI SOCIETY of India, writing from Sarnath, tells us that at the celebration of the birthday anniversary of the late Ven'ble Dharmapala, founder of the Society, the following were the speakers - Ven'ble Acharya D. Sasanasiri Thero; U. Dhammaratana, M. A., Tripitakacharya Dharmarakshi; U. Mahawathada Pandit (Burma); Rev. Yao Yutha (China); Mr. Dhamapriys, B.A.; Mr. Kamalapati Tripathi presiding.

> "All paid glowing tributes to the memory of the greatest Ceylonese
> of the twentieth century. In his illuminating speech the presi-
> dent referred to the qualities of head and heart of the great scion
> of Lanka. He said that Ven'ble Dharmapala was not only a national
> leader but a cultural ambassador from the east to the west. Honour
> for the revival of Buddhism in the land of its birth goes to him.
> If not for the awakening brought about by him among the people of
> this country the Asokan wheel would not have found its rightful
> place in the National Flag of India. He said it was a great
> pleasure to see the Maha Bodhi Society, founded by him, carrying
> on its activities for the spreading of the message of the prince
> of peace here and abroad."

-*- -*- -*- -*- -*- -*- -*- -*- -*- -*- -*- -*- -*- -*- -*- -*- -*- -*- -*-

Bhikkhu Anuruddha, General Secretary of the INTERNATIONAL BUDDHIST STUDY CIRCLE and Editor of its publication "The Buddhist Herald", writing from Ceylon, sends us a very interesting statement of the Objects of the I. B. S. C., -

> "1. To promote a conception of the real nature and meaning of life
> and the method of transcending it in accord with the teachings
> of the Buddha, the Enlightened One.
>
> "2. To propagate Buddhism as an 'Ethico-Philosophy' which unre-
> servedly accepts the 'Supremacy of Reason' verifiable by ex-
> perience and independent of any arbitrary assumption of authority.
>
> "3. To help all to realize that the salvation taught by the Buddha
> can be obtained in this life and upon this earth by the correct
> exercise of one's own faculties.
>
> "4. To form a nucleus of such persons as are prepared to study,
> disseminate and live the fundamental principles of Buddhism."

> "Persons above the age of 21 years residing in any part of the world,
> desirous of promoting the objects of the I. B. S. C. and its work
> in general, are admitted to membership."

Through the kindness and courtesy of Bhikkhu Anuruddha, a copy of "The Buddhist Herald" is enclosed as a holiday gift to our readers.

-*- -*- -*- -*- -*- -*- -*- -*- -*- -*- -*- -*- -*- -*- -*- -*- -*- -*- -*-

News comes in from China of the establishment of an organization under the leadership of Mr. F. C. Shao, called WORLD BUDDHIST DISSEMINATION. Pending further details of this world-minded group of Chinese brothers, we tender greetings and best wishes.

WILL: (December, 1947, p. #196)

The Will has been confused quite often with the Determination, but the latter operates at lower levels. ÂTMA alone expresses the Will, and Will is therefore a Spiritual Power or Expression. It is the steady pressure of the Will that carries the being onward through Evolution.

ESOTERIC: (December, 1947, p. #197)

A term long misused. The esoteric is the hidden, the unknown, the to-be-discovered. It does not mean secret in its true sense. It means beyond grasp or beyond knowledge, and as such applies most truly to the hidden truths of Nature. A student should use this word carefully and precisely.

EXOTERIC: (December, 1947, p. #197)

This is the opposite of esoteric. It is used to indicate Truth already discovered, laws of Nature already known to Man. It has its root in the word "exoter" - outside - therefore it may be applied to easily procured information.

GOLDEN FACES: (December, 1947, p. #204)

This term is ancient. It continued to be written, as a fact, down to Atlantean days, and "The Secret Doctrine", speaking of that time, renders the title "Lords of the Dazzling Face". Literally, it describes the Glory round the head of Adepts, perceptible then to the less material sight of Man. This Glory identified and guaranteed the Adepts; there was no hiding of rank in those days. No imposture, no untrue claims of Adept rank could be perpetrated. There would seem to be none left to the race, because now the aureoles are hidden from the materially-blinded eyes of a much-changed race. The Lords - both Radiant and Dark - walk unperceived by Man.

LOGOS: (Greek)   (December, 1947, p. #208)

This word is used to replace "God" in some students' minds, but this should not be. The Logos in occultism is the Cosmic Deity or Universal Source, true; but if the term is qualified by "Solar" or "Planetary", it means the Overseeing Intelligent Semi-Deity who is an Agent or Intermediate Ruler for higher Intelligences. The plural, Logoi, refers to the Semi-Deities (but at their height they are deities to Man), responsible for the planets and suns.

SOLITUDE: (April, 1946, p. #50)
ALONENESS:

These are English equivalents for the Sanskrit KAIVALYA. It is a term meaning one who reaches the Heights, a definition very unfamiliar to the crowded mass within the Valley. Aloneness is not selfish separation, but the solitary duty of the Heights, like a sentry on a lonely mountain pass. The few who venture upward are close comrades, but there is no alleviation of the lonely flight into the Realm of Spirit.

THE SUTRA OF 42 SECTIONS

THE SUTRA OF 42 SECTIONS AND TWO OTHER SCRIPTURES OF THE MAHAYANA SCHOOL, newly translated from the Chinese by Chu Ch'an, is a welcome addition to the available Buddhist literature. The thinking of English-speaking people has been influenced greatly by the Hînayâna School, largely because of the remarkable systematic work of The Pali Text Society in publishing translations based upon the Pali, but translations from the Mahâyâna sûtras are few, so that THE SUTRA OF 42 SECTIONS is the only one available to the general reader. To The Buddhist Society of London belongs the merit for publishing this important introduction to the Mahâyâna.

The translator, Chu Ch'an, is gifted in that he has a mastery of English, a sound knowledge of Sanskrit terms and their use, an adequate insight into the Dharma, and is a son of old China, so that he is well equipped to bring into the West these excellent translations from the Chinese Tripitaka. In his "Introduction" he describes the works he has translated and the future holds promise, for he writes: "This volume forms the first of a series of translations from the Chinese."

"A Record of the Mysterious Way in which Buddhism Came from the West in Response to our Needs", the first Translation, serves as a brief historical introduction to "The Sutra of 42 Sections". It touches upon the life of the Buddha and the time of the Emperor Ming Ti who was the Royal Patron of Chinese Buddhists 61 A. D. Obviously the Dharma was long established and was the cause of the Emperor sending for Bhikshus to come to China.

"The Sutra of 42 Sections", the second Translation, previously was translated by the Rev. Samuel Beal, and by the Japanese professors, D. T. Suzuki and M. Matsuyama (for the Buddhist Propagation Society, Kyoto). This new translation is the best, except where it contains sectarian additions, which are indicated in the footnotes.

"The Imperial Edict Concerning the Wide Promulgation of the Sutra of the Doctrine Bequeathed by the Buddha", the third Translation, is a brief introduction -- an edict by another Royal Patron, the Emperor T'ai Tsung (627 A.D.).

"The Sutra of the Doctrine Bequeathed by the Buddha" was partially translated by the Rev. Samuel Beal, who called it "Vinayasamakase - The Substance of the Vinaya", and stated it formed a part of the PARINIRVÂNA SÛTRA. Chu Ch'an states that this Sûtra and "The Sutra of 42 Sections" contain a summary of some of the most fundamental points of the Buddhist doctrine. This Sûtra is said to be the Buddha's last instructions and deals with Discipline - Vinaya.

"The Sutra of the Eight Awakenings of the Great Ones", the fifth Translation, is in line with the teaching in the previous Translations, and provides an appropriate conclusion to the work.

Throughout the book the translator includes helpful footnotes for the student's guidance. This addition to Buddhist literature is warmly recommended.

THE SUTRA OF 42 SECTIONS is available from The Golden Lotus Press, price $.75 including postage. It is a paper-backed pamphlet.

A N N O U N C E M E N T

The fourth year of THE GOLDEN LOTUS ends with this December number.   The new Fifth Volume, Year 1948, is to be different.

Some changes in the operation of the magazine have become necessary, because of the increasing pressure of the correspondence with friends and readers, the growing demands upon the Sales Department for books and information, and the time consumed in meeting these demands.

1.   The custom of personally acknowledging subscriptions and book orders will be discontinued.

2.   The custom of personally acknowledging renewals will be discontinued.

3.   The Index, previously sold to subscribers, will be furnished only on order, but will be included with all complete unbound or bound Volumes - 1944, 1945, 1946 and 1947.

4.   Uncomplicated questions will continue to be answered in The Question Page.   Complicated personal problems are - if you please - a burden we cannot assume.

5.   Delay in answering letters indicates that we are under pressure, and in some months the late issuance of the magazine itself may remind you of it.   Please have patience.

Continue to write us on points of inquiry, business, books and questions, but help us by making correspondence brief and to the point.

With the Season's Greetings,

THE STAFF
1947

www.ingramcontent.com/pod-product-compliance
Lightning Source LLC
Chambersburg PA
CBHW062040090426
42740CB00016B/2966